Graphic Design Is (...) Not Innocent

D1003451

Not

Valiz

(Ed.)
Ingo Offermanns

Graphic Design
Is (...)

Innocent

Contributors

Karo Akpokiere
Christian Bauer
David Bennewith
Friedrich von Borries
Clémentine Deliss
Sandra Doeller
Daniel Martin Feige
Annette Geiger
Matthias Görlich
Jianping He
Anna Lena von Helldorff
Martin Ludwig Hofmann
Jun Kay
Anoushka Khandwala
Klasse Grafik
Christoph Knoth
Francisco Laranjo
Degeng Li
Eva Linhart
Madoka Nishi
Ingo Offermanns
Sophia Prinz
Markus Rautzenberg
Konrad Renner
Conor Rigby (Feminist Internet)
Isabel Seiffert (Offshore)
In-ah Shin (Feminist Designer Social Club)
Pierre Smolarski
Markus Weisbeck

Graphic interlude by Mairen Hernandez

Designers' Notes
Critics' & Commissioners' Notes

DN

CN

Table of Contents

Designers' Notes
Critics' & Commissioners' Notes

DN

CN

Point of No Return
A Polemic?

Without political education, a soldier is a potential criminal.
> Thomas Sankara (officer, socialist revolutionary, and one-time president of Upper Volta)

By virtue of their social role, graphic designers are among the first to come into contact with different forms of social exchange and the associated conflicts of values. They are wanderers between different ways of thinking, communicating, and living, and they do this not (only) in protected spaces (such as the White Cube), but in direct interaction with our everyday social and economic life. At best, they try to build a living bridge that enables communication between different shores. Design theorist Annette Geiger outlines this cross-disciplinary interaction: "Design aesthetics is less a theory of beautiful things than a theory of reflected life with things. ... It asks how people use the aesthetic approach to artifacts and scenarios to design a different possible world. ... Criticism and resistance are part of it by definition, because all good form aims at reforming the given in the sense of the human being."[1]

The interdependency and interconnection of visual communication and society thus make graphic design a constituent element of public life—an entity that erodes to the extent that society breaks

1   Annette Geiger, *Andersmöglichsein: Zur Ästhetik des Designs* (Bielefeld, 2018), p. 100 f., 126.

down into particular interests and singularities.[2] Interestingly, visual communication is an integral part of meaningful social and intercultural communication, as well as of its decay, since it not only supports the discursive element of public life, but also the monological, ruthless competition for attention in economized societies. In other words, visual communication potentially works just as well on social participation as on social exclusion. What surely applies to various cultural practices applies in particular to communication design, since "today graphic design in its differentiation into many specializations and depending on constantly evolving technologies and media permeates all areas of life and has been the tool for communication, information, and visualization par excellence in our society since the digital revolution. Its impact extends from package inserts for tablets to the design of books, posters, and websites, corporate identities, and the formation of cultural trends at a wide variety of interfaces."[3] Between the findings of the humanities (such as sociology and psychology)[4] and the potential of aesthetic and ethical placements, in visual communication possibilities for society are formulated which require a critical and constructive questioning. What references are available to graphic designers in order to develop meaningful graphic design and at the same time critically question it? What is the critical and reforming capacity of visual communication for society, and where do the chasms of its manipulative possibilities lie?

Even if in my view these questions have too little tradition in graphic design and its theory, they are not new. For example, upon reading the *First Things First* manifestos from 1964[5] and 2000,[6] it becomes clear that an uneasiness about the power of visual communication and, consequently, an awareness of responsible graphic design developed along with the discipline itself. Consequently, designers should not be compliant and externally controlled executors of questionable content, but act critically and with strong opinions. But is this sufficient as a commentary and guideline? In any case, I often wonder whether my (self-)reflexive ability for criticism and my sophistication/education are sufficiently developed to be able to act in a meaningful way with strong opinions.[7] Also, how can and should I let my potentially strong opinions flow into my creative work as a graphic designer? Is it enough to work for morally opportune content and clients, so that you don't have to critically examine your own creative work? How can I not only become critical and opinionated as a citizen, but also as a graphic designer?

Universalism,[8] strollology (respectively societal design),[9] social design,[10] and critical design[11] offer different approaches in older and more recent design history for developing frames of reference for (self-)reflexive design. Such approaches are often strongly influenced by product design, fashion design, architecture, or urban planning, and it must be consid-

2   Cf. Andreas Reckwitz, *Die Gesellschaft der Singularitäten: Zum Strukturwandel der Moderne* (Berlin, 2017).
3   Eva Linhart: 'Grafikdesign denken,' in this publication, pp. 49–56.
4   Martin Ludwig Hofmann explains how the findings of various humanities disciplines can be made productive for design in his book *Neurodesign: Was Design und Marketing von Neurowissenschaften und Psychologie lernen können* (Paderborn, 2019).
5   www.designishistory.com/1960/first-things-first.
6   www.eyemagazine. com/feature/article/ first-things -first-manifesto-2000.
7   The Islamic studies scholar Thomas Bau-

er comments: "Having an opinion is almost a prerequisite. ... Since everyone has an opinion on everything, distrust of science grows. Why do you need real experts when you've already understood everything yourself? ... Academics are hardly invited to talk on television anymore because they only make things more complicated, and sometimes even use foreign words that have to be explained so that everyone can understand everything immediately. My personal revenge for this escalating pseudo-expertise is to mutate into a soccer expert along with everyone else during the World Cup and annoy the other soccer

experts with particularly naive but at least clear comments about a sports topic that I don't know much about." From: Thomas Bauer, *Die Vereindeutigung der Welt: Über den Verlust an Mehrdeutigkeit und Vielfalt* (Ditzingen, 2018), p. 110 f.
8   Cf. *Max Bill, Sicht der Dinge, Die gute Form: Eine Ausstellung,* 1949, eds. Lars Müller with Museum für Gestaltung Zürich (Zurich, 2015).
9   Cf. Lucius Burckhardt, *Warum ist Landschaft schön? Die Spaziergangswissenschaft* (Berlin, 2006).
10   Cf. Claudia Banz (ed.), *Social Design: Gestalten für die Transformation der Gesellschaft* (Bielefeld, 2016).

11   Cf. Matt Malpass, *Critical Design in Context: History, Theory, and Practice* (London, 2017).

ered whether and (if so) how such approaches can be transferred to the specifics of visual communication—a design discipline that does not exist without a linguistic substrate, meaning it is always embedded in (verbal) language, works mainly with (precise) verbal statements by others, largely depends on commissions, and its artifacts can be appropriated to a lesser extent by its users than, for example, those of fashion or architecture. But how can the multifaceted specifics of visual communication be described today? And how could a forward-looking critical theory of graphic design be developed that is separate and at the same time constructively linked to the theories of other design disciplines?

But perhaps my call for a more engaged and nuanced discourse on visual communication or on graphic design is exaggerated. Perhaps the majority of its representatives are already on the right track. Quite a few mission statements at least suggest this.[12] But on closer examination, doubts may be justified. When I look at these mission statements, it is often postulated that designers are interested in a true exchange, in exploring the unknown, and in (cultural) diversity, and consequently would only favor design solutions that, independent of their personal style, are precisely tailored to the content to be designed. Such mission statements are very enjoyable to read; they sound serious, nuanced, sensitive, sophisticated, even humble, and the politically opportune sound of these words somehow suggests critical quality. Still, the question arises as to how these postulates relate to the unmistakable (Western-influenced)[13] visual uniformity of the commercial as well as the 'hipster' mainstream and the striking stylistic consistency of many active designers. After all, visual translations—the artifacts—are meant to make the content, parameters, and processes of communication tangible in their diversity, as a multifaceted echo and reverberation of these aspects, and thus enable the senses to perceive poly-phonic meaning.

Has an overly unsuspecting approach to well-meaning claims turned the actors' rhetorical whitewashing into common sense? Is the placement of positively connoted terms perhaps only (still) carried out in order to be able to market all the participants more readily with a pleasing framing? To put it bluntly: When dealing with euphonic terms in a superficial way, does a supposedly critical stance become a matter of taste in which specific simulations of being critical are chosen depending on the respective context in clothing, gestures, and appearance?

An outlook: "A graphic design that does not also ask what its objects are for and in what way they are made for something is a privation of graphic design—a practice that does not do justice to a full understanding of what graphic design could achieve in our society. This is because, in such a position, the quality of the craftsmanship is only coincidentally linked to

12   Cf. ww.2×4. org, ww.bureau-da-vid-voss.de, ww.design-gruppe-koop.de, ww. fabrique.nl, ww.fon-shickmann.com, ww. lamm-kirch.com, ww. mirkoborsche.com, ww. ok-rm.co.uk, ww.please-donotbend.co.uk, ww. thonik.nl, ww.veryvery. de, ww.vier5.de, ww.zak. group, and others.
13   Even if Stefan Zweig's description of international uniformity and monotony may irritate us networked and widely traveled (Western) designers, it may still be worth considering: "The most potent intellectual impression ... of every journey in recent years is a slight horror in the face of the monotonization of the world. Everything is becoming more uniform in its outward manifestations, everything leveled into a uniform cultural schema. The characteristic habits of individual peoples are being worn away, native dress giving way to uniforms, customs becoming international. Countries seem increasingly to have slipped simultaneously into each other; people's activity and vitality follows a single schema; cities grow increasingly similar in appearance. ... An equivalence of souls unconsciously arises, a mass soul created by the growing drive toward uniformity, an atrophy of nerves in favor of muscles, the extinction of the individual in favor of the type." From: Stefan Zweig, 'The Monotonization of the World' (1925), The Wei-mar Republic Source-book, eds. Anton Kaes, Martin Jay, Edward Dimendberg (Berkeley, 1994), pp. 397–400. Original text: Stefan Zweig, 'Die Monotonisierung der Welt,' Berliner Börsen-Courier, February 1, 1925.

the ethical quality. A correctly understood aesthetics of graphic design does not mean ... a self-contained consideration of how it was made ... but a consideration of the means and ends it their particular forming through the objects of graphic design. ... a correctly understood graphic design is by no means external to its purposes; rather, the objects of graphic design themselves work on the contours of the purposes."[14] Is this contrary to when the designer Matthias Görlich questions the effectiveness of today's communication designers in principle? I don't think so. After all, when Görlich points out that perhaps completely different forces are responsible for the current graphic design of our societies, and graphic designers (can) only serve as the trendy fig leaves for these actors, he focuses on similar basic principles. However, it becomes clear here that simple answers to the range of questions outlined cannot be found. Following the human instinct for convenience, simple answers may be desirable, but certainly not helpful and in any case hypertrophic.

Graphic Design Is (...) Not Innocent is thus both a disappointment and a challenge. The publication does not aim to establish a canon of criticism or a set of rules; instead, it aims to contribute to an increased linguistic ability of the discipline in order to outline *possible* frameworks for criticism. In the assumption that responsible visual design must relate equally to context, task, object, process, and artifact, that its critical and resistant qualities must always be determined within a complex network of relationships, and that they imply pragmatic as well as moral qualities, this publication places a critical questioning of the *operations* of visual communication at the center: How does contemporary graphic design or contemporary visual communication operate—not function!—viewed from inside and outside, meaning from the perspective of reflexive (visual) speaking-thinking and think-

14   Daniel Martin Feige, 'Ästhetik des Grafikdesigns,' in this publication, pp. 213–219.

ing-speaking, or from the perspective of the significant and its various authors?

The publication thus aims to initiate a dialogue
between designers, academics, clients, and critics
who outline the potential, responsibility, limits, and
risks of designing visual communication. *Graphic Design Is (...) Not Innocent* combines field research and
academic work and thus attempts to lay the foundations for basic research. The publication is a 'road trip'
between different concepts of challenge and practice. It is a temporary stock-taking, without any claim
to completeness. It is just as much a question mark
as an exclamation mark—but above all, it aims to contribute to critical thinking in graphic design.

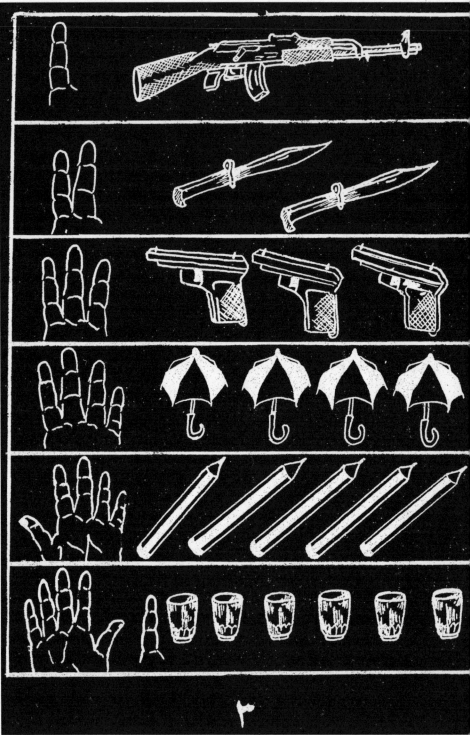

Graphic interlude by Wahab Mohmand. US-published, CIA-sponsored textbook
for 1st grade Afghan kids, 1980s

Ingo Offermanns

Anti-Ambiguity vs. Translation
Design despite Complexity

When translating, one should go as far as the untranslatable; only then does one become aware of the foreign nation and the foreign language.

Johann Wolfgang von Goethe[1]

Wandering and the 'science of strolling'[2] were yesterday. Surfing is the present and only the present. Complexity and crisis are like water and wind, and the winner is whoever rides the wave the longest and smartest without being devoured by it. The important thing is not to be in the water, but on the wave. And one must find exactly the bay or niche that allows for a perfect staging. Contemporary graphic design follows this example. In this sense, design, when dealing with complex subjects, is more like a smart gliding on the surface of turbulence than a decelerated and (self-) reflective committing and penetration of contradictions. Is Sloterdijk right when he says that design is nothing more than a "sovereignty simulation" that helps "to stay in shape in the midst of the decomposition of form?"[3] After all, design provides us with the means to (superficially) master devices and situations with a structural complexity that overwhelms the competence of most individuals. It is an offer that we are all happy to accept, because we modern experts in diversified specialist societies are increasingly good at fewer and fewer things, and therefore need means

1   Johann Wolfgang von Goethe, *Maximen und Reflexionen* (Wiesbaden, 2012), p. 172.
2   Lucius Burckhardt, *Warum ist Landschaft schön? Die Spaziergangswissenschaft* (Berlin, 2006).
3   Peter Sloterdijk, 'Der ästhetische Imperativ,' in: *Schriften zur Kunst* (Berlin, 2014), p. 144.

and gestures (interfaces, style coaches, kitchen appliances, rhetoric trainers, art advisors, and so on) in order to approach what we have not mastered not powerlessly, but in an accelerated manner and with instructions.

We are witnessing a world that is approaching the limits of globalization, in which there is no longer any outside, and in which the communal is increasingly being eroded in the face of a self-referential frenzy of production and growth. The commercialized networking (both analog and digital) leads to an accumulation of data and products that is as uniform as it is rampant, and design or graphic design helps to perceive this indifferent accumulation not as unpredictable and thus as overwhelming, but as enjoyable. Unpredictability, and the associated loss of friction and time, does not fit into a system that elevates productivity to the highest virtue. That is why any lubricant is welcome.

Pleasure and relaxation arise when a balance of stimulus and smoothness is achieved, which stimulates calculable affects and assimilates the unfamiliar into the familiar (uniform). But does this describe the task of contemporary design? Or is this just one of the possibilities that the discipline offers, but which does not exhaust its potential for meaningful visual communication?

Graphic design (or communication design, or visual communication) claims to convey, advertise, and seduce through the professional use of a visual language. In itself it is neither good nor bad to convey, advertise, and seduce, even if the latter has an inherent element of insincerity. A moral evaluation—if one wants to bother at all—only applies when it becomes clear in whose service the conveying, advertising, and seducing is done, or how this service relates to the society in which one acts. However, according to my thesis, an evaluation should include *logos* as well as *pathos* and *ethos*, since "a correctly understood graphic design is by no means external to its purposes; rather, the objects of graphic design themselves work on the contours of the purposes."[4] This means not just conveying functionally (literally); instead, translations are developed and implemented within and between societies and from that a responsibility arises that cannot be understood based only on the logic of standardized work processes (sensation, omnipresence, volume, trends, exclusivity, legibility). After all, translations are always also interpretations, since they attempt to bring foreign *logos* to society and society to this *logos* through dialogue, exploration, analysis, criticism, and invention, as the writer and translator Karl Dedecius explains in his book *Vom Übersetzen*.[5]

The Possibility of Being Different
through Translation

The architect and design theorist Friedrich von Borries ascribes a political—that is, critical and interventionist—potential to design, which arises from the "inherent tension between being rooted in everyday social and economic life, speculative production of desires, and artistic imagination."[6] I understand this in the sense of designing a "possibility of being different," as the design theorist Annette Geiger describes in her book *Andersmöglichsein: Zur Ästhetik des Designs*:

Design aesthetics is less a theory of beautiful things than a theory of reflected living with things.... It asks how people use the aesthetic approach to artifacts and scenarios to design a different possible world.... Criticism and resistance are part of it by definition, because every good form aims at reforming the given in the sense of the human being.[7]

Contemporary graphic design often seems to me to be less contradictory. Looking at a large number of graphic design forums (festivals, biennials, symposia, prizes, blogs), I tend to be confronted with individual

4   Daniel Martin Feige, 'Ästhetik des Grafikdesigns,' in: Ingo Offermanns (ed.), *Graphic Design Is (...) Not Innocent* (Amsterdam, 2022) p. 218.
5   Karl Dedecius, *Vom Übersetzen* (Frankfurt/M 1986), p. 45 f.
6   Friedrich von Borries, *Weltentwerfen* (Berlin, 2016), p. 136.
7   Annette Geiger, *Andersmöglichsein: Zur Ästhetik des Designs* (Bielefeld, 2018), p. 100 f.

showcases, similar to those at trade fairs, where it is seldom about questioning, analysis, or criticism, and instead about assertions of power within a professional field with the help of sophisticated staging techniques. I get the impression that the forces of desire production and imagination are primarily directed toward self-design[8] driven by fear of deficits and failure—that is, personal survival in everyday economic life, and not toward the possibility for individual and social striving to be different. Primarily, forces are mobilized in order to competitively attain attention, individuation, and desire for designers and clients instead of—in regard to graphic design—speculatively breaking up positions in the *translation*, and instead of a monological exchange of blows seeking out an experiment in dialogue.

Translation aims at a dynamic and not precisely identifiable in-between. It is dialogical[9] and deals with the distance instead of the difference between various parties in order to identify commonalities, to keep the parties in tension and at the same time to

8   Friedrich von Borries makes a distinction between the liberating or 'designing' and the 'subjugating' potential of self-design. He describes the subjugating self-design that I have in mind here as follows: "Self-design, which is self-optimization, obeys capitalism's logic of growth. The self should also grow in its possibilities, exhaust its potential, and generate profit of whatever kind. Thus there is a threat of self-design in which and through which people make themselves a product, reinterpret themselves in product development cycles, adapt to the market situation, and attempt to position themselves op-timally in the various sales markets through design." From: Von Borries 2016, p. 103 f.

9   François Jullien, *There Is No Such Thing as Cultural Identity*, (Hoboken, 2021) p. 68: "In Greek dia means both divide and crossing. A dia-logue is all the more fecund, as the Greek already knew, for having a divide in play (as in the potent dialogue between Socrates and Callicles). If we say more or less the same thing, the dialogue turns into a monologue for two, and the mind makes no progress. But *dia* has another meaning: path that crosses a space, with the space perhaps offering up resistance. A dia-logue is not instantaneous; it takes time.... Meanwhile, *logos* speaks to the common of the intelligible, which serves paradoxically as both the condition and the aim of dialogue. In other words, a common is engendered through the divides themselves. Each language, each line of thought, each position allowing itself to spill over because of the other, a mutual intelligence can emerge in an *interspace* that has become active—even if said intelligence is never fully realized (the potential in the *intelligible* speaks to this). The common is no matter of resorption of divides or forced assimilation. Rather, it is *produced*, as the internal tension of the divides occasion work. Neither imposed nor held to be given from the start, it is *promoted*."

10   Ibid., p. 24.

11   Thomas Bauer, *Die Vereindeutigung der Welt: Über den Verlust an Mehrdeutigkeit und Vielfalt*, (Ditzingen, 2018) p. 73. The Islamic scholar Thomas Bauer observes the same thing with regard to industrially produced pop music, which replaces *logos* with *pathos*: "Similar to the fact that the increasing number of chocolate bars does not correspond to a real increase in diversity of food items, these industrially produced pop songs are also more a symptom of a clarification of the world than of artistic diversity."

mutually break up their positions and bring them together. The philosopher and sinologist François Jullien specifies this relationship as follows:

> Both divide and difference mark a separation, but difference does it through *distinction*, the divide through *distance*. *Difference*, then, is classificatory—its analysis proceeding by resemblance and difference—and at the same time identificatory. It is by proceeding "from difference to difference," as Aristotle says, that we arrive at a final difference. This final difference delivers the essence of the thing, expresses in a definition. The *divide*, by contrast, is not identificatory but exploratory, giving rise to some other possibility. Thus a divide has no classifying function—does not set up typologies, in the manner of a difference—but consists precisely in the overflowing of classes. Rather than an orderly array, it produces disarray *non pas un rangement, mais un dérangement*.[10]

In contrast, advertising aims primarily at classificatory disambiguation in order to achieve exclusivity with the help of a brand (or a visual identity) and to convert (supposed) needs into demand. The exclusivity comes from variations of the similar instead of heterogeneous diversity in order to satisfy the logic of efficiency and exploitation of globalized capitalism.[11] In the competition for attention, sensation, omnipresence, volume, trends, exclusivity, and readability are its references—all calculable quantities[12]—and manipulative affect production is its goal. This is also a form of conveying, but conveying in the form of a one-way street without detours.

Since the history of graphic design is closely linked to the emergence of our current economic principles, however, the question arises to what extent graphic design can even make the tension outlined by

12   Here is an example of how even simple algorithms can make use of these references today: www.brandcrowd.com, https://placeit.net/online-poster-maker?gclid=EAlalQobChMIoLaShM_16QIViMmyCh30-AU-gEAAYASAAEgJbevD_BwE. And AI research is just getting started.

Von Borries and Geiger its own. After all, graphic design is a design discipline that is largely dependent on (commercial) commissions, works predominantly with (precise) verbal statements by others, is always embedded in (verbal) language, and uses artifacts that can be appropriated by its users to a much lesser extent than those of fashion or architecture, for example. Furthermore, it should be clear that the purpose of (visual) rhetoric is to efficiently use seductive heuristics to form attitudes and influence actions.[13] Still, persuasion requires choices. And here I see the potential for an increased focus on other possibilities: designing does not mean following supposed inevitabilities, but rather exploring, perceiving, and revealing options. It means exploring (communicative) freedoms from the point of view of the different authors and making them permeable—whereby the designer also becomes the author through the translation and thus interpretation.

Authorship, Dialogue, and Diversity

Now one can ask how much authorship graphic designers can and should produce. After all, the statement brought to them from the 'outside' is usually at the center of the communicative free space. It is the narrative ignition and remains the most important reference. The translation and thus interpretation of the statement then immediately demands authorship, which moves subjectively between the statement and the recipients. After all, every statement can be interpreted in very different ways, as we are familiar with from theater or music. The statement to be (visually) communicated is thus the subject of negotiation.

In the best case, the interpretation is part of a *permeable* dialogue with the basic conceptual impulse, the clients (whose impulses—for example, in the case of a job from a publisher or a gallerist—do not necessarily need to coincide with the basic conceptual impulse), the designers, as well as the inter-

13 Gui Bonsiepe, 'Visuell-Verbale Rhetorik,' in: Arne Scheuermann (ed.), *Design als Rhetorik* (Berlin, 2008), p. 28 f.

est of the recipients. In the worst case, the translation by the designer distorts the perception of the original impulse to such a degree that the interpretation claims something that is completely different from the original statement.

Graphic designers analyze the narrative of the statement brought to them, make an inventory of its narrative potential, and accentuate certain aspects of the statement or give them a character in order to make them accessible and permeable, and thereby activate the dialogue between the basic conceptual impulse, the client, the designer, and others. Assuming that content is potentially diverse in our differentiated and networked world, one should assume that the process just described leads to equally diverse (visual) expression. After all, as stated above, translation should bring foreign *logos* to society and society to this *logos* with the voice (and the authorship) of the designer. In this sense, translation does not mean forcing the unfamiliar into the known; it does not mean assimilation or focusing on similar things, but rather the search for commonalities and creating tension between unique aspects.

If I look at the visual uniformity (of Western character) of the commercial as well as the 'hipster' mainstream in graphic design, which is widespread internationally, I ask myself how many designers actually follow this ambition. Instead, we see efforts either to synthesize a uniform visual language—at least one that functions imperatively and 'universally' for an era or a generation—or to retreat into the hermetically subjectivistic or identitarian. But where is the awareness of the plural, the porous, the simultaneity of the non-simultaneous—which global networking can potentially also produce? Where is the resonance, exploration, multilingualism, ambiguity, and nuance? The impression arises that many designers tend to surrender to the constraints of everyday economic life rather than to allow themselves to develop

Anti-Ambiguity vs. Translation

a polyglot translational intelligence that emphasizes diversity, variety, and polyphony in dialogue.

What I believe to notice about the present time was described in the early twentieth century by the writer Stefan Zweig:

> The most potent intellectual impression... of every journey in recent years is a slight horror in the face of the monotonization of the world. Everything is becoming more uniform in its outward manifestations, everything leveled into a uniform cultural schema. The characteristic habits of individual peoples are being worn away, native dress giving way to uniforms, customs becoming international. Countries seem increasingly to have slipped simultaneously into each other; people's activity and vitality follows a single schema; cities grow increasingly similar in appearance.... It is not with impunity that everyone can dress the same...: monotony necessarily penetrates beneath the surface. Faces become increasingly similar through the influence of the same passions, bodies more similar to each other through the practice of the same sports, minds more similar for sharing the same interests. An equivalence of souls unconsciously arises, a mass soul created by the growing drive toward uniformity, an atrophy of nerves in favor of muscles, the extinction of the individual in favor of the type.[14]

Interestingly, large parts of society are now very concerned about diversity elsewhere—namely, biodiversity. Here people increasingly recognize that diverse habitats are more stable and adaptable than monocultures. Therefore, diversity means taking precautions: evolution under changing conditions is only possible with biological diversity.[15] So when the WWF's Living Planet Index shows that species diversity has

14   Stefan Zweig, 'Die Monotonisierung der Welt,' in: *Zeiten und Schicksale: Aufsätze und Vorträge aus den Jahren 1902–1942* (Frankfurt/M, 1990), p. 30 f.
15   murmann-magazin.de/society/2017/05/biologische-vielfalt-darum-ist-das-thema-wichtig.

Book design by Ingo Offermanns, 2018.

Morgue und andere Gedichte von Gottfried Benn

Mit Zeichnungen von Georg Baselitz

Klett-Cotta

Morgue

I.

Kleine Aster

Ein ersoffener Bierfahrer wurde auf den Tisch gestemmt.
Irgendeiner hatte ihm eine dunkelhellila Aster
zwischen die Zähne geklemmt.
Als ich von der Brust aus
unter der Haut
mit einem langen Messer
Zunge und Gaumen herausschnitt,
muß ich sie angestoßen haben, denn sie glitt
in das nebenliegende Gehirn.
Ich packte sie ihm in die Bauchhöhle
zwischen die Holzwolle,
als man zunähte.
Trinke dich satt in deiner Vase!
Ruhe sanft,
kleine Aster!

5

Book design by Ingo Offermanns, 2012.

decreased by 27% between 1970 and 2005,[16] counter-measures are called for in many societies.

At the same time, the Society for Endangered Languages has found that almost one-third of the approximately 6500 languages spoken around the world will become extinct within the next few decades.[17] The knowledge about this cultural loss, the loss of perceiving and talking about the world in different ways, in a more multifaceted manner, is probably less widespread than the knowledge about the loss of biodiversity, and it can be assumed that problematizing this loss is also less widespread. Many cling to the hope of a universal language that allows people to communicate more easily and efficiently with one another, even if that would mean a hegemony of that language (or a monoculture). But what would we give up? François Jullien writes:

> If we begin to speak only one tongue, if the fertile divides between languages are lost, then languages will no longer be able to reflect off one another: they will no longer enable the perception of one another's *resources*. Soon we will be unable to think outside of the same standardized notions, and begin to mistake mere stereotypes of thought for universals. 'Babel' is, in fact, a stroke of good fortune for thought.[18]

In my view, what applies to spoken language also applies to visual language. But if one reacts to diversity and ambiguity—according to globalized capitalism's logic of efficiency and exploitation—by designing visual uniformity (misunderstood as something shared in common) as well as exclusive and equally valid visual identities,[19] and if one follows the striving for clarification, prerogative of interpretation, and lack of alternatives, one does the (exploratory) dialogue a disservice, since the cultural is characterized by the fact that it

16   Gesellschaft zur Erhaltung alter und gefährdeter Haustierrassen: Rote Liste der bedrohten Nutztierrassen in Deutschland 2016, www.g-e-h.de/images/stories/news/pdf/rotliste.pdf.
17   Gesellschaft für bedrohte Sprachen e.V., www.uni-koeln.de/gbs.
18   Jullien, op. cit., p. 41.
19   Jullien, op. cit., p. 58: "On the other hand (otherwise), we can rank cultural difference first, with each culture folding back into its supposed identity. Here we cannot help but shut these cultures into worlds. This is 'culturalism,' which prepares the way for a *lazy relativism* that never seeks to exceed its own bounds (*se dépasser*)."

is simultaneously diverse and unique. That is why I advocate for focusing more on the translational potential of visual communication. There we can find elements of speculative production of desires and the power of artistic imagination, so there we can also find the possibility of being different.

Conveying, Transferring, Adapting, and Disinclination toward Oneself

Creative translators are wanderers between different ways of thinking, communicating, and living. They anthologize, collect, and seek several answers at the same time, in the hope that one of them will resonate. It is not about transgression, taking possession, submission, or conformity, but about a back and forth, similar to the job of a ferryman who enables communication between opposite banks.[20] Translation is not a monological one-way street; instead, it keeps all participants in view in a dialogical manner.[21] It also seeks the universal, but it seeks it in the common, and not in the totalitarian (essentialist) one, or in the superficially similar, assimilable.[22]

Translation deals with the in-between, with the transition. It is not a compromise, not a lowest common denominator, but rather a creation of tension in order to open up the different (visual) languages, to get them out of their conformity, and to test their potential. The communicative achievement, the creative translation, must not be limited to refined briefings, brainstorming, and (verbal) derivations or concepts. Rather, it must be expressed at least as much in the final visual artefact, sine this is precisely where the naming of foreign, previously nameless (faceless) beings takes place. This is precisely where the foreign is made recognizable and understandable for both sides.[23] The artifact makes content, parameters, and processes tangible, is a sensual echo and resonance of these aspects, and thus enables an understanding of meaning through the senses. To respond to ambitious, complex communicative concepts with variations of trendy visual uniformity would exaggerate the ambitions.

In this respect, it is at least as much about the 'how' as it is about the 'what.' The writer and translator Esther Kinsky remarks:

> Every translation is first and foremost the result of a process of designing language as material which does not arise from dealing with an object, but rather from dealing with the tension between two types of treatment of an object. This is a process in which the 'what' takes a back seat to the 'how.' ... The 'what' is only interesting insofar as it reveals layers of the 'how' that go farther and deeper than most readers suspect.[24]

Language is not a value that can be calculated or owned, but a resource that can only be tamed to a limited extent and from which everyone can draw. Language is a system of abbreviations that is imprecise as a whole. It runs alongside the what, is just behind it, sometimes ahead of it, but rarely overlapping with it.[25] What Karl Dedecius describes about spoken and written language applies even more so to visual language, since graphic design translates spoken and written language into the retinal space. But it also harbors the potential of specification on the one hand and permeability on the other. The visual translator also has access to (visual)

20   Dedecius, op. cit., p. 27.
21   This becomes obvious for instance in the Biblia Polyglotta (Antwerp, 1568–1573, by Christopher Plantin), a Bible in five languages that run parallel to one another in order to achieve a nuanced understanding of the text by comparing the languages.
22   Totalitarian (identitarian) ideologies seek to make everything exactly as it is imagined by the respective ideology. In the discourse of authenticity, everything is good when everything is as I imagine it to be—meaning a person's dignity is made dependent on their resemblance to oneself.
23   Dedecius, op. cit., p. 21.
24   Esther Kinsky, Fremdsprechen (Berlin, 2019), p. 8 f.
25   Dedecius, op. cit., p. 35 f.

language(s), topic, ideas, time, author, work, space, form, interpretation, and meaning as frames of reference.

Being open to the (visual) language of others means taking an inventory of mental and symbolic resources and this leads to the cultural creation of relationships. This creation of relationships is translation and, in my view, should be the focus of graphic design.[26] The striving for a linguistic international, just like the striving for identitarian isolation, is therefore as idealistic as it is destructive:

> A single language would be much more convenient, certainly, but it would also impose its uniformization. Exchange would be made easier, but there would be nothing, or nothing effectively singular, left to exchange. Once all is arrayed in a language / line of thought—every culture—will, as I have said, be reduced to stubborn declarations of its identitarian 'differences.'[27]

In the spirit of Karl Dedecius, I would like to suggest an, admittedly somewhat rough, differentiation of the term 'translation,' which may be helpful for design practice: a differentiation between conveying, transferring, and adapting. Conveying is about reproducing information precisely ('verbatim'), but without contextual and contradictory expansion. In contrast, a speculative expansion begins with the transfer of content. The artistic imagination finally takes hold in adaptation, which—just as in the relationship between thinking and reflecting—includes reflection, speech, response, dialogue, criticism, interpretation, and integration. Here I understand the artistic as "an aesthetic practice of reflecting ourselves in the medium of idiosyncratic shaping,"[28] which through its practice produces an opposing (i.e., critical) element to social reality. This differentiation of the term 'translation' is not intended to sketch

26   Wilhelm von Humboldt, 'Einleitung zu Agamemnon,' in: Aeschylos' Agamemnon metrisch Übers., Gesammelte Schriften, Abt. 1, Werke, vol. VIII (Berlin, 1903–1936), p. 132: "As long as it is not foreignness but what is foreign that is felt, the translation has achieved its highest purpose, but where the foreign appears in itself, and perhaps even obscures the foreign, the translator reveals that he cannot measure up to the original."
27   Jullien, op. cit., 2021, p. 72.
28   Daniel Martin Feige, Design: Eine philosophische Analyse (Berlin, 2005), p. 18.

an either/or, but rather to show three aspects of translation that come into play in every translation, and that must be weighted anew with every translation in order to ensure the coordination of discipline and freedom, relatedness and foreignness, meaning and form.

Since, as stated above, cultural symbolizations are always part of social relationships, just as social relationships cannot exist without cultural symbolizations, in my view the exploratory and artistic element should be taken particularly seriously. Here lies the potential to wrest alternatives from the constraints of everyday economic life—that is, the possibility of being different. In addition to the effort to convey, it is about including the operative, open, and ambiguous elements of visual translation. In this way, the self-determined, idiosyncratic appropriation of a text or information by the reader—a productive 'poaching'— could be stimulated.

Such a permeability would open up different mental paths, and it would allow us to recognize ourselves and our environment in a more multifaceted manner in the awareness of diversity and foreignness:

> Widely accepted information treats the foreign as a third party—clinically, superficially. Literary translation aims at what Sigmund Freud achieved in contrast to conventional medicine— namely, the doctor's dialogue with the patient; it is based on partnership. It sees the foreign as a second party. Through dialogue, translation leads to backgrounds that leave third-party information hidden.[29]

The precise contouring of a (visual) form of language can therefore only be an effort to make oneself 'vulnerable.' It can only be useful as a temporary dialogue that seeks to change with the response of the other party. François Jullien understands translation in this

29   Dedecius, op. cit., p. 45.

sense as inherently ethical.

When Friedrich von Borries speaks of the production of desire and imaginative power inherent in design, which "crosses boundaries and creates new possibilities of the world,"[30]—according to my thesis—graphic designers should not submit the statements they deal with to a visual style. In other words, not apply a synthetic or an identitarian and essentialist visual language of understanding the world, but rather design the possibility of being different in the translation (adaptation), or visual language. They should cultivate a desire to design and a disinclination toward themselves. They should cultivate an enjoyment of transformation, the possibility of living several lives in one life.

If one wants to take these words seriously, graphic design should be echoing instead of imposing and (non-transparently) manipulating. Multilingualism, resonance, ambiguity, nuance, exploration, speculation, porosity, imperfection, and the will to transform could therefore be key concepts of a creative attitude that focuses on the inherent potential of translation.

Likewise, one must critically question individuation, the darling of many clients and graphic designers, as a form of one-dimensional and monological self-isolation, since individuation stands in the way of the possible opening up to the social outside and its polyphony. One must have the courage to oppose the neoliberal, egocentric individuation with the will to plurilogical and culturally transversal 'dividuation,'[31] as offered by the aesthetic theorist Michaela Ott as a concept for a new understanding of the self. After all, it is about to removing the 'in' from 'individuation,' which refers to 'undividedness,' and instead accentuating what is shared, this voluntary and involuntary participation, and combining it with the demand to recognize this as much as possible and to moderate it sensibly. Only when we know that we

30   Von Borries, op. cit., p. 136.
31   Michaela Ott, *Dividuationen: Theorien der Teilhabe* (Berlin, 2015).
32   Jullien, op. cit., p. 75.

are inextricably embedded in transnational linguistic communities can a non-universalized, lateral—that is, spreading in all directions—translation community develop, as dreamed of by those philosophers who are at home in different cultural spheres at the same time:

> ... if every era has its own resistance, then let us posit that our era's struggle is to cede not an inch of ground to the twin perils of uniformization and identity, and to inaugurate, through the inventive power of the divide, an intense common.[32]

IS GRAPHIC DESIGN SUPERFICIA
ARE WE ONLY PRODUCING
VISUALLY PLEASING ARTEFACTS
SOMETIMES YES, BUT
SOMETIMES NOT. I ASKE
MYSELF THE QUESTION MANY
TIMES. BUT I COULDN'T FIND TH
RIGHT ANSWER FOR THAT. FOR
THIS REASON, I WOULD LIKE TO
SAVE AT LEAST THE PRINT INK.
USED THE ECO FONT VERA SAN
FOR THE POSTER, WHICH USES
20% LESS INK.
TECHNICAL DETAILS:
PAPER: PLOTTER PAPER
SIZE: 841 X 1189 MM
ECO FONT VERA SANS
REGULAR, SIZE: 140 PT,
LINE SPACING: 144 PT,
KERNING: OPTICAL, -10
COLOR: RGB TO CMYK
COLOR PROFILE: ISO
COATED V2 300 % (ECI)

Graphic interlude by Sam Kim

Matthias Görlich

Point of Departure, Point of No Return[1]

I interpret the discussion that this publication initiates as a productive discomfort and as a good sign that graphic design has now reached a point where it can no longer ignore the fact that it is socially relevant and thus has a social responsibility. I have approached the topic with more questions than answers, and I would like to share my thoughts and how I arrived at them. I think it is important to mention that in all of this I am aware that I cannot completely avoid a Westernized, white male gaze, especially against the postulated disciplinary competence in regard to interculturality. This publication presents many examples that demonstrate the social relevance and effectiveness of graphic design, and here I would like to add an example that illuminates graphic design from another perspective: www.youtube.com/watch?v=iRTTkmC6vBk.

Assumption: Graphic Design Is Apparently Impactful

The video shows an excerpt from the speech given by Israeli Prime Minister Benjamin Netanyahu to the United Nations General Assembly in New York on 27 September 2012. In this speech, Netanyahu uses not only spoken, but also visual language in the form of a diagram to support his argument.[2] This speech received worldwide attention, both positive and negative.[3]

Against the background of our topic, one could ask to what extent this example can serve as a further

1   This text is a revised version of a lecture give at the symposium 'Point of Departure: Point of No Return' on 25 January 2019. Due to the format and the limited time for the lecture, I could only outline points. This revision represents a first 're-concentration' with an awareness that these ideas must be continuously updated. The original text of the lecture remained untouched, but was supplemented, specified, or corrected in various places marked by the footnotes with notes and references.

I would like to take this opportunity to express my thanks for the intensive and insightful exchange with the designer Sandy Kaltenborn, who has already integrated the above considerations into his practice at various points and in different constellations. For details, see image-shift. net.

indication that graphic design has the claimed relevance and effectiveness. As questionable as the intention, the graphic quality, and the one-dimensionality in this specific case may be, one can assume that the speech was accompanied by a diagram—precisely this diagram—for very deliberate reasons and with full intent. The reactions to the speech at least lead to the conclusion that it achieved its goal quite successfully, because it was perceived—not least because of the diagram—as 'liberatingly clear and unambiguous' in Israel in particular.[4]

 This is not the place to go into this example in more detail, and many more examples from international politics could be cited to show that the use of graphic design has led to 'empowering,' 'mobilizing,' and 'colonizing.'[5] Ultimately, this forms the basis for the justification (and responsibility) of the entire discipline. If it could not change anything, it probably would not exist.

 The assumption from the introduction can apparently be affirmed: Yes, graphic design has an im-

2   The purpose of Netanyahu's speech was to convince the international community of the urgency of taking action against Iran. A 'red line' that must not be crossed was drawn once again. See news.un.org/en/story/2012/09/421552.

3   I would like to emphasize very clearly that I do not in any way follow Netanyahu's argument or support his cause. In this example, my aim is to draw attention to the use of images that has or can have a specific impact on the population of a country.

4   It goes without saying that the example shown can and must also be cited as an example of how im-

ages can be used to manipulate.

5   From my own practice, I can cite the correction note made as part of a United Nations project that gave precise instructions on what kind of dashed line to use to depict the borders in the Middle East. It goes without saying that the map had to be changed to agree with different political convictions depending on where it was to be used.

6   Here I understand the term 'graphic design' to mean the deliberate use of images to convey something in a social context. See also the following statement by Vincent Perrottet (Les Graphistes Associés):

"I have the impression that every image is social. Every picture was made to socialize people. Interestingly, though, one could say that there are non-social images in the sense that they tend to create a distance between people. And there are images that bring people together, that inspire discussions, brotherliness, and even love. One shouldn't expect too much, but it is possible. When two people meet and then fall in love with the same image ...Thus, there are images that exist in order to separate people and others that exist in order to bring people together. So when we create social or cultural images, it is to cre-

pact and plays a role on the international, diplomatic stage. Whose interests graphic design represents and whose interests it does not, or what goals are pursued with it (and which are not), is the crucial discussion that should be held.[6]

Do Graphic Designers Have Anything to Do with Graphic Design?

Next, we will examine the assumption made in the introduction that we graphic designers are crucially involved in the creation of graphic design.[7]

Would something fundamentally change in our visual culture, in the impact of graphic design, if all graphic designers disappeared overnight? Is graphic design done by graphic designers at all?[8] What graphic design is done by graphic designers and which is not?

One could ask whether it is graphic design that is relevant or the graphic designers themselves. Perhaps we are not important at all. Perhaps we only make a minimal contribution—and that in a non-crucial place.

ate relationships and discussions. If we fail to do this, these are still images that ask questions of the individual. And these questions are always related to the individual's place in society."
    Translated from: NGBK working group, Sandy Kaltenborn, *Engagement und Grafik: Politisch/Soziales Engagement & Grafikdesign* (Berlin, 2000), p. 33.
7   From the introduction to the symposium (2019): "What applies to verbal language of course also applies equally to visual language, which today is significantly shaped by graphic designers."
8   The contributions to visual culture that are currently being made in the digital realm often come from non-professional graphic designers, whether on Instagram, TikTok, various image boards, or YouTube. The same of course also applies to the analog world—for example, the role of images or visual information in urban spaces.

Just look at the world of PowerPoint templates, website themes,[9] clipart, color schemes, online publishing, system fonts, and automatic typesetting, or the contribution that art, architecture, and club culture make to graphic design. Aren't we overestimating our role in the process of creating graphic design? Are there participants in this field who may know very well about the impact of graphic design and who consciously develop and use it—deliberately without the help of graphic designers? Perhaps it makes sense not to ask too much of us graphic designers. We also have to prove our assertions.[10] We have a long way to fall, and do we really want to be measured by that?

Next question: are we really honest? As Ingo Offermanns mentioned in his introduction, the oft-proclaimed responsible behavior in the discipline seems flimsy, and projects do not deliver what is promised elsewhere.[11] Are we really seriously interested in making a relevant social contribution from our discipline? Aren't we actually quite happy with the situation we are in? Our clients from business and culture pat us nicely on the back; one can make a decent living from the job; books, flyers and websites designed by us circulate around the world; and the confirmation within the discipline seems very reassuring thanks to social media and other formats that we have developed ourselves. So why change? Everything is so nice and peaceful, and it works.

Incidentally, one could also ask what interest lies behind the 'sedation' of our discipline. Don't we first have to 'empower,' 'mobilize,' and, to quote the design collective Brave New Alps,[12] "decolonize" ourselves and our discipline?[13]

Discontent

What if we want to acknowledge and exercise our newly discovered responsibility? What if we understand

9   Konrad Renner and Christoph Knoth in this volume, see pp. 169–174.
10   The assertion of impact and the assertion of a resulting responsibility.
11   Introduction to this volume, see pp. 11–17.
12   The work of the Brave New Alps collective is certainly a very important contribution: www.brave-new-alps.com.

Exhibition design (and publication series) *Wohnungsfrage* by Matthias Görlich,
Haus der Kulturen der Welt HKW, Berlin, 2015.

Book design by Matthias Görlich

Book design *Studienhefte Problemorientiertes Design* by Matthias Görlich, co-edited with
Jesko Fezer, Oliver Gemballa. Adocs, Hamburg, since 2012.

the network of dependencies—strong actors with their possibly questionable political, economic, or social interests—as an invitation to consciously engage with it in order to make a contribution?

What possibilities open up for us if we want to critically engage with these realizations? What are the options for us if the discomfort exceeds the sedation?

Possible Action: Giving Up

One option (and perhaps not the worst) would be to stop designing in light of what it can do.[14] This is not meant to be as polemical as it sounds. It is based on the recognition that a relevance to society as a whole can only develop in a network of strong actors and interests as described above. The roles in this network may be assigned, and interests are looked after. (But the question is, whose interests?)

Giving up is understandable here and may do less damage than a graphic design that cuts its teeth on its own excessive demands.

13   The designer Sandy Kaltenborn offers a dissenting opinion in a discussion and cites an excerpt from the publication *Der Kotti ist kein Ponyhof*:
"And NO, on the contrary, we have to team up with others and change ourselves and our practices as a result. A good designer sees the (social) mandate as more important than the discipline, I would say! What can art (or design) look like as an urban practice that laughs at the character of the work due to its market-based nature and which operationally marginalizes authorship? How can we use the economically determined reference systems of cultural production and their operations for a practice that equally leaves them behind? For a practice that is inscribed over years, that makes itself dependent on everyday scuffles, and that seeks a different mandate than the project? An art that cares about the issue of housing, the right to the city, and does not want to be a confirmation mirror game must invest in conflict. Investing in conflict means accepting a sociopolitical mandate and aligning your creative work with it.

This mandate can deviate from the economy to which one is subject per se. The creative desire then potentially moves in other vanishing lines, complicities, and reference systems. It also changes work. Productivity can also be a cup of tea that people don't really have time for. And art can be wrong."
Translated from Julia Brunner, Stefan Endewardt, Sandy Kaltenborn, *Der Kotti ist kein Ponyhof: Gestalten im sozialen Handgemenge*, 2019. Available online: www.hebbel-am-ufer.de/fileadmin/user_upload/HAU_ponyhof_heft_2019_FIN_A_WEB.pdf.
14   Tom Holert, *Civic City Cahier #3: Distributed Agency, Design's Potentiality*, eds. Jesko Fezer, Matthias Görlich (London, 2011), p. 27.

Possible Action: Rejection

Furthermore, the radical rejection of existing economic, cultural, political, and social contexts would be conceivable in order to confront what exists (an anti-position). Often, this ignores the fact that we are part of the system and, for example, the capitalist system has repeatedly shown how creatively it integrates the anti-position into its own mechanisms and makes it productive for its own purposes.[15] So perhaps it is not so easy. One option would be a 'selective anti-position' where appropriate.

As a direct reaction to the *First Things First* Manifesto, the American typeface designer Jeffery Keedy recommended to his colleagues: "Designers can make their biggest social and political impact by not designing." And: "If you are a corporate tool, at least be a good one." "Everyone knows the difference between engaging and deceptive messages. If you are doing work that you feel conflicted about, however, don't kid yourself that some pro bono work or anonymous culture jamming will even the score. It doesn't, and stop pretending you're an artist, because you're not."[16]

Possible Action: Retreat

In the sense of a 'classic understanding of authorship,' one option would be a retreat into the subjectivist, isolationist, into the maximum minimization of dependency in the expectation of the greatest possible freedom and independence. The question arises as to where this freedom lies and whether this does not simply create another form of dependence (possibly a more fatal one). Think of the precarious working situations in the field of culture and art. Also, especially with this option, one must ask to what extent we demobilize and disempower ourselves in a kind of 'anticipatory obedience' with this strategy.

15   Tomás Maldonado's remarks from the early 1970s, for example in: *Umwelt und Revolte: Zur Dialektik des Entwerfens im Spätkapitalismus* (Reinbek, 1972).
16   Jeffery Keedy (Mr. Keedy), 'Hysteria TM,' in: *Adbusters*, no. 37, 2001.
17   Gui Bonsiepe: "... the designer encoun-

Possible Action: Euphoria
Another possible action is a euphoric design practice:
the full recognition of being embedded in economic,
cultural, political, technological, and social forcefields
and, based on this, the demand for the maximum
opening of the discipline seem necessary to me. Opening not only in the sense of letting the world in, but in
the sense of a proactive approach to the world,[17] with
the knowledge that graphic design is created and has
an impact through dialogue, and with an awareness of
the actors, their interests, the contexts, and rituals.

Occupying Spaces, Transformative
Rather than Descriptive
Based on this position, the proclaimed responsibility of graphic designers can be examined and spaces can be identified and possibly occupied in which
their impact can take shape—an impact that is transformative and not just descriptive.
          Even more than the one revolutionary moment,
it seems to me to be the increasingly impatient questioning of the role and practice of design that breaks
up established traditions and patterns and thereby
opens up new spaces for action.[18]

Process, Problem-Oriented Rather
than Solution-Oriented
All of this requires that we develop a culture of 'getting your hands dirty,' that we be ready to seriously
doubt[19] and, consequently, also to seriously fail (some-

ters the difficulty of not simply being able to stick to a critical atti- tude toward reality and to remain in this posi- tion, but rather to in- tervene in this reali- ty with their actions in design. After all, design ultimately means the willingness to change reality by getting in- volved..." Translated

from: *Entwurfskultur und Gesellschaft: Ge- staltung zwischen Zen- trum und Peripherie* (Basel, 2009), p. 29 f. 18   I would like to ex- press my thanks to the digital and analog fo- rums that have emerged in the conflict-rid- den months since the symposium for the ex- change and for estab-

lishing a critical design discourse. 19   The design histo- rian and critic Jörg Stür- zebecher criticized the proclaimed but not se- riously pursued doubt within the design dis- cipline in March 2000 on the occasion of the symposium 'Die Kunst des Zweifelns' (The art of doubting), noting that

the manifestos of mod- ernism consist almost exclusively of state- ments; questions, by contrast, never appear in them.

thing that is so inherent to the design process) and free ourselves from the ideology of problem-solving on the path toward a deeper examination of how problems arise.[20]

Opinionated Design, Allowing Graphic Design to Change

We could, and we should, take sides for people and issues that we consider important, stand beside those who have not been adequately represented, and stop striving for (supposed) independence or even neutrality.[21] We should learn from our partners and allow our graphic design to change as a result.[22]

Perhaps this also requires placing the process above the idea of the work. Perhaps we need to kill some of our darlings.[23]

It is crucial that we be prepared to discuss it in formats like this publication, which is not only aimed at an audience interested in design, but creates this audience in the first place. However, this discussion

20   And also to accept and address the involvement in certain expectations, power relations, dependencies, interests, conflicts, etc. as something inherent in design practice, instead of concealing or supposedly resolving these conflicts. See also Chantal Mouffe, *Agonistik: Die Welt politisch denken* (Berlin, 2014).

21   Unfortunately, the postulate that there is a neutral infographic or a universal typeface or generally a neutral or universal design remains persistent. In my opinion, this is neither possible nor desirable.

22   Gestalten im sozialen Handgemenge' in: *Lechts und Rinks: Eine Auseinandersetzung mit dem Design der Neuen Rechten (Ta-gungsdokumente)*, eds. Michelle Christensen, Jesko Fezer, Bianca Herlo, Daniel Hornuff, Gesche Joost (Hamburg, 2020).

23   Here again I would like to point to the role of social media, to the mechanisms of competitions, exhibitions, and many publications that proclaim a social claim, but the works presented often do not have any effect on society outside of their own expanded discipline.

we want to work in social contexts, completely different questions arise in regard to visual authorship, personal style, distinction, and visual codes.

24   This does not speak against this privilege, but rather demands that it use this privilege properly to explore other forms of practice.

25   Wim Wenders, *The Act of Seeing: Texte und Gespräche* (Frankfurt a/M 1992), p. 32.

must be carried from here (with an awareness of the privileged, limited perspective of the university[24]) to the outside world, to the juries, magazines, neighbor-hoods, administrations, and decision-making bodies.

We are at a beginning. At an important one.

I would like to conclude with a quotation by Wim Wenders[25]:

"The most political decision you make is where you direct people's eyes. In other words, what you show people, day in and day out, is political... And the most politically indoctrinating thing you can do to a human being is to show him, every day, that there can be no change."

Graphic interlude by Paul Rutrecht

Thinking
Graphic Design

After the fine arts were singularized to 'art' in the German-speaking world in the middle of the eighteenth century,[1] they left applied art behind as the negative of their autonomy—an art whose creativity did not seem worthy of the effort of aesthetic reflection and which still has the reputation of not being real art. The reasons for this are attributes such as the fact that the works are commissioned, are products, have a purpose, and are reproduced, as well as the compensation practice associated with this 'commercial art.' All these are elements that were contrary to the then new ideal of artistry in the spirit of "disinterested pleasure" and "purposeless play of forms" (Kant).[2] After all, in view of the approaching democratization, it was about giving the artist the task of embodying the model for the citizen, who trusts in his creative powers.[3] Artistic creativity under the sign of autonomy was the strategic weapon to achieve the emancipation from the role of the subject to that of a free

1   While German and Czech refer to 'art' in reference to the autonomous fine arts, the term 'fine' is still used to characterize art in English, Italian, French, and Dutch. However, the question of why and possible historical and political developments must remain open here. The specif-

ically German development has not only influenced the terminology, but also cultural ways of thinking that are discussed here.
2   Immanuel Kant, *Kritik der Urteilskraft* (Darmstadt, 1963), § 16, p. 69 ff.
3   Jochen Schmidt, *Die Geschichte des Geniegedankens in der*

deutschen Literatur, Philosophie und Politik 1750–1945, vol. 1 (Darmstadt, 1985), p. 9 f.

citizen. According to the ideology, creativity, a natural resource and an innate potential, offered everyone, regardless of their social status, the same opportunity to shape their lives independently. Exaggerated to the ingenuity of a subject, the creative has become the emancipatory instance of the enlightened bourgeois world, and the establishment of art museums is a consequence of this.

It is therefore essential to address the question of the impact of graphic design through the historical conditions from aesthetics and art, since the hierarchy between fine and applied art has developed in this very founding context. To this day it still dictates the criteria and shape of the arguments.

The State of a Disproportion

In every major city in Europe and beyond, there are several museums and/or exhibition venues that are dedicated to fine art as autonomous art. Museums with a focus on the 'applied,' on the other hand, are much rarer.

Museums of the latter type were founded in the second half of the nineteenth century. Most of them were created as museums of applied art out of discomfort with the design of industrially produced goods, which was seen as being of poor quality. Their initiators saw the creation of model collections as the appropriate countermeasure for designers and the general public to train and improve their taste for outstanding objects in art history such as paintings, sculptures, and vases. The first was the V&A (Victoria & Albert Museum) in London, formerly the South Kensington Museum, followed by the MAK (Museum of Applied Arts) in Vienna, which was initially called the Museum für Kunst und Industrie (Museum of Art and Industry). In this context, graphic design began to become a discipline of collecting in the twentieth century, especially with a focus on books in the mindset of bibliophilia, the art of printing, and ornamental engravings and prints. This orientation was expanded in the second half of the century to include poster collections and artist's books. Graphic design was consequently spread across a few museums with a focus on 'applied' art and shared attention, mostly as book art and/or graphic art, with other departments such as European handicrafts, East Asian art, design, and fashion. As applied art, it was consequently subject to the production-aesthetic paradigm of handicrafts, applied art, design, and industrial design: handicrafts as the production of unique pieces by hand had the criterion of authenticity since the time of industrialization; applied art as serial production via manufacture; design, where idea and execution need not be done by the same person; and industrial design, which adapts the design to mechanized production in large quantities.[4]

Graphic design thus plays the role of one discipline among several, and in the context of museums it has a significantly lesser presence than autonomous art.

In contrast, reality clearly speaks a different language. After all, today graphic design—in its differentiation into many specializations and depending on constantly evolving technologies and media—permeates all areas of life and has been the tool for communication, information, and visualization par excellence in our society since the digital revolution. Its impact extends from instruction leaflets for pills to the design of books, posters, websites, corporate identities, and the formation of cultural trends at a wide variety of interfaces.

This disproportion between presence in reality and the reflection of the relevance of graphic design can be traced to the universities and art schools. After all, neither applied art nor graphic design are part of the curriculum of a degree in art history, nor do design schools teach the history of design, and instead mostly focus on the history of visual autonomous art.

4   Eva Linhart, 'Buchkunst im Museum,' in: Imprimatur: Neue Folge 14, 2015, Ute Schneider (ed.) for Gesellschaft der Bibliophilen (Munich, 2015), p. 157 ff.
5   Cennino Cennini, Trattato della Pittura, (Florence, 1859).

One cause of this is the hierarchy of fine and applied art. There are reasons why this has developed. After all, fine art developed art theory at the Italian courts in the early Renaissance for the purposes of legitimation and in the context of renegotiating political power relationships. The first treatise that marks this turn is by Cennino Cennini,[5] who expands the tradition of instructions for craftsmen with art-theoretical considerations on the imitation of nature and the role of the artist.[6] He justifies—or, more precisely, constructs an argumentation for—why art is not a craft and not a "service" or way of "earning a living," but rather a discipline of the seven fine arts: consequently, it is an intellectual activity worthy of the free man.[7] To this end, he developed arguments such as that an artist should not be paid, but honored, because his wonderful achievement is neither measurable nor calculable.[8] These discursive strategies of social emancipation, ennobling of artistic achievement, and its staging in centers of power were predestined to see art as the suitable projection medium for realizing bourgeois ideals of freedom.

A Question of False Classification

The development from the fine arts to 'art' moved the realization of creative genius into the core of aesthetic endeavors. In view of the infinite potential of the gifted, this was presented in terms of production aesthetics as a process tending toward open ambiguity. The associated mental concepts relieved art of

6   Erwin Panofsky, *Idea: Ein Beitrag zur Begriffsgeschichte der älteren Kunsttheorie* (Berlin, 1982), p. 23.
7   Martin Warnke, *Hofkünstler: Zur Vorgeschichte des modernen Künstlers* (Cologne, 1985), p. 52 ff.
8   Ibid., p. 55. On the construction of the argumentation regarding the upgrading of art alongside the imitation of nature and talent, cf. Eva Linhart, 'Zum Begriff der Naturnachahmung bei Cennino Cennini,' unpublished essay, 1987.
9   Günter Oesterle, 'Vorbegriffe zu einer Theorie der Ornamente: Kontroverse Formprobleme zwischen

the task of imitating nature (mimesis) in order to use ornaments to posit a non-figurative art and later to realize it as abstraction.[9] Its focus is the inner world of the artistic subject. According to the claim to authenticity, it has since been about the "turn of art on itself" (Boehm), which deals with the questioning of the means used as their own creative process[10]—an understanding that also shaped the critical introspection on the exaggerated gestures in art in the twentieth century.

In view of industrial production methods in the late-nineteenth century, autonomous artist subjects, who must answer only to themselves, positioned themselves in opposition to mass society, the "factory goods of nature" produced "by the thousands" (Schopenhauer).[11] The ideal of an unappreciated genius developed.[12]

By contrast, the social relevance of graphic design comes from completely different sources. The profession initially known as commercial or advertising art developed out of the profession of printing. Its role is defined in terms of a productive transmission of information in a socially constructive manner with the mandate to form a visual culture for a successful communication, while interpreting the possibilities of innovative reproduction technologies and media.[13]

This juxtaposition of autonomous art and graphic design makes it clear that there are two different contexts of pictorial productions, whose quality standards would have to be subject to very different

Aufklärung, Klassizismus und Romantik am Beispiel der Arabeske,' in: *Ideal und Wirklichkeit der bildenden Kunst im späten 18. Jahrhundert* (Berlin, 1984), pp. 119–139.
10   Gottfried Boehm, 'Mythos als bildnerischer Prozess,' in: *Mythos und Moderne: Begriff und Bild einer*

Rekonstruktion (Frankfurt/M, 1983), pp. 528–544.
11   Jochen Schmidt, op. cit., vol. 1, p. 467 f.
12   Eva Linhart, *Künstler und Passion: Ein Beitrag zur Genieästhetik der frühen Moderne, entwickelt an den Christusdarstellungen von James Sidney Ensor (1860–1949)*, en-

sor-christus.com/Dissertation.pdf.
13   Eva Linhart, 'Perspektiven,' in: 172 neue Buchobjekte: *Buchkunst und Grafik im Museum Angewandte Kunst weitergedacht*, exh. cat. and documentation of the collection of the book art and graphics at the Muse-

um Angewandte Kunst (Frankfurt/M, 2017), pp. 7–14.

systems of evaluation. The more acute problem, however, is that because applied art has so far not formed its own criteria and theory, an orientation toward the traditional standards of fine art is taking place.

The difficulties begin at one common interface, namely the production of images and their creativity. Although this allows for comparison, the lack of purpose of the one becomes a negative verdict of functionality for the other. It is not an original, not a unique piece, and the visual aspect works in the sense of the effectiveness of its mandate. This perceived deficit of graphic design is echoed in the presentation strategies of museums when the staging, in order to emphasize the uniqueness of designs, presents objects as unique pieces on pedestals or in frames.[14] Yet this doesn't work in terms of what, for instance, a poster has to accomplish. After all, it is not just a single printed image on paper, but must exist in the public context alongside other posters. Likewise, its expressive power must be integrative enough to effectively address its concerns to the respective target group. Furthermore, it must be so stimulating that it motivates sympathy. The degree of distribution as well as the client and the motivation play a decisive role, to name just a few criteria for its relevance.

A Plea for Rethinking

It is a fatal strategy for graphic design to enter into the dichotomy of form and content, even if only for methodological reasons. This division suggests that the two components are independent of each other. Yet the separation is not neutral, but rather, since Plato, the bearer of a tradition of thought[15] that assumes the content to be the mental and unalterable element as opposed to the accidental and interchangeable element of form.

This shows its effect in the concept of 'applied art' when it is understood as an art that garnishes the practical purpose in the sense of an accessory or imbues everyday objects with beauty or good form. Transferred to graphic design, this then results in a categorization that devalues its visual achievement as opposed to the content in terms of merely illustrative importance.[16] The intention behind this is to control it in order to dampen its sensual effect and its captivating power of suggestion. It is demonized as the 'seducer of the soul,' which is why Plato banished the arts from his ideal state.[17]

It is not necessary to refer to the Nazi era or advertising to show that graphic design is powerful. Its presence in the field of information and communication already shows the 'persuasive potential' that we 'actually' grant its visual quality. However, if we think of it as an interchangeable form that, depending on its skill, conveys the content more or less effectively in the sense of its topic, then it is only a means to an end without the corresponding shared responsibility and would then in fact only be a service.

Conversely, however, as the media and design theorist Christof Windgätter concludes, there is "no

14   The exhibition 'Give Love Back: Ata Macias und Partner: Eine Ausstellung zu der Frage, was angewandte Kunst heute sein kann' in 2014/15 at the Museum Angewandte Kunst dealt with these strategies. See Eva Linhart and Mahret Kupka: 'Gimme! Gimme! Gimme!@: Die Kuratorinnen der Ausstellung im Gespräch über Ata, das Museum und angewandte Kunst,' in: newspaper for the exhibition, (Berlin, 2014).
15   Cf: Heinz Paetzold, 'Der Mensch,' in: Philosophie: Ein Grundkurs, Ekkehard Martens (ed.), (Hamburg, 1985), p. 445.
16   On the importance of visuality under the primacy of the logo, cf.: Gottfried Boehm. 'Zu einer Hermeneutik des Bildes,' in: Seminar: Die Hermeneutik und die Wissenschaften, Hans-Georg Gadamer and Gottfried Boehm (eds.), (Frankfurt/M), 1978), pp. 444–471.
17   Heinz Paetzold, op. cit.
18   Christof Windgätter, Epistemogramme: Vom Logos zum Logo in den Wissenschaften, lecture at Hochschule für Grafik und Buchkunst Leipzig (Leipzig, 2012), p. 12 f. The author shows how the concept of form and content with regard to an optimal reading expectation results in an anti-perceptual functionalism that leads to the widespread error of understanding content instead of seeing printed materials. Marc Rölli, 'Design als soziales Phänomen: Wider das funktionalistische Paradigma,' in: Social Design: Gestalten für die Transformation der Gesellschaft, Claudia Banz (ed.), (Bielefeld, 2016), pp. 27–34.

specialized knowledge without design knowledge"[18]: graphic design determines the culture of information, communication, and imagery of our everyday life. In the sense that it is always intentional and concerned with enforcing its interests, it shares responsibility for the quality of the co-authorship. The comparison to autonomous art is productive for determining the extent to which this is the case. For the sake of self-determination and in a methodical exaggeration of the production-aesthetic reflection on its means, it declares form its content.

However, if autonomous art from the delimited area of the white cube only relates to life[19] as a model, as an aesthetic transformation, then the traditional place of graphic design is everyday life. Here it has an immediate, context-dependent, and varied effect. Therefore, a reflection on its potential impact is all the more urgent if its reception is not to be unconscious. It is a responsibility of civil society as a whole to see through connoisseurship by means of the ability of the complex and power-constituting context of the effectiveness of graphic design if we as consumers are not to be merely seduced by its effects.

19   Günther Oesterle, op. cit.

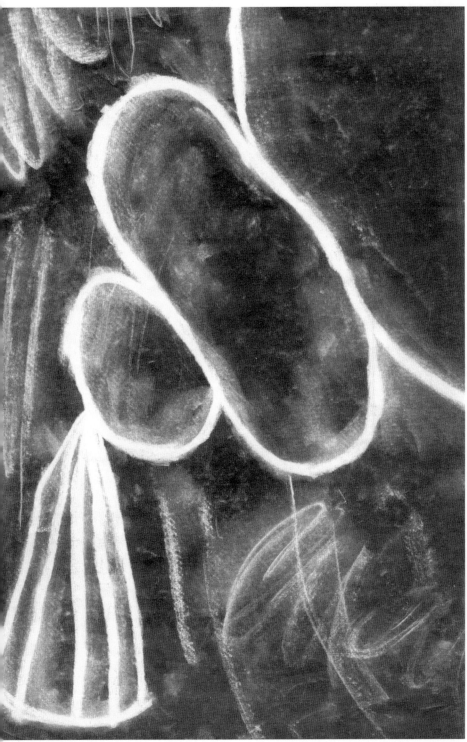

Graphic interlude by Maud Serradell

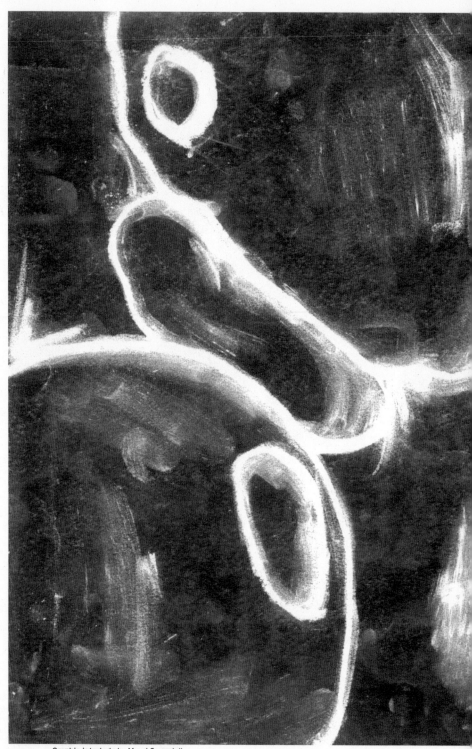

Graphic interlude by Maud Serradell

Anoushka Khandwala

On The Encroachment of Modernism
Class, Culture and Colonialism

When we go to art schools and get an elite education, we automatically say, "our design is better than yours."

Amy Suo Wu (2020)

In most countries, students pay universities in exchange for an education. This exchange of money for knowledge fuels the illusion that thanks to this elite education, these students know more about design than their clients. However, placing images and words together is not something that requires a degree. Actually, the client is paying for the designer's ability to sculpt a visual language to grab the attention of the consumer. As a result, the client's product or service will be more engaging and easier to use, ultimately becoming something that the consumer wishes to purchase.

This is palatable design. Design that differentiates but still fits in, that is desirable but not too intimidating—design that constructs an ideal that the consumer wishes to buy into. Today, this palatability often manifests as a modernist aesthetic that heralds the clean-cut typeface, sharply edged grid lines, and white space. It praises scarcity, and shuns maximalism.

This aesthetic, with its overarching desire to neatly box information in, to de-clutter, to do 'less with more,' encroaches on our visual culture until there is little personality left. 'While much of this stems from the proliferation of digital devices that require designs to function on multiple platforms, somehow, this urge for simplicity has evolved from a sensible design decision to a stifling industry standard. We see it in the 'new build' architectural developments that snake into increasingly gentrified cities, the clients who desire a 'timeless' feel for their brand, the interfaces that seek to tidy up information in the name of 'improving the user experience'.

In an article published on *Elephant Magazine*'s website in 2020, Louise Benson described how "middle class modernism" took over the world. "The original ideology of these modernist and brutalist objects and buildings remains at odds with their contemporary use. Many were designed in the wake of the destruction endured during the Second World War, a time of austerity and scarcity." Today, Benson writes, a house formerly designed by London County Council can sell for more than a million pounds, divorcing the homes from their original utopian aims of improved housing for all—"their history reduced to little more than a footnote in a sales brochure." By repurposing this aesthetic for consumer profit, while disavowing the conditions that produced it, we detach the design from its purpose, and subsume modernism into nothing more than a desirable trend.

In an interview I conducted with designer Elizabeth Critchlow for AIGA Eye on Design (2018), she articulates how a fetishization of minimalism can be an indicator of class. "People can afford to be minimalist because they can afford to throw things away, but know that they can re-buy it should they need to again in the future. They have that financial stability. I was raised in a way that you don't throw anything away, because you might need it again in the future, and going out and buying it again isn't an option." Critchlow explains that the idea of 'less is more' is connected to the guise of expensiveness. In short, scarcity costs more.

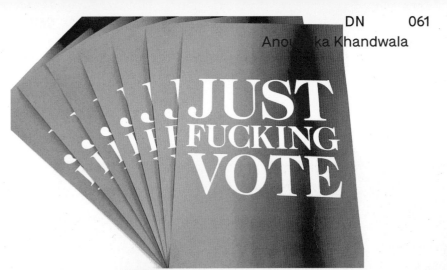

Poster design by Anoushka Khandwala encouraging young people
to vote in the 2017 U.K. General Election.

Illustration by Anoushka Khandwala for a roundtable discussing indigenous
approaches to design for the climate crisis.

Website design by Anoushka Khandwala for Gaysians, an organization
that brings together resources for queer South Asians.

Website design by Anoushka Khandwala in collaboration with Kelly Walters to archive an exhibition entitled 'Open Dialogue: Artists and Designers of Afro-Caribbean Descent', Central Saint Martins, 2018.

In a roundtable entitled 'Decolonizing Means Many Things To Many People—Four Practitioners Discuss Decolonizing Design' published on AIGA Eye on Design in 2020, Ramon Tejada echoes these sentiments, explaining how these aesthetic trends intersect with graphic design—"Design has taught us to concentrate everything into these sleek clean things, which usually is not what most of our cultures look like. The reality of everything is incredibly complicated, diverse, beautiful, messy." Not only is this 'clean' aesthetic symbolic of the rich, it is also dismissive of many visual traditions around the world. It's an ideal to be chased, a representation to be coveted, the pinnacle of 'good taste.' By praising this particular modernist aesthetic as 'good design' and relegating visual languages of different cultures to the labels of 'kitsch' or 'tacky,' this way of thinking has successfully wormed its way into mainstream discourse and established itself as the dominant way to communicate information.

Consider the concept of design thinking, and the ideology it promotes, the idea that it is a 'solution-based' approach to problem solving. By framing a brief as a problem to be solved we ultimately fall into a binary way of thinking, which again seeks to algorithmize the graphic design process into set boxes. Design work is never finished. Society and culture are in constant flux, which means that new 'problems' are created every day. There's a finality to the term 'solution,' which is disingenuous. Ian Lynam speaks to Emily Gosling in an interview for Creative Boom, and declares that "In regard to design… I am not interested in outcomes or 'solutions'—that is the rhetoric of genocide… I want untidy endings."

If we think about the history of colonialism, the relationship between settlers claiming the land of indigenous communities has parallels with modernist ideology dominating design.

Consider missionaries, who would travel to countries where they believed the indigenous people needed to be 'saved' by religion. Often, this intent was used to disguise the fact that they were sent to civilize native populations, thus making them easier to control by colonial powers. Today, similar attitudes manifest in the white savior complex, where guilt leads to people attempting to help those deemed 'less fortunate' than themselves. This help, however, is often supplied on the terms of the saviors themselves—I will help you if you convert to this specific religion, if you choose to accept my version of the truth, if you give up your 'false idols.' By stating the terms of the transaction, the savior seeks to retain the power in this relationship and to drain the recipient of any agency they may have possessed.

Put this scenario in the context of modern-day cities, where gentrification often seeks to displace immigrant/poor communities in order to impose a high street of soulless coffee shops, smoothing over any visual diversity that existed before. This aesthetic, again, rears its ugly head in an attempt to clean up visual languages that are seen as 'bad design.' Ishwari Giga writes in her 2020 dissertation about the connections between gentrification and colonization, and how the effects of this can be seen in the design of the city. Giga observes the similarities between the design of the shopfronts in Southall, South London and those in India. From the garish typography in curly, 'ethnic looking' fonts, aimed to coax in a South Asian shopper by reminding them of home, to the chaotic layout of the wares inside, the store is designed to create a familiar, almost nostalgic experience for the customer. By dotting a Zara on every corner of the city, these experiences, which are pertinent to a particular culture, are flattened into a homogenous style, deeming a different kind of consumer—who tends to be richer and whiter—as more important. "At the heart of gentrification, is the method of designing a sleek and clean future where capitalism plays a central role and community is manufactured." (Giga, 2020)

Anoushka Khandwala

Modernism, in the context of design, increasingly feels like a tool to aid capitalism. And the problem doesn't just lie with this particular style—it is rooted in how we teach design. In an attempt to rationalize the place of communication design in the world, students are often taught that design has the power to change the world, resulting in an inflated sense of self-importance. The ideology of design thinking then emboldens students to frame themselves as agents of design—saviors of a kind—who enter the world to identify 'problems' that they can design 'solutions' for. This results in a god complex that shapes the culture of the industry, and how we view ourselves. Clara Balaguer urges designers to fight against this instinct in an interview with Walker Art's The Gradient. "Challenge yourself to dismantle what the (Ivy League?) man has told you is ugly, uncouth, primitive, savage. Finessing popular voice into a missive of power... doesn't mean you have to dumb your design education down. It means you get to throw out the notion that the populace is dumb... and that the formally educated have all the answers."

working and searching

working and searching
working and fighting
working and finding

working and searching
working and fighting
working and finding
finding and seeing
seeing and communication

working and searching
working and fighting
working and finding
finding and seeing
seeing and communication
challenge the past
challenge the present

but first of all

but first of all
designers must be true
to themselves

working and searching
working and fighting

working and searching
working and fighting
working and finding
finding and seeing

working and searching
working and fighting
working and finding
finding and seeing
seeing and communication
challenge the past

working and searching
working and fighting
working and finding
finding and seeing
seeing and communication
challenge the past
challenge the present
challenge the future

but first of all
designers must be true

but first of all
designers must be true
to themselves

design is attitude
helmut schmid

Graphic interlude by Frieder Oelze

In-ah Shin (Feminist Designer Social Club)

What Is a *True* Designer?

It is necessary and empowering to talk about possibilities of graphic design itself. However, do we feel the same way when we are asked whether the working conditions allow experimentation and exploration of exciting possibilities of this professional field? Many would feel differently. The numbers say so. 78.1% of designers responded they are working more hours than they are paid for while only 8% of designers are members of a trade union.[1] According to a recent survey, the *2019 Design Census*,[2] job satisfaction decreased from 82% (2017) to 65% (2019) due to the unstable nature of the industry. What is more, designers based in rural areas are more dissatisfied with their conditions.

     As a graphic design student, I was trained to be a citizen designer, to acknowledge my obligation to the community, and to be always mindful of the impact that my work might have. I guess I was a good student. The first thing I did after getting fired from my first job at a design agency was emailing non-for-profit or social enterprises for work opportunities. Working at a design agency, I was mostly unhappy. I was usually working from 10 am to 4 am the next morning and spent most of my time retouching photographs, turning tacky spaces into luxurious backdrops. I wanted to at least work at a place where designing did not involve deception. But I ended up being just as unhappy at non-for-profits and social enterprises. They didn't

1   *Graphic Design Surveyed*, (London, 2015).
2   www.aiga.org/ 2019-design-census.

What Is a *True* Designer?

see the value in quality design. Then, reality hit with the #sexual_abuse_in_the_art_world hashtag in 2016. People started to wonder 'where have all the female designers gone?' leading to the calling out of gender inequality in the design industry.

There I realized that only a few lucky designers get to shine in design magazines while numerous studies show that talent is not the only determining factor in who makes it. I came to the conclusion that the design community never cared to mentor female graphic designers, nor did they make an effort to advance diversity. Everyone is simply too busy dealing with the 10 am to 4 am routine, believing the exorbitant hours would make them into sincere and dedicated, or true designers. This notion served as a big threat to me. I had no ambition other than to stay in my lane and continue my career as long as I possibly could. But the question 'where have all the female designers gone?' sounded like 'have you seen any seasoned female designer? Do you think you can be so lucky?'

Besides, while reading the interviews looking for the secret recipe to a long-lasting career, one thing I noticed was that you need a topic of interest that you could experiment and play with forever. Unfortunately, I couldn't settle on any design style or a subject matter to dedicate my entire career to. One thing that interested me at that time was Korean culture that felt foreign to me after eleven years of living overseas. I made good friends writing short pieces about contemporary Korean culture, a few of them being colleagues such as Heewon Beak, Smila Park, and Juon Kim. They are core members of the BIYN Basic Income 'Youth' Network who envision new possibilities that look at a basic income for young Koreans, while also advocating the importance of handling the matter from a feminist perspective. They do not compromise when it comes to what they think is right and keep on finding their own way of doing things. As I listened to them discussing new ways of initiating social movements, I was able to clarify what I was look-ing for. While I easily become bored with things, the habitual ennui could be channeled toward a drive to try new things. What I wanted was change and I was itching to see what design could do in the process. My main concern back then was that I, myself, might be contributing to solidifying the patriarchy by main-taining the status quo and blindly following the prec-edents. That 'spark of joy' in me seemed like some-thing that I can count on for always.

So, in July 2018, I founded the Feminist Designer So-cial Club (FDSC) with Somi Kim, Yuni Ooh, and Mean-young Yang. I was responsible for drafting the key prin-ciples behind FDSC. In doing so, I twisted the question 'where have all the female designers gone.' Although the question calls out gender inequality, it could also be a threatening epigram for aspiring female design-ers, painting a dead end for them. I replaced 'where' with 'how' and listed seven reasons why with com-mon phrases we hear every day:

1.   long working hours and toxic work environ-ments where staying up all night is considered an indicator of dedication (Don't tell me you're headed home already?", "She's no more con-cerned about the work, but about her kids");
2.   poor salary or unpaid internship ("You're not here to work, but to learn");
3.   tendency to blindly praise only a handful of male designers, lifting them up to a god-like-status ("He is a legend, period. No words needed");
4.   stigmatizing femininity ("I don't like to talk in front of people. It is not in my nature");
5.   bro-culture based on university ties and re-gionality ("Be careful, the design scene is a very close-knit and small community");
6.   sexual abuse ("Who are you trying to impress dressed like that?");

What Is a *True* Designer?

7.   defending the status quo ("It's how it's always been and always will be").

FDSC's mission statement is simple. We're reversing the above.

1.   We keep our working hours to 9–6. Working all night should not be an indication of our professional dedication. It is a form of discrimination against a socially underrepresented group. We work together to improve our working conditions.
2.   We do not work for free. We will take pride in the work we do and ask for the compensation we deserve. Also, we value the work of others like we do ours.
3.   Women are raised to be modest in social situations. As we work hard to improve our skills, we will make sure others recognize them.
4.   We stand against bro-culture based on university ties and regionality. When we hire or find collaborators, we will make sure we provide equal opportunities to socially underrepresented groups.
5.   We will critique on fair grounds. When we talk about a good design, we should provide good reasons and be open to anyone who wishes to contribute to the discussion.
6.   We will not tolerate any form of sexual abuse.
7.   We recognize that we were born and raised in a patriarchal society. Following precedents may seem natural and we may find the alternative ways to be uneasy and time-consuming. While we work together to build a new community, we will make sure no one suffers for the greater cause. We will create a safe space where everyone can be themselves. We treat one another with respect and support.

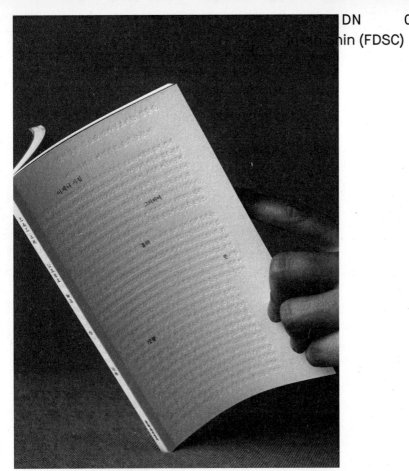

Book design by In-ah Shin (FDSC)

Book design by In-ah Shin (FDSC)

What Is a *True* Designer?

Poster design by In-ah Shin (FDSC)

Website design by In-ah Shin (FDSC)

These principles provide the members with a bigger picture with directions for the future and steps to be taken. However, the last thing we'd want to do is to burden our members for the sake of maintaining FDSC. The change might not be applicable for everyone immediately, but that should not be grounds to shame anyone. Therefore, the actual activities of FDSC are designed to provide substantial benefits and enjoyable experiences to participating members. I believe the change on an individual level can occur more effectively where as a group of people may require more time and effort. So FDSC should provide a glimpse of a possible feminist society, which would accelerate the changes on an individual level.

To put the above philosophy into practice, we designed the following framework;

A.   FDSC is not a club hosting good-willed social gathering. Rather, it is a community that is beneficial to its members. In other words, we require our members to be ready to share what they have and participate more actively, which does not necessarily mean flaunting spectacular portfolios. So FDSC is not an 'open community' where anyone can join any time, nor an exclusive club of fancy designers. Rather we have a certain admission process. Those who are willing to join FDSC should apply for and attend 'Open Day,' which we host twice a year. On 'Open Day' we introduce our context and principles, and what they can expect from FDSC.

B.   Though perhaps in a modest way, we try our best to compensate for any type of contribution rather than rely on volunteers. To join FDSC one has to pay a membership fee of 30 USD per month. Some find it surprising, however it was necessary to secure rewards. FDSC now has

19 members in the administrative team, each taking on specific roles like managing FDSC's online platforms, finances, emails, gatherings, activities, and more. Members can organize small gatherings and they are also asked to set up a fee and take minimum of 50 USD for their work.

C.   We write and update our Code of Conduct twice a year to reflect changes. FDSC started with 50 members and quadrupled just in the past two years. A community of 50 compared to 200 requires quite a different set rules and management. This document started out as a single-page, now it has extended to nine pages!

D.   Our Code of Conduct states that the members are to eat good food and have a great time after any form of meeting or gathering. We also use language that lightens things up and focus on making sure participating in FDSC activities are fun. In doing so, we also purposely maintain the typical Korean customs but reappropriate them in our own way. For example, we hosted a sports day called 'Woondonghae' ('Woondonghae (운동해)' can be interpreted as 'sunny sports', 'do sports' and also 'sports day'). Activities included typical Korean sports day games such as 'tug-of-war', 'three-legged race' and 'breaking baskets.' Last Christmas season, we also hosted a general assembly as an end-of-year party with a dress code of 'over the top.' It was like a Halloween party where designers turned out as dragons, shamans, or aliens and sang karaoke together. This year with Covid-19, we hosted an online general assembly with a theme of 'FDSC Airlines.' Attendees dressed up as tourists in front of their cameras, while a series of presentations were designed as in-flight entertainment and continued to 'Group Bus Tour' and 'Campfire.'

FDSC is known to the public, thanks to our activities such as the podcast *Design FM*,[3] online conference *FDSC STAGE*,[4] workshop *Fflag-high*,[5] blog *FDSC.txt*,[6] portfolio reviews, recent participation at MMCA(The National Museum of Modern and Contemporary Art, Korea) exhibition *2020 MMCA Asia Project: Looking for Another Family*, '40 Designers You Should Know'[7] program, as well as our presence in online channels such as Instagram(@fdsc.kr), Facebook(@fdsc.kr), Twitter(@fdsc_kr)[8] and Youtube(@fdsctv). Yet I am proudest of our community when I notice the changes within our members. It is moments like when I see a member who suddenly shows growth in skills (which often means a positive change in attitude), or when they get work through the FDSC network or when they collaborate together outside their university connections, or when networks germinate. There are many such moments within FDSC, which are all positive signs of change for me.

Despite being proud of FDSC as a community and what we've achieved so far, it doesn't mean we

3   *Design FM* is a podcast that talks about topics around our principles. We invite FDSC members to talk about their professional life. This show was designed to present many ways of being a designer as there seems to be quite a distorted notion of a 'true designer' in South Korea.

4   *FDSC STAGE* literally provides FDSC members with a stage to speak about their work. The first stage was launched in June 2020 with 450+ audiences. Due to the measures in response to Covid-19, it was held online. Yet we hope to see this stage come to life later on and become a major design conference.

5   *fflag-high* is a summer vacation student workshop. In this workshop, students form small groups to design a flag in collaboration with one another using contemporary Korean feminist phrases. It was designed to provide FDSC members with a chance to become a mentor and to address the competitive learning environment that most students face. You can check the results by searching #fflaghigh on Instagram.

6   *FDSC.txt* is a Notion blog featuring results from our internal writing club or pieces about FDSC. ww.notion.so/fdsc/4891810e6f-6c44f4ad09082d1 59f436b?v= e8263d-1369c24842b 14a5a807861c3dc.

7   MMCA invited FDSC to participate in *2020 MMCA Asia Project: Looking for Another Family*. FDSC proposed a work called *FDSC NEWS*, a news desk showcasing our activities in a news format and hosted a program called *40 Designers You Should Know*. In this program, FDSC designers were asked to speak at the *FDSC NEWS* set and introduce the work of other female designers they think deserve attention. They were asked to choose a designer whom they are not friends with and to use this opportunity to highlight the designers who are not yet well known. It was distributed via YouTube, and is archived on FDSC YouTube channel.

8   We use our online channels to promote works by FDSC members (using the hashtag #페디소 meaning 'Introducing feminist designers') as well as promoting activities by FDSC.

are perfect. Our current task is to write up a managing manual so the community may run more autonomously. Recently we also initiated a team called the 'Violence Prevention Vigilante,' to prepare manuals for any potential violence or conflict. The team will host regular feminist workshops to examine how we could define 'violence' in FDSC and in doing so fine-tune the understanding of FDSC's core values and principles. The process so far has been an eye-opening experience for me, unexpectedly providing me a space to face my own weakness. The journey with FDSC has always been like this, it continuously unfolds

new possibilities for me. It comes as no surprise, after all, that there's no place on earth that has achieved equality and that the path toward it will always open up new possibilities. Wouldn't that be what *true* designers aspire to see? Today, when someone asks me 'where have all the female designers gone', I say "look, they're here" as I learnt from FDSC. Likewise, now I know I'm going to stay in my career as long as I want. There's no dead end. Even if there's no precedent, I'll find a way, like I did with my friends in FDSC.

In-ah Shin (FDSC)

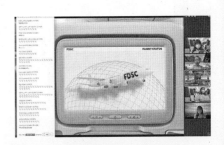

FDSC's end of year party.
Photo Soyoung Jeon.

WHAT MOVES YOU?

TURBOCAPITALISM

WHAT IDEALS DO YOU FOLLOW?

NEOLIBERALISM

WHAT IS THE VALUE OF YOU WORK?

IDEOLOGY

DO YOU HAVE ANY SOCIAL RESPONSIBILITY?

NONSENSE

WHERE DO YOU POSITION YOUR DESIGN WORK?

Graphic interlude by Leon Lechner

Sophia Prinz

Ficticious Characters

The political dimension of graphic design is not limited to the task of making catchphrases, slogans, and protest symbols visible and legible in struggles for cultural hegemony. The aesthetic material itself—that is, the form of the writing and its surfaces—also contributes to the political statement. Moreover, one could go so far as to claim that the political, understood as the opening of a space for processes of negotiation beyond established practices and discourses,[1] only becomes reality when established orders of knowledge, perception, and practice are broken down. Thus, the political can lie particularly within a removal of meaning.

Here it is worthwhile to take another look at the fundamental relationship between power and writing. As has become clear since the post-structuralist turn toward the materiality of text, writing cannot be viewed as a simple expression of a pre-existing meaning or idea. Rather, it must be assumed, conversely, that writing in the broadest sense—that is, understood as differentiating forms and putting them into relation—precedes conceptual thinking and acting. Only through concrete, practical engagement with the external world—meaning the discursive, material, and sensory formations of the dispositive—do people develop a functioning perceptual and practical knowledge that enables them to orient themselves intuitively in the socio-material world.

1   The following remarks are primarily based on Foucault's concept of power and criticism. A similar understanding of politics, which locates the 'political' beyond established social orders and power relations, can also be found in the works of Ernesto Laclau/Chantal Mouffe and Jacques Rancière.

Writing is therefore not a passive bearer of a political message or a mere representation of a knowledge of power, but rather brings out the orders that underlie all perception, thought, and action. But what exactly does this fundamental insight mean for the thesis that the political aspect of writing does not lie solely or even primarily in its legibility, but also in the removal of meaning?

Xu Bing's *Book from the Sky* (1987–91) could provide some indications of this. In one version of this work, the artist printed black characters on three vertical-format scrolls of Chinese newspaper. These logograms are not legible: they come from a pool of 4,000 fictitious characters that Xu developed based on existing character elements, called radicals, and carved into wooden type. Since Chinese comprises around 90,000 characters, of which a maximum of 4000 are in active use, even highly educated Chinese people cannot easily identify the fictitious characters as such. It is thus a specific form of illegibility that remains related to the basic practices of the production of meaning, but resists understanding.

The political dimension of this illegibility can only be understood against the background of the Chinese governmentality, which has always been closely linked to a culture of writing. Without a sophisticated 'graphic regime'[2] supported by the elite class of the literati, the establishment and maintenance of the centrally organized Chinese empire would not have been possible. And even after the communist Cultural Revolution, during which intellectuals were disempowered and 're-educated,' 'writing systems' (Kittler) played a central role, albeit in a different form. At first glance, Xu's duplication of characters can therefore be interpreted as a criticism of the Chinese machinery of propaganda and censorship: the overprinted newspaper reports appear as empty of content as Xu's fictional characters—though in another guise. While the latter seem to keep the meaning unresolved, the newspaper aims to narrow down the written content to a single reading—the truth approved by the party. But we would do the work injustice if we interpreted it merely as a negation of the ideological games with the truth. After all, it also refers to other power effects of writing—these include not least the reforms implemented by the Chinese government to simplify and standardize Chinese characters, which reduced the number of strokes within a single character to a maximum of 35 and specified a certain number of standard characters for general use. Even if Xu Bing himself is not uncritical of the script reform,[3] *Book from the Sky* does not take a clear position on it: it could be understood as a satire on the decadent excesses of meaning of the ancient Chinese culture of writing and as a criticism of the sprawling imperial government administration (which, however, continued under the communist government). Conversely, it could also be interpreted as a reminiscence of the calligraphic tradition of the cursive script cultivated by the literati, which largely distanced itself from its designative function in favor of the aesthetic impression of the gestural stroke. Such an interpretation would also make sense insofar as many of the simplified characters, which previously originated in the elitist cursive script, served as the basis for the communist script reform. In contrast to the literati, however, Xu deliberately dispensed with individual expression.[4] The appearance of the characters he designed is based on a widespread typeface that has been used since the Song dynasty in

2   Cf. Hajime Nakatani, 'Imperious Griffonage: Xu Bing and the Graphic Regime,' *Art Journal*, vol. 68, no. 3, 2009, pp. 6–29.

3   In a conversation in 1999, Xu explains why the script reform was particularly memorable for his generation: "My generation of artists has a very strange relationship with words. During the Cultural Revolution, Mao was promoting simplified characters. We spent a lot of time memorizing new words. Then they would change the words the next year. And then they would change them again.... It was really confusing. Not only with respect to language but culturally." (Simon Leung, Janet A. Kaplan, 'Pseudo-Languages: A Conversation with Wenda Gu, Xu Bing, and Jonathan Hay,' *Art Journal*, 1999, vol. 58, no. 3, pp. 86–99, p. 94.

4   In the same conversation Xu makes clear: "I'm not particularly attracted to calligraphy because it is too self-expressive, too individualistic, too emotional for my purposes." (Simon Leung, Janet A. Kaplan, op. cit. p. 89).

the twelfth century for book and newspaper printing and must therefore look familiar to a broad Chinese audience.[5]

Even though these interpretive approaches only scratch the surface of the multiple cultural-historical allusions of *Book from the Sky*[6]—the history of Chinese written culture is extremely complex— they can be used to draw some conclusions about the question posed earlier of the political effects of writing and non-meaning. As was already alluded to, Xu Bing's play with legibility and illegibility demonstrates that writing can open up a space of possibility for critical practice even if it does not itself convey a literal statement.

Here, with Foucault, 'critical practice' is understood as a performative attitude which, based on the perceptual and practical knowledge gained in a dispositive, relates itself to that dispositive in a critical and distancing manner. A critical practice can therefore never claim to be final, but always exists in relation to the historically and culturally specific

5   The choice of printing technique can also be seen as a critical commentary on the Eurocentric history of media and technology, which declares printing with movable type to be a European invention, even though this technique was developed in China 400 years earlier.

6   For an up-to-date, in-depth examination of Xu Bing's oeuvre, see Sarah E. Fraser, Yu-Chieh Li, (eds.), *Xu Bing: Beyond the Book from the Sky* (Singapore, 2020.)

7   Michel Foucault, 'What is Critique?', Sylvère Lotringer (ed.), *The Politics of Truth* (New York, 1997), pp. 23–82, pp. 29, 28.

8   For example, Roland Barthes says:

"To create meaning is very easy, our whole mass culture elaborates meaning all day long; to suspend meaning is already an infinitely more complicated enterprise— it is an 'art.'" (Roland Barthes, 'Literature and Signification,' *Critical Essays* (Evanston, 1972), pp. 261–279, p. 272).

9   Theodor W. Adorno, *Aesthetic Theory* (London/ New York, 2002), p. 78.

10   Christoph Menke characterizes this failure as follows: "Aesthetic experience is a negative event because it is an experience of the negation (the failure, the subversion) of (the nevertheless unavoidable effort at) understanding." (Christoph Menke, *The Sovereignty of Art. Aesthetic Negativity in Adorno and Derrida* (Cambridge US/ London, 1999), p. 24.

complexes of power and knowledge. In this sense he also describes criticism as an "art of not being governed quite so much"—that is, "not to be governed *like that*, by that, in the name of those principles, with such and such an objective in mind and by means of such procedures, not like that, not for that, not by them."[7]

The non-meaning or the subversion of meaning in the sense of a critical practice can consequently not be limited to a banal insignificance or incomprehensibility, as is frequently the case in everyday practice. Rather, it is a very specific form of removal that intervenes in the prevailing practices and orders of meaning.[8] Such an intervention can only succeed if it makes use of the media that—like the conventionalized characters—normally function as bearers of meaning in the respective dispositives. Xu's *Book from the Sky* can therefore only be perceived by viewers as a critical examination of Chinese governmentality because it adopts and shifts its formal elements and mechanisms at the same time. Or, to put it another way: the practice of non-meaning is only an "art of not being governed quite so much" if it makes the way in which the existing forms of meaning function in relation to power and technology understandable through these very forms.

With reference to Theodor W. Adorno's negativity-theoretical aesthetics, it could be asserted that an aesthetic element is always inherent in such a critical writing practice of non-meaning. After all, according to Adorno, an artwork is characterized precisely by the fact that it adopts formal elements of the 'empirical' world but does not combine them into a coherent, identifiable unit. The artwork thus appears as "a script with broken or veiled meaning,"[9] which stimulates a process of understanding that, unlike the intuitive understanding of conventional mass-cultural forms, can never be completed.[10] This infinite postponement of understanding causes intuitive identification of the visible to recede in favor of an explicit attention to the formal properties of the aesthetic material. In summary, in an aesthetic experience, not only the fundamental relationship between meaning and materiality itself becomes apparent, but also the implications of intuitive understanding, which are taken for granted.[11]

This idea can be reformulated in terms of practice theory with reference to Foucault: by shifting, manipulating, or rearranging the forms on which the sensorial order of a dispositive is based, the subjects' implicit perceptual and practical knowledge is appealed to, but at the same time disoriented—and only in this disorientation can the power effects of the sensorial order of the dispositive, which are not explicitly perceived in undisturbed practice, be aesthetically experienced as such.

While Adorno restricts his analysis of the aesthetic to the artwork in the narrower sense, these considerations can easily be applied to graphic design: since writing is not only conceptually but also formal-aesthetically linked to a governmentality, a critical practice that opposes precisely these forms of governance cannot reproduce existing design practices in an unreflecting manner. Instead, it must work on the existing discursive, material, and sensorial formations of a dispositive in order to be able to introduce a critical distance to them. This critical distance cannot— as in the case of artworks—consist in a mere failure of intuitive understanding. In political disputes, it is essential that non-hegemonic positions are made audible and visible. However, graphic design can show that these positions not only call for a shift in the governmental space of possibility on a discursive level, but that their "art of not being governed quite so much" necessarily entails a transformation of the sensorial order. Still, such a transformation can only take place if the medium of writing reveals its own function in regard to the technology of power.

11   Ibid., chapter 2.

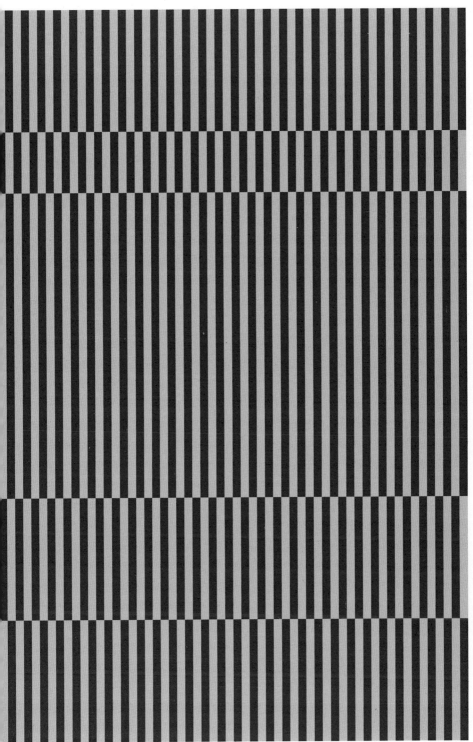

Graphic interlude by Laurens Bauer

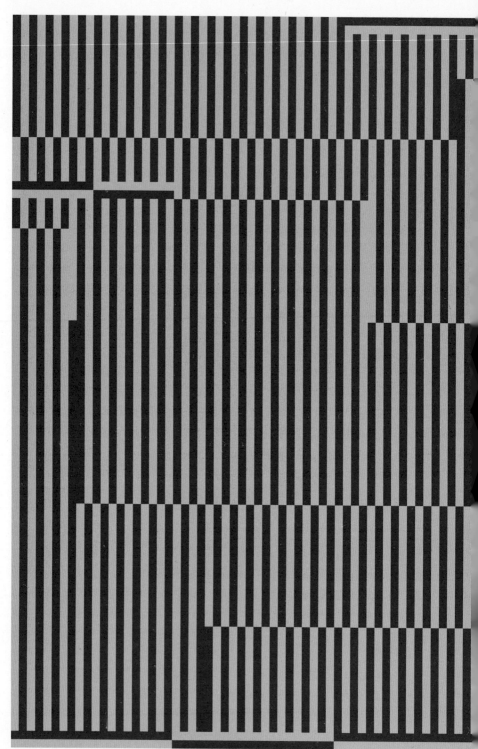

Graphic interlude by Laurens Bauer

Learning to Live with Complexity
Perspectives for the Communication Society

The Age of Backlash

Today no one can say how designers will work in the future. But we can already sense that their tasks will become even more complex. Simply giving form an appearance is no longer enough. Making advances in functionality and sustainability is already considered a standard service. Innovation is included, according to current expectations. We require a product to work well, but merely working well is far from being good design. After all, on closer examination, there are many things we could do without. Consumer research has long shown that numerous items at discount retailers are only purchased because they are priced so cheaply when they go on sale. Customers feel they cannot miss the opportunity and have to take advantage of it. Products bought in this way are often not even taken out of their packaging, let alone used. They would certainly have worked, but that no longer seems to be the point. They were bought to be owned, to feel good about being able to own them.

Such items have lost their actual purpose, but consumers supposedly do not notice this. For this reason, a variety of marketing positions have been created, all of which David Graeber would classify as "bullshit jobs"[1]: The products are made to tell nice stories as identification offers for the buyer. We still believe in Roland Barthes' "myths of everyday life,"[2] those narratives that are meant to give us a sense of home and history, identity, and confidence. But the politics of symbols brought about by advertising alone is proving to be less and less credible. It lacks "resonance,"[3] to cite Hartmut Rosa. It is all just rhetoric, a nice appearance, so that we can function better in the community, so that everyone has their accustomed place in society. However, in the age of self-optimization, such an assigned identity only makes people 'tired'[4] and the desire to have and be something is followed by burnout.

So consumers can tell their own story on social media, where they are the main actor of their own series. Selfies form a well-crafted plot, a design task for everyone. The borderless internet, freely accessible and uncontrolled, initially promised great freedom for personal development. A new age of tolerance was foreseen, open to all ways of life, according to our hope for a new "culture of digitalism"[5] (Felix Stalder). But this spirit of optimism once again led to a backlash. It seems to me that we have not yet fully understood our disappointment about the failed mediatization of the social. After all, who could find a home in the digital world? This might work well as a channel of information and entertainment, but who wants to believe in the identity that they themselves constructed on the Internet? One can fool oneself and others about many things, but real life—contrary to all prognoses—has by no means been subsumed into the bubble of beautiful appearances. Just because we can be someone else on social media, this does not make us happier with who we actually are.

This double life in several realities has instead tended to produce borderliners who are not at home in either world. Influencers and communities are now radicalizing lifestyles and worldviews. To prevent the digitally augmented self from breaking apart, they offer the simplest possible lessons to imitate. A society based on knowledge is reverting to a society based on belief, with a plentiful selection of ideologies to choose from. Complexity is taboo and ambiguity is unbearable in the shadow of the age of backlash. 'Backlash' refers not only to conservatives now campaigning against leftist liberal identity politics from feminism to LGBTQ. On the contrary, we must understand all endeavors to construct status and identity, to create a home and origins for oneself, as well as to fight for recognition and equality, as identity politics. It is practiced by *everyone*, by conservatives and liberals, right and left, the radical fringes and the integrated center. With the potential arbitrariness of the internet self and selfie avatars, the vehemence of this means of securing identity in real life increased. Some fight, rightly, against discrimination and oppression, while others secure their privileges and supremacy. Both, it should be recognized, are an expression of the same impulse.

If we are honest, everyone maintains a personal identity politics account, in both directions: On the one side, entries are made where we feel unrecognized, disadvantaged, or even exploited and oppressed. On the other side is a list of what we have attained and are unwilling to give up. For some it is about life and death (Black Lives Matter, the threat of climate change, and so on), while for others it is only about luxury problems or the defense of property that is historically illegitimate (colonialism) or was acquired unfairly (class privileges). Warnings have long been made about increasing inequality (for example, by

1   David Graeber, *Bullshit Jobs: Vom wahren Sinn der Arbeit* (Stuttgart, 2018).
2   Roland Barthes, *Mythologies* (New York, 1972). [original French edition 1957].
3   Hartmut Rosa, *Resonanz: Eine Soziologie der Weltbeziehung* (Berlin, 2016).
4   Byung-Chul Han, *Müdigkeitsgesellschaft* (Berlin, 2010).
5   Felix Stalder, *Kultur der Digitalität* (Berlin, 2016).

Learning to Live with Complexity

Pierre Bourdieu and Thomas Piketty,[6] but we sense this more clearly than ever today: The celebrated freedoms online are ultimately worthless if they do not exist in real life.

    What do these social developments mean for design? Today's identity politics articulates a fundamental unease with universalism. People mistrust reason, which was meant to realize social, economic, and technical progress since the Enlightenment. The certainty that freedom and equality reign is no longer trusted in view of the structural disadvantages, whatever the constitution may say. Rather, one suspects that it was precisely the Enlightenment ideal of equality for all people that produced inequality in the first place. After all, people do not have the same qualifications and conditions. We are different from the start and are made even more different due to socioeconomic conditions as well as labor and educational policy. The accusation is made that equality is only claimed, but not achieved. Since Kant, "immaturity" has been portrayed as being 'self-imposed,' as if people could have freed themselves from their misery if only they had worked harder. There are efforts in society to compensate for the disadvantages (support programs, quotas for women, and so on), but they do not represent the fundamental system, and are little more than a drop in the ocean.

Hence the backlash: the foundation of universalism, of the rational, good nature of human beings, from which the equality of all necessarily results, is increasingly being called into question. Society does not treat us equally, and so people want to be recognized for these differences. Compensating for disadvantages must become the topic of the future, around the world. Securing advantages, on the other hand, needs to be questioned more than ever if it is systematically undertaken by groups and classes, and others experience structural disadvantages as a result. The "dialectic of Enlightenment"[7] (Theodor W. Adorno, Max Horkheimer) has now produced reactions that should be taken seriously. The old dream of a universal reason for everyone has lost its social basis, and design will have to respond to this.

The Problem Is Problem Solving

Can the current crisis of universalism be resolved through more identity politics? The representatives of the latter think so. For example, in her book *White Fragility*,[8] Robin DiAngelo emphasizes that all social progress achieved so far has been achieved through identity politics. Indeed, for instance, one might ask where women would be today without the history of the women's movement. We still need the dedication of civil rights movements and all efforts for equality and equal opportunities more than ever. But is today's identity politics the right actor for this? It is currently causing social fragmentation in communities, because it only stands up for the interests of the group it represents. It loses sight of the interests of *everyone*.

To me, identity politics and universalism seem like two sides of the same coin: each side is too one-sided and runs the risk of neglecting the other side to such an extent that it becomes a blind spot in one's own perception.[9] But society should always keep both sides in mind—individuals and groups—and their specific concerns and needs, as well as the whole. Furthermore, the idea of compensation for disadvantages is as such universalist. We must all take care of

6   Pierre Bourdieu, *Distinction: A Social Critique of the Judgement of Taste*, (Cambridge US, 1984) [original French edition 1979]; Thomas Piketty: *Capital in the Twenty-First Century*, (Cambridge US, 2014).
7   Max Horkheimer, Theodor W. Adorno, *Dialektik der Aufklär-ung* (Amsterdam, 1947).
8   For instance, DiAngelo writes: "The term *identity politics* refers to the focus on the barriers specific groups face in their struggle for equality. We have yet to achieve our founding principle [of equality], but any gains we have made thus far have come through identity politics." Robin DiAngelo, *White Fragility: Why It's So Hard for White People to Talk About Racism* (Boston, 2018), p. XIII.
9   On the 'blind spot' as a sociological term, see Niklas Luhmann, *Soziale Systeme* (Frankfurt/M , 1984).

one another, according to the basic idea of the welfare state and the principle of subsidiarity. This idea is incompatible with the identity politics logic of representing interests.

Therefore, two things are needed today: a new understanding of the existence and legitimacy of identity politics, since it is a fundamental driving force of all people. No one can be free from striving for recognition or from securing what has been achieved. And two, universalism is in need of a fundamental reform or a 'critique'[10] in Michel Foucault's sense: Our discourse of universal reason has degenerated into a hegemonic thinking, led by the elites and used as a form of rule that no longer serves everyone.

Contemporary design must also face this challenge: according to the traditional understanding, design is a top-down way of thinking. There is the planner and the user. Their relationship is usually asymmetrical when read as a distribution of power. Furthermore, design usually only follows a single school of thought: there must be *one* solution for *everyone*. Designers submit to one reason, common sense, from which the good and correct solution to the problem they are working on necessarily results—causally deducible, rationally justifiable. Good design is only what solves a problem as a universally applicable form, according to this discourse. Such design is still based on the utilitarianism of an end-means relationship; the design solution is considered convincing when it is free of doubt and uncertainty, free of ambivalences and contradictions. The universalism of design always presupposes that good and correct knowledge and action are possible. But can today's problems still be solved? Who could discern what people actually need? What can people hope for in Western consumer societies, which have lived far too long at the expense of others?

The call for a return to the virtues of the universal, as formulated by Mark Lilla,[11] seems almost naive

10   Michel Foucault, 'What Is Critique?,' in David Ingram (ed.): *The Political: Readings in Continental Philosophy* (London, 2002) [original French edition 1978].

11   Mark Lilla, *The Once and Future Liberal: After Identity Politics,* New York: Harper, 2017.

12   For more, see Armin Nassehi, *Das große Nein: Eigendynamik und Tragik des gesellschaftlichen Protests* (Hamburg, 2020).

today. After all, what is left for common sense to be based on? These days, even the search for an urgently needed vaccine results in anti-vaxxers.[12] So what single principle of reason can we all collectively rely on? Today, what some see as a good solution is not a good solution in the view of others—and this also applies to design solutions. So far, in design it has been common to develop a thing or a tool, a medium or a strategy for solving problems. What people cannot do themselves is taken over by an artifact. We have machines work for us, to everyone's benefit. For a while, the dream of the common good seemed to work. But what can we expect from new technologies and innovations today? The development of problem-solving tools is correct and important in the logic of technology. But in design it runs the risk of replacing the actual job of design, because the mechanization of the social is far too simple a solution for today's problems.

In the future, smart technologies could become as intelligent and eloquent as Samantha from Spike Jonze's science fiction movie *Her* (2013): she is just a voice from a tiny box, a speaking operating system. But for the main character, Theodore, who falls in love with the digital Samantha, she serves as a replacement for a partner in flesh and blood. She does not need a body. The device  she resides on fits in his shirt pocket and can share what he experiences anytime and anywhere (Fig. A). She is very efficient, always available, therapeutically tailored to him, to overcome his depressive mood and creative crisis—an excellent solution in terms of functionality. But what would human beings be then?

In determining his own identity, Theodore enters into a highly narcissistic relationship with himself, because the operating system tailored to him is perfectly oriented toward his needs (though this

A   Theodore happily sitting next to Samantha on a park bench in *Her* by Spike Jonze (2013). ww.moma.org/calendar/events/3341.

changes over the course of the movie). Theodore has no need for the relationship to be recognized by the world around him. He is tautologically connected to himself, and that is enough for him. Is that a good design solution? The human-like Samantha ultimately helps Theodore out of his crisis. The AI is highly functional in regard to his healing.

But, according to the dystopia formulated here, intelligent media relieve people from their duty to work on themselves. We only use our reason under the guidance of another entity—according to Kant the greatest sacrilege to the ideal of the Enlightenment. The technical solution would rob us of our humanity, and Theodore's identity of its meaning. Under Samantha's direction, it mutates into an easy-to-use, affordable product that one wouldn't even take out of its packaging. In short, problem solving is a problem in design because it tends to keep problems small so that they can be solved. Anyone who is always looking for the most efficient technical solution with an emphasis on design thinking will only produce 'social technology': The complexity of the task is reduced, the internal contradictions are stifled, and all doubts are left out. The most important thing is for it to fit on a Post-it note on a mind map wall. Design differs from technology in that it must also consider problems that cannot be solved with things and media, technologies and strategies. Today's problems of identity cannot be solved with an app, because all the devices and programs in the world will not be able to tell us what human beings are.

Design as a Space for Open-Mindedness

Kant posed four major questions for philosophy: "What can I know? What ought I to do? What may I hope? What is the human being?"[13] These are certainly not insignificant questions, for how would one find answers to them? Those who want a simple solution

13   According to Kant, this encompasses no less than the areas of metaphysics, morality, religion, and anthropology. Immanuel Kant, 'Logik, Physische Geographie, Pädagogik,' in: Kants Werke, vol. 9 (Berlin, New York, 1962), p. 25. (korpora.zim. uni-duisburg-essen.de/ Kant/aa09/025.html)

to such problems will obtain only simple 'truths,' and usually those that verge on the ideological or esoteric so as not to overwhelm us. This is a hindrance to any complexity. Design, on the other hand, has the task of stimulating and implementing complex thinking in society. Design should ask questions that are hardly smaller than Kant's, even if one does not have an answer to them, and instead must develop the tolerance of complexity that is lacking in many places today. Design must remain open to ambivalences and be ready to endure its own inability to know something. We must increase the degree of uncertainty in the system. Only then will we find interesting answers to social and design problems.

Of course, this does not mean that we should strive toward ignorance—otherwise we would remain ignorant. This is not to propagate the relativization and deconstruction of all knowledge, but rather to advocate for a new culture of "tolerance of ambiguity"[14] (Thomas Bauer, Else Frenkel-Brunswik). We must expand the conceptual spaces of design so that they also include the imponderable—for example, as "heterotopia" or "other spaces"[15] (Michel Foucault) that are not determined or designed without an alternative, but can always also take a different shape.[16] To this end, we need play and speculation, fantasy and fiction. All knowledge first needs imagination to increase the perception of complexity. Only then will we escape the rampant lack of imagination in many design solutions. However, 'critical design' or 'specu-

14   The Arabist and Islamic scholar Thomas Bauer shows in his study *Die Kultur der Ambiguität: Eine andere Geschichte des Islams* (Berlin, 2011) that a high degree of tolerance for ambiguity was originally cultivated in Islam. Only under the influence of Western colonial rule, which presented universal, secure knowledge as superior, was this openness abandoned. In cognitive psychology, the tolerance for ambiguity also plays a central role in personality development with regard to belief in authority and racism or cultural prejudice. Among others, see Else Frenkel-Brunswik, 'Intolerance of Ambiguity as an Emotional and Perceptual Personality Variable,' in *Journal of Personality* 18, 1949, pp. 108–143. Frenkel-Brunswik was also instrumental in Theodor W. Adorno's study of the structure of the authoritarian personality. See Theodor W. Adorno, Else Frenkel-Brunswik, Daniel J. Levinson, R. Nevitt Sanford, *The Authoritarian Personality* (New York, 1950).
15   Michel Foucault, 'Of Other Spaces: Utopias and Heterotopias' [original French edition: 1967]. web. mit.edu/allanmc/www/foucault1.pdf.

lative design'[17] still has a bad reputation in Germany, or is not even known. According to one accusation, they are irrelevant gimmicks, and according to another, just cynical commentaries bordering on art. In the land of engineers, straightforward, expedient design work is still preferred. This may be more economically viable, but it makes us blind to the complexity of today's problems.

From now on, the Enlightenment motto *sapere aude* [dare to know] should first strengthen the imagination before it strategically narrows again: What relationship should humans have to the planet and the environment, for example? How should we organize our coexistence with "nonhuman people"[18] (Timothy Morton), meaning animals, plants, and things that are non-human and yet relevant to us? How could we look back from a fictional future into the current moment in order to change the present today? Projection and imagination are highly effective for courage and self-consciousness or the ability to face the unbearable current problems in a new and different way. For example, in Afrofuturism as an emancipation movement: today's technologies cannot be a solution because they function in a racist manner. First we need a revision of tech culture, which in turn can be imagined and anticipated as science fiction.[19]

Visualization in particular can be understood as a cultural technique of speculation: pictures and letters

16   I developed this idea in Annette Geiger, *Andersmöglichsein: Zur Ästhetik des Designs* (Bielefeld, 2018).
17   See Matt Malpass, *Critical Design in Context: History, Theory, and Practices* (London/New York, 2017); Anthony Dunne, Fiona Raby, *Speculative Everything: Design, Fiction, and So-* *cial Dreaming* (Cambridge US, 2013).
18   Timothy Morton, *Humankind: Solidarity with Nonhuman People* (London/New York, 2017).
19   This perspective was presented by Alondra Nelson (ed.), *Afrofuturism: A Special Issue of Social Text* (Durham, 2001) and Alondra Nelson, Thuy Linh Tu (eds.), *Technicolor: Race, Technology, and Everyday Life* (New York, 2002). For a current overview, see e.g., Isiah Lavender III, *Afrofuturism Rising: The Literary Prehistory of a Movement* (Columbus, 2019).
20   Claude Lévi-Strauss, *Wild Thought* (Chicago, 2021) [original French edition 1962].
21   Charles Jencks, Nathan Silver, *Adhocism: The Case for Improvisation*, (London, 1972).

Annette Geiger

mean what they say—or not. Does Figure B read 12, 13, 14, or ABC? We actually love this game because it has no goal and no end; there is always a new round to play. Claude Lévi-Strauss' *bricoleur*, a role model cherished in the design discourse, is certainly not an efficient problem solver, because he cultivates "wild thinking."[20] This is never certain, always provisional, tending toward spontaneous activism or even "adhocism"[21] (Charles Jencks, Nathan Silver) without claiming absoluteness and conclusiveness.

12
ABC
14

In the open conceptual space of design, we ultimately no longer need to differentiate between independent art or high culture and applied design or low culture. With the expulsion of the traditional, causally conceived end-means rationality from design the difference becomes superfluous. After all, when we isolate the images of high culture in museum temples, beyond all accessibility, as pure identity politics for educated citizens, when universalism retreats into the gold frame of supposed sophistication and the popular is condemned as barbaric, a little Zorgh will come around the corner as a backlash and smear swastikas on the wall again (Fig. C). Universalistic educational measures may then run after him with a stick, but

—ZORGH! NOT THE WALLS!

they will not bring back the breakaways motivated by identity politics, the disobedient, radicalized dropouts from the logic of *one* reason and culture this way. Such pedagogy remains at a Stone Age level; it will only further divide society. We need a design that communicates with relish, in a humane and humorous way, that there is no such thing as the one simple solution, but rather only complex ranges of possibilities for an eternal rethinking process.

B   Typographically ambiguous figure. www.pinterest.de/pin/8162843045287037/?nic_v2=1a2taclr2.
C   Samuel Nyholm, *Untitled*, 2010. Courtesy of the artist, 2020.

Graphic interlude by Karo Akpokiere

Not all Africans Are Criminals, Not all Koreans Eat Kimchi

Chris is the creative director of an advertising agency in Lagos, Nigeria. He is a young, black Nigerian writer.

At the moment, Chris is in South Korea for an advertising conference. Apart from the thrill and uncertainty of being in this part of the world for the first time, Chris has also been confronted with the very recent news of the FBI 77. The FBI 77 is a list of 77 individuals indicted for fraud and money laundering activities.

The 77 individuals are all Nigerian.

In an age where the stereotyping of Nigerians and Africans happens to be rife due to the widespread activities of 'Nigerian Princes' and love scammers, the publishing of the list naturally got Chris agitated.

Determined to not let the list put a burden on his shoulders, he decided to do something about his agitation. Chris had a T-shirt designed and printed with the statement: "Not all Africans are criminals, Not all Koreans eat Kimchi" in both Korean and English. The statement acknowledges that stereotyping is in fact an equal opportunity phenomenon that cuts across cultures, race, etc., and at the same time, it challenges those same concepts in the most basic, accessible, and effective way by employing graphic design. He intends to wear the T-shirt for the duration of his stay in South Korea. So far, it has proven to be a conversation starter online and, most importantly, offline as well.

Chris' experience can be broken down into three parts: stereotypes, conversations, and most importantly, narratives. Narratives provide material for conversations and for the crafting of stereotypes. They form the core of our existence as humans, shape our identities, and give us a worldview. I am interested in how the human can be brought to bear on the discipline of graphic design via narratives. By 'the human' I refer to the emotions and experiences that represent our journey through life and run the gamut from the good, not so good, and the outright nasty. Experiences such as those of Chris.

Looking beyond the news of fraudulent individuals and the stereotyping it fosters, my thoughts go back to my primary school days... I vividly recall history being one of my favorite subjects at the time, as it presented narratives of wars, intrepid explorers, and inventors, and so on. In one of these stories, the young Scottish Doctor Mungo Park 'discovered' one of the most important rivers in West Africa—the Niger. As I got older, I realized that the story (amongst others), wasn't only untrue but also ridiculous as the existence of the River Niger predates the existence of Mungo Park and was a vital source of sustenance and a conduit for trade for the inhabitants of the region before his 'discovery.'

Stereotyping and misinformation are cut from the same cloth as deception and perception engineering. As a graphic designer now living and working in Europe (Hamburg, Germany), the misinformation and stereotyping are more widely felt and as such, the need to assert oneself is even more pertinent; asserting in a manner that seeks to show the broadness and richness of one's experiences and interests and not in a way that panders to political and social trends that only serve to give birth to new stereotypes and portray people as one-dimensional. The tools that graphic design provides and the flexibility and accessibility

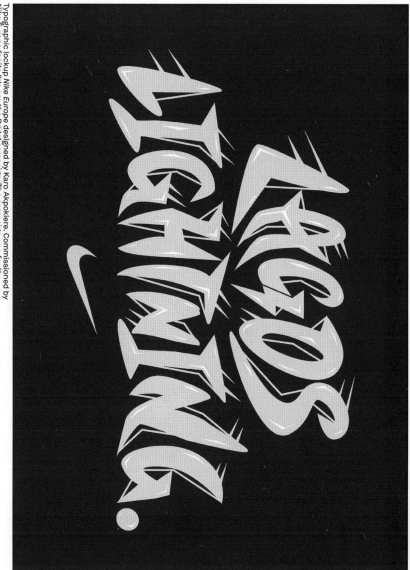

Typographic lockup *Nike Europe* designed by Karo Akpokiere. Commissioned by Nike Europe for its 'We are the Pride' campaign. The campaign was for the launch of Chelsea Football Club's 2017/2018 Nike Vapor Kit Jersey. 'Lagos Lightning' represents Chelsea player Victor Moses and his roots in Lagos, Nigeria.

Poster design by Karo Akpokiere. *Love Note to Difference*, 2018, Open edition. When I'm in a new city, one of the things I'm immediately drawn to is the graphic design there as it represents an oasis of familiarity in a mass of difference and it also offers a way to engage with a city. In Seoul, I was immediately confronted with and drawn to the Hangul symbols and though I had no idea what they meant, I could see the value inherent in them being used not as a tool to make oral and written communication possible, but as a tool to form new drawings and patterns based on their visual and aesthetic strength. *Love Note to Difference* represents my fascination with the Hangul symbols and, in a wider sense, it represents the importance of accepting and appreciating all that is different and foreign to us because, in acceptance and appreciation, value can be seen and potentially new and significant ways of communicating can be developed. The poster was part of my contribution to the group exhibition 'MMCA Report' at MMCA, Changdong, Seoul from 23.11 – 2.12.2018.

it offers to merge intent and approach to make messaging of any kind possible, gives the graphic designer the agency to craft and to share (without borders) alternative narratives (that represent the aforementioned broadness and richness of experiences and interests and could be from the graphic designer's own experiences or from the experiences of others.) to the dominant narratives that produce the stereotypes we are confronted with.

We are not individuals freefalling in an abyss of helplessness. We can use the discipline to our advantage, to tell our stories and share them. Graphic design revolves constantly around the confluence of agency, sharing, conversations, and the need for connection. It provides conditions for these human needs to thrive and this is what makes it a tool for empowerment.

Graphic design as a tool for empowerment isn't a new phenomenon, as all through history the discipline has featured heavily in political, social, and personal movements but, at a time when issues regarding stereotyping, inclusion, and diversity are at the forefront of many discourses, the importance of its power cannot be overemphasized.

A quote by Dori Tunstall sums up the empowering quality that graphic design has:

"The superpower of [graphic] design is that it's actually one of the tools that you have to change your world and the world of people around you."[1]

Let's get to work.

Not all Africans are criminal
Not all Koreans eat Kimchi

1   Taiguri, Lily Saporta, 'Dori Tunstall: Decolonizing Design,' A/D/O, 23 August, 2019. a-d-o.com/journal/ dori-tunstall-decolonizing-design-interview.

Graphic interlude by Caspar Reuss

Markus Weisbeck

Graphic Design is Fluid

A fictitious interchange between a graphic designer (B) and an artist (A)

B   What are you working on right now?

A   My thoughts revolve around current social changes and the resulting phenomena. I've been researching in various Internet forums and libraries on this topic for quite a few years, especially regarding forms of artistic participation and corresponding collectives.

B   That sounds extremely process-based. How do you approach it artistically?

A   For me, these investigations are a kind of instinctive selection and categorization: films, photographs, texts, diagrams. Information changes its meaning through new classifications and contexts. So, the artistic approach is to rearrange content and add your own elements.

B   You don't want to be precise about the respective content and sources?

A   In general, the subjective approach of my interventions is more important to me than scientific meticulousness. The way I deal with the selected content and information can also be viewed as an examination of general behavioral patterns. By combining media, adding and editing them in an associative manner, my own artistic work gradually emerges, which also conveys the content from my research.

Graphic Design Is Fluid

Do you also work with such methods in graphic design when there is no specific task or job?

B   I can't answer that for all designers. Howev-
         er, my own visual investigations are ongoing.
         After all, it's also about advancing your own
         development. Graphic methods are constant-
         ly expanding, with new tools and channels of
         information. Trying these out and discovering
         new things is essential for design research. For-
         mally, I'm now mainly interested in spatial tran-
         sitions from black to white that are not sim-
         ply based on linear gradients, but result from
         technical glitches in the images and mistakes
         in digital reproduction—contrasts that are hard
         to understand at first glance.

A   So, it's a purely formal task based on, say,
playful experimentation, right? I see different
creative approaches: the experimental one,
which is used for personal development, and
the conceptual one, which is used as graphic
design.

B   In both cases I would see the beginning as
         something playful. Something unusual has to
         emerge here that will surprise you as much
         as possible. It's always good to follow several
         designs in parallel, to create overlaps, and to
         sharpen them through continuous selection.

A   When I work in the studio, I usually don't
pursue any goal at all at first; instead, I ob-
serve how things develop and condense, enter into a dialogue with the material and myself.
Sometimes you're lazy and fall into routine patterns; other times you're braver and try out new
methods. This results in new considerations,
which in turn lead to new series of works. If you
work in a similar way, how do you combine your
graphic design experiments with applied jobs?

B   First of all, it's often the case that the client
         doesn't have all the materials. That means a

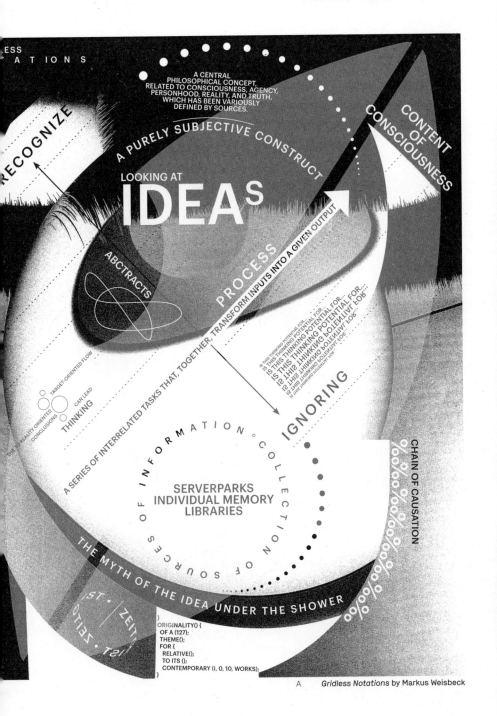

A   *Gridless Notations* by Markus Weisbeck

Gridless Notations by Markus Weisbeck

transdisciplinary approach to working is necessary right from the start, which is not straightforward but requires filling in gaps, condensing, and improvisation. It's important to always keep the task in mind and to continually adjust ideas and design parameters accordingly. If, along with a new conceptual approach, I also need additional graphic elements, I first search my files for fragments and then weave them together with the idea of the content. For me as well it's those moments of combining that create something interesting.

A   And when is a job finished for you?

B   With conventional commissioned work, an extended dialogue usually takes place that motivates possible changes to the concept or individual design elements. Sometimes the exchange makes you aware of aspects that you simply ignored during the design process. To allow input and criticism in this phase and to integrate them into your own process is a challenge, but at the same time also a great opportunity and requirement for good graphic design. A completed work combines the demands that are made of the design by different parties into a functional unit.

A   With regard to art, the idea is perhaps a little more unspecific, since it's about many interlinking, meandering ideas that determine the direction in which the work ultimately develops. These dynamics and forces gradually shape the individual artistic vision. They drive the working process, which otherwise I personally like to let run its course in order to then make the work more concrete within the respective concept.

B   A coherent idea (Fig. A) often works even when it's not implemented well. A small technical mistake usually doesn't ruin things. The situation is different with works that are 'well'-made but 'sloppily' conceived. As far as the interaction between form and content is concerned, the latter is clearly the focus in visual communication. After all, the information must be legible. This also makes it easier to decipher the time and context that the works of graphic design come from. Despite its diversity of media, our vocabulary doesn't form an autonomous body of knowledge, but always functions as part of the wider culture of communication.

A   Regardless of the respective context, of all the coincidences, discoveries, and possible combinations, one question remains that probably affects both of us: Are our means sufficient to create something truly new from the collective fossil soup? At what point does the visual search stop, and where does finding begin, the idea?

B   And above all: How resilient is this idea then? How does it behave as it ages? What if you tear it out of the context in which it is so securely embedded? To what extent do we, as designers, also have to empathize with viewers outside the specific field of a work?

A   In contemporary art, there isn't much space outside of one's own circle. As soon as we leave this circle, we hear voices that completely reject our work or make fun of it, so we like to stay under the warm blanket of our own discipline for self-protection and live in parts of the city that are bustling with like-minded people.

B   And yet you can warm yourself quite well in the light of the mythical and the inconceivable. Since your work cannot be clearly determined by worldly functions, you avoid the pressure of having to explain yourself.

A   And we feel very good about that. We only have to justify our subjects to ourselves,

C   *Gridless Notations* by Markus Weisbeck

and we can change direction from time to time in our personal expectations by developing new series of works and defining new parameters.

B   And what do these works have to say then? Or rather, what do you have to say yourself? (Fig. C) When we approach a new idea with a new task, with our own ideas, memories, and terms, what we have previously learned or thought always has an impact on the result. Shouldn't your own portfolio be consistent with yourself?

A   The design constant is probably almost more essential for you, since a certain reliability is expected of you, especially with commissioned work—even if the ideas have to be surprising. On the other hand, we as individuals may increasingly be asked to be our own brand. After all, your profession is to communicate brands. From this perspective, you graphic designers are your own brands that produce brands.

B   The vision of our work comes first, followed by the strategy. Interestingly, contemporary artists like communication design from a bygone era, in which the content is no longer read in the context in which it is used, so the function has virtually disappeared. With us applied designers, it's usually the other way around when we look at art. For us a work has to reflect current trends of the present so that we find them relevant. In dialogue with the here and now, we understand the fossil mixture of your thoughts best.

Graphic interlude by Qifan Zhou

Graphic interlude by Qifan Zhou

Translocating Historic Graphic Design to Encode Contemporary Curatorial Communication

My practice consciously plays with the transgression of roles, of narrative forms, and of institutional contexts within art practice. I studied contemporary art, then social anthropology, became an independent curator and a researcher, and then a publisher. For the greater part of my career, I moved incessantly to different cities to live, work, and print. *Metronome* was one outcome of this transitional modus: a publishing organ that I initiated in 1996 in Dakar as a collective artwork, and a curatorial methodology.[1] Through *Metronome* I could practice a form of direct and autonomous collaboration with artists, free from the constraints of museum curating or exhibition making that were increasingly aimed at large, mass audiences. Too backstage for museums to finance, I sought support from foundations, educational institutions and individuals, and secured my own survival through contracts with art colleges, taking up artists' residencies, and moving from London to set up base for six months or more in Dakar, Berlin, Basel, Vienna, Frankfurt, Oslo, Stockholm, and Tokyo. *Metronome* was very subjective and very much 'under the counter.' There was no editorial team or regular time structure to an edition, and I designed my own system of names and numbers for the total of seventeen publications. For example, *Metronome* 4-5-6 consisted of one issue, whereas 8A and 8B split into two. All these were ruses, which I deployed to aggravate the focus and articulation of *Metronome*'s circulation. Artists had to trust me to produce an artery of ideational and visual flow out of their semi-formulated research ideas, which included drawings, plans, photography, scenes of action, manifestos, and fiction. In its idiosyncratic and analogue manner, it brought artists across the world into direct contact, beyond the presence of explanatory contextual information. What emerged was the editorial trace of our conceptual intimacy. For this reason, *Metronome* was more often compared to an artwork than a publication.[2]

I called it an 'organ' because it was generative and fragile. Each issue was contingent on my ability to mobilize contributions that I would graphically re-encode according to earlier organs generated by individuals or collectives. Whenever I was invited to produce *Metronome*, I began by searching on site for an earlier publication that once manifested the need of artists and writers to disseminate their stance. There was *Metronome* 8A and 8B, the 'Stunt and the Queel' based on the eponymous rag of Chelsea School of

1   *Metronome*: Dakar (1996), London (1997, 2003), Berlin (1997/for Documenta X), 'Tempolabor or a libertine laboratory,' Basel (1998), 'Backwards Translation,' Frankfurt, Vienna, Bordeaux, Edinburgh, Biella (1999), 'The Bastard,' Copenhagen, Oslo, Stockholm, Bergen, Malmö (2001), 'Le Teaser' and 'Metronome Press,' Paris (2005), 'Future Academy – Shared, Mobile, Improvised, Underground, Hidden, Floating,' Oregon (2006), and 'What is to be done?,' Tokyo (2007). Two special issues of *Metronome* were produced for documenta 12 magazines: *Metronome* No. 10, co-edited with artist Oscar Tuazon, a survivalist guide to future art academies with tips on mobile living and getting by with minimum expenditure; and *Metronome* No. 11, a bilingual Japanese-English edition on translation, mobility, and future faculties of knowledge in art academies. Connected to *Metronome* was Met-ronome Press in Paris, co-directed by Clémentine Deliss and Thomas Boutoux between 2005–2007.
2   In 2000, Chantal Crousel invited me to show at her gallery with Rirkrit Tiravanija and Alenka Pirman.

Art in 1929, which featured subversive scenarios for amateur dramatics; Metronome Nos. 4-5-6 replicating the pro-Europe, politico-literary *Edinburgh Review* from 1870; and *Metronome* No. 10 recasting a mimeographed zine called 'Dwelling Portably' that I reprinted in Oregon in collaboration with artist Oscar Tuazon. For *Metronome* No. 3, 'The Tempolabor', I poached the layout of a specific edition of Justine by the Marquis de Sade published by Jean-Jacques Pauvert in 1968 with a preface by Georges Bataille. The graphic design, size, and binding of *Metronome* No. 3 was a loyal copy of this earlier publication, and its contents corresponded accordingly to an act of mimetic appropriation. Slitting each page open with a knife, the reader would be drawn into the dramaturgical transcription of the 'Tempolabor,' a meeting that took place behind closed doors, which I curated for the Kunsthalle Basel in 1998. Artists, activists, curators, and gallerists were invited to discuss the enigmas and dilemmas they faced in different art situations worldwide. Rather than produce a reader, with its appropriately sanitized and explanatory structure, I chose to work with the tropes of mid-eighteenth-century libertine literature and disguise the political potential of this *bureau d'esprit* by turning the transcription into a play with scenes and asides. I had no need for a graphic designer, only the craft of the typesetter who would translocate all the stylistic elements of the original onto *Metronome*. A dictum that I carry with me and which originates from 'Le Sofa' (Crébillon fils, 1742) encapsulates the process in one line: "It is harder to know where to stop than to invent."

Metronome No. 9, which I produced a few years later in Paris together with Thomas Boutoux, adopted the graphic layout of 'The Stripteaser,' a neat promotional pocketbook of sixty odd pages printed at night—to beat the censorship police—by underworld publisher Maurice Girodias. In the 1950s, Girodias' publishing house, Olympia Press, offered young French literati, international beat poets, and friends of the penumbra a performative adjacency between life and work. By translocating this historical organ, I wanted to test the vitality of the debates fifty years on, and put a question to artists: what would lead you to withhold your authorship, remove your name, or use a pseudonym? With its eroticized choreography, the original 'Strip-teaser,' accompanied the reader through sequences of women getting undressed and pages of short texts by authors such as Alexander Trocchi, Jean Genet, and William Boroughs, all in authorial disguise. According to the success of the tease, the reader could then locate the book they wished to purchase from Olympia Press. With this prototype in hand, I was able to ask artists and writers in 2003 whether they felt the desire or necessity to withhold their name, and why? Liam Gillick, Tom McCarthy, Michael Archer, and Ina Blom transitioned into Nancy Strasbourg, Susannah Mabbitt, Bella Woodfield and Bill Moan, respectively. One of the most complex of the seven guest artists invited to define a visual section of 'Le Teaser' handed me a stack of color snapshots taken in a flat he occupied at the start of the new millennium. Calling it 'Adresse Anonyme,' the artist sought a redefinition of the locus of art by renting an apartment and living, performing, and documenting the extreme corporeality of his definition of anonymity. I collated the series and, as always, replicated the original graphic design of the prototype organ. For the launch, Boutoux and I hired all the rooms and the lobby of a typical old-style three-star hotel near l'Opéra in Paris and handed the keys over to the artists and their friends for twenty-four hours. I pursue this homage to publishing organs because I try to sense the energy of earlier artists' movements and reformulate this drive within today's context. The only issue of *Metronome* that was not based on the graphic layout of an earlier organ is aptly named 'The Bastard' and was designed by Liam Gillick. Finally, in Tokyo, for an exhibition I had at Masato Nakamura's gallery CommandN in 2007, I produced an edition of sandals, which I made from second-hand books. I picked them up around Kanda district in Tokyo and they included a nineteenth century illustrated bible, a cookbook, an atlas of the world, a biography of Sigmund Freud, Japanese technical dictionaries, soft-spine Manga comics, and several cheap thick French novels. I used these books to make flipflops by going to a printer to punch holes in the mass of pages through which I passed a knot of thick silky cord. A hardback provided a longer-lasting sole. A pocketbook indicated the size of a child's sandal. Every visitor to a Japanese home could tear off the worn page and enjoy a hygienic slipper, as well as read anew. This *Metronome* edition was called 'Think with your feet' and while it referenced a line from Jacques Derrida, it bore no kinship to an earlier graphic design.

My relationship to artists' books has always been quite selfish. I like making them. I like operating through their medium to curate new artworks or initiate pieces of writing, but I am not a bibliophile and I do not collect other artists' books or magazines for their graphic ingenuity. Instead, I suffer from the boxes full of printed matter that accumulate in my life and that I am responsible for. After eleven years, I ceased publishing *Metronome*. By 2007, the internet had become ubiquitous, offering default dissemination between artists, whose participation in the litter of biennials seemed to resolve the problem of how to identify a trusted interlocutor within the global field. Now everything had to be visible to be apprehended as contemporary art. With the lights on permanently, even the nocturnal mythic fell prey to the potency of illumination and the promise of heightened communication. As a curatorial platform, *Metronome* had become briefly redundant.

It was while I was curating the Dilijan Arts Observatory in Armenia in 2016 that I returned to printing organs. I needed to communicate locally at a site where Facebook was not a viable option. I found the only shop in a radius of fifty kilometers that had an offset printer and imitated the local newspaper, producing a thin, one-page sheet in black-and-white containing information on the project in Armenian, Russian, and English. I wanted a grandmother to let the contents of the broadsheet slip into her consciousness as if it were the local newspaper that she had read all her life. For this to work, the various graphic details were faithfully reproduced. The model worked and we printed eight editions that were distributed by a local man to all the families of Dilijan. Using this conduit, we were able to communicate what our international group of artists, historians, and designers were doing in the abandoned electronics factory at the edge of town. Moreover, this medium proved all the more relevant when, a short while later, I came across a remarkable collection of Armenian literary and political organs at the Berlin State Library. I presented these diasporic publications, printed during existential translocations around the world in New York, Addis Abeba, Athens, Damaskus, and many other cities, together with the results of the Dilijan Arts Observatory at the exhibition 'Hello World. Revising a Collection' at the Hamburger Bahnhof in 2018.[3]

A few months later in Paris, together with art students from the Ecole nationale supérieur d'arts de Paris-Cergy, I set out to research the existence of printed organs produced by communities of Korean, Armenian, Senegalese, Congolese, South American, Algerian, and Chinese immigrants who had come to Paris throughout the twentieth century. The basis for this new project named 'Organs & Alliances' was a series of questions which I directed to the students: "What is the network that you connect to and that you trust? Who do you address through your work? What constitutes a bond of engagement? How close is your collaborator geographically speaking? When you arrive in a foreign place, what media do you use to communicate your presence?"[4] Unlike the well-known Surrealist and Lettrist publications, there was barely anything to be found in the Parisian state or city libraries. In effect, locating these printed vectors would have necessitated an extensive dialogue with older persons from the generation of immigrants who, somewhat poignantly, were still alive and presumably holding onto their material past. Although forays were made into Algerian feminist journals from the 1970s and Korean artists' collectives of the 1980s, the necessary fieldwork would have required more time and support. Such archives, which denote contentious moments of migration require sensitive remediation. Is graphic design able to heal and transfer past experiences? Can this model of curatorial practice convey former channels of aesthetic communication that occurred during transitioning social and political contexts?

'Organs & Alliances' eventually extended to the Academy of Fine Arts in Leipzig, where the project shifted from locating historical tracts to the collective acquisition of the means of production itself: the offset printer. Students in Paris and Leipzig pooled their personal funds and bought a bootleg Tiegel machine produced in the Czech Republic in 1968. This was the first act of aesthetic, financial, and social commitment between them. The machine was the organ, not printed matter. It determined engagement with other people through design understood as an experiment in life. As Jonas Roßmeißl described it: "I think infra-

3 'Portable Homelands. From Field to Factory,' in Udo Kittelman, *Hello World: Revising a Collection* (Nationalgalerie im Hamburger Bahnhof, April–August 2018). See catalogue for the juxtaposition of contemporary and historical publishing organs.

4 'Organs & Alliances,' 2018, consisted of Ismail Alaoui-Fdili (Morocco/France); Kévin Blinderman (France); Anne Dietzsch (Germany); Thibault Grougi (France); Seongju Hong (Korea/France); Paul-Alexandre Islas (Mexico/France); Rosalie Le Forestier (France); Philip Markert (Germany); Bocar Niang (Senegal/France); Jonas Roßmeißl (Germany); Araks Sahakyan (Spain/France); Clara Wieck (Germany). It was curated by Clémentine Deliss, Visiting Professor, Ecole Nationale Supérieure d'Arts de Paris-Cergy (ENSAPC) with the participation of Markus Dreßen, Professor of Graphic Design at the Academy of Fine Arts (HGB), Leipzig.

structure can create a collective work too. Because it's not a manifestation of content. Instead, through infrastructure, roles can become autonomous. It's about a production process. And instead of worrying about content, we focus on the infrastructure that will influence the frame within which we shall work and print. The infrastructure will frame the content. The machine creates presence. And out of this presence, we emerge. Behind the machine. But until the point when the first page comes out, we cannot define it."

The plan was to transport the Tiegel in a purpose-built van complete with generator, petrol, water, ink, and accessories and to produce everything on the road from the cliché to the poster. Travelling from Leipzig to Paris through the wealthiest parts of Western Europe, the team of students aimed to stop over at slaughter-houses, hospitals, dispatch centers, in villages as well as in towns, offering a service to the different com-munities encountered along the way. With two thou-sand sheets printed in one hour, the team would en-gage in performative systems of distribution. One of the students, Thibault Grougi, tested this out in Nice where he walked along the Promenade des Anglais handing out pages with a slogan in thick black font, which read EUROPE OR DIE. This became the title of a limited edition, a launch event and a debate hosted by the Goethe Institute in Paris in October 2018 and aimed at raising funds to build the transporter van for the Tiegel. We printed a limited edition of single sheets authored by each member of the group. In ad-dition, Lydia Ourahmane, Paul B. Preciado, Tom McCar-thy, and Luke Willis Thompson sent us new text works that we produced as offline statements and includ-ed in the edition. Designer Markus Dreßen and one of the students from Leipzig determined the matrix for each single sheet, adapting an identical layout only minimally according to the length of the text. It was an intentional part of the project that none of the twen-

ty-five statements would be uploaded onto web platforms. This regulation was key to the project and it
raised the question as to why an artist or writer would
wish to produce printed matter that is strictly offline?
Luke Willis Thompson suggested to me recently that
alliances are as fragile as the "sharing of breath, anal-
ogous to the Hongí, a literal exchange of air dubbed in
global media as the Maori kiss." Offline communication
is evanescent too, it passes, but through a different
social tissue and speed of engagement than the corporeal or digital. Thompsons original 'Letter to an Editor' for Organs & Alliances, subsequently reproduced
as the analogue film *Black Leadership* was a succinct
deployment of the offline organ. With the right measure of pathos, Thompson wrote a letter in which he
critiqued the opportunism of art journalism that reproduces unresearched missives, thereby cancelling
out a protagonist who questions racialist claims to
the rights of representation. At the conference EU-
ROPE OR DIE, which included the team from 'Organs
& Alliances', Thompson, Ourahmane, Dreßen, and art
consultant Martin Heller, we discussed the question
of trust, the complexities of working collectively as
an artist today, operations of trans-border communication, and the autonomy of print and its role as a
medium today.

    In 2019–2020, the question of conceptual in-
timacy generated through close-knit channels of exchange is relevant once again. But should we read
this critically as an anachronistic flashback to an
avant-garde, a craving for clandestine encoded art
publications that confront society and address the
role of the artist as aesthetic disrupter or closet revolutionary? Or, are we facing an acute state of non-directionality? Of not knowing which transmission can
be trusted, which medium, infrastructure, and graphic language to use to translocate concept-work and
cross borders? And if content is less vital than transmission, then should we question the nature of our

addressee with more rigor and vigilance? What is the democratic intellect in 2020? What have the mass media done to our understanding of dialogical communication, and how does this affect curatorial relations and graphic design? To deploy a methodology of translocation is to transplant the organ within a contemporary corpus, which may not be built around the same sets of identifications that we have known until now. It may suggest a notion of trans that mirrors the construction of a differentiated syntax, one that emancipates itself from a normative metabolic order, while remaining humble toward the fragile, politicized ramifications of today's trans-corporeal human condition.

Graphic interlude by Julian Mader & Max Prediger

Graphic interlude by Julian Mader & Max Prediger

A Platform for Implementing Visual Language
Collaboration with Graphic Designers in *IDEA* Magazine

It has become commonplace for graphic designers to publish a book or produce an indie magazine or zine to pursue independence and autonomy in their work. Every year, droves of visitors flock the art book fairs worldwide (especially in Asian countries in recent years), where more art and design publications are on exhibit than can be seen in a single day. While such fairs provide designers with new opportunities for presentation and communication, they also tend to fuel transitory design trends and graphic culture consumption. How can we work together to foster new possibilities that benefit both sides of design and publishing? By reflecting on the seventy years of history of collaborating with graphic designers at *IDEA*, a design magazine where the author is the editor, this article will explore how magazines can continue to serve as a platform for implementing visual language.

A Platform for Implementing Visual Language

A Design Magazine for Designers, by Designers

IDEA was first published in 1953. Kikumatsu Ogawa, the founder of Seibundo Shinkosha publishers, had been interested in advertising and propaganda art since before World War II. He published *Kokokukai* (1923–1941), which later became *IDEA*. An economic inspection tour around the world led him to plan the first issue of a new design magazine. As Japan recovered from the war and leaped forward into a period of rapid economic growth, he named the magazine, '*IDEA*: the magazine of the world,' to introduce Japan's culture, aesthetic sensibility, and manufacturing philosophy, topics that were beginning to garner worldwide attention. The logo was designed by Yusaku Kamekura, one of Japan's leading graphic designers at the time.

Although the word 'design' was still alien to the Japanese vernacular, Kamekura organized GRAPHIC '55 (1955) as a design exhibition led by the designers themselves. Kamekura is also known as an advocate for the social recognition of graphic designers and a leader in the postwar Japanese design industry. While Kamekura was also a contributor to *IDEA* since its inception, he and other designers led the magazine to become publicly recognized as a platform for graphic designers to question and exchange ideas of their own volition.

Collaborative Editing with Designers

Due to the circumstances surrounding its inception, the magazine continued to collaborate with designers, attracting numerous submissions and texts from Japan and abroad. The present two hundred-page, full-color edition owes much to technological advances in printing design, including the proliferation of color printing and DTP. Since the 1990s, *IDEA*'s page design became more graphics-oriented, and its collaboration with designers shifted from a text- and project-based approach consisting of contributions and group discussions to a style of communication that relied primarily on visual language. IDEA, a trade magazine that had ideologically led the graphic design industry, became a platform for implementing visual language, weaving together graphics and text and focusing on paper and printing as a mode of expression.

Implementation
since 2000

Since the 2000s, as the internet allowed digitized works to be handled much more efficiently, up-and-coming design movements in Europe and projects that featured young designers were published with a minimal time lag. The old-school design magazine became connected to the progressive movement and established a unique position as a journal specializing in graphic design. This was made possible by design editors such as Kiyonori Muroga, former editor-in-chief of *IDEA*, and Toshiaki Koga, a former editorial staff member who focused on typographic research and design criticism, and others who have kept their eyes on the forefront of Western graphics culture. Later, *IDEA* has intermittently taken up the context of critical design, which was becoming increasingly prevalent in Europe and the United States. It has introduced designers who question design from outside the boundaries of capital and production and engage in autonomous activities to explore problems independently. Issue 391, which was released in September of 2020, was titled: 'Alternative Reality—Design and imagination in dangerous times: where fantasy and reality intersect.' The first half of the issue was titled 'Phantom Spoon,' which featured contributions from designers around the world. It showcased promotional materials for exhibitions and events that were either canceled or postponed due to the pandemic and introduced them as 'phantom' design projects. By presenting each graphic alongside the circumstances of the shutdown and the story behind its production, the issue created a visual archive of the time vacuum caused by the global lockdown. The project was developed in collaboration with the London-based design collective Åbäke and the California-based designer Jon Sueda. These designers, who have explored the relationship between society and designers through not only client work but also in exhibitions, publications, and educational activities, share a commonality with the role of graphic designers that Yusaku Kamekura and others aspired to when the magazine was first published. One of the unique aspects of *IDEA* is that it has remained a design magazine co-edited by graphic designers even after seventy years since its first publication. On the other hand, the reality that the practices and discussions of such designers are still not thoroughly ingrained in society may be one reason why media like *IDEA* are still in demand.

After the Pandemic

More than the pandemic itself, its limitations on physical communication subverted the conditions and environment that provide the basis for the design work. In graphic design, the suspension of economic and cultural activities in cities around the world has forced many designers to halt their activities. This indicates that today's graphic design has not yet escaped the framework of modern design, which has developed as an inextricable part of the capitalist economy. It also brings into focus the environments within each country where the practice and discussion of postmodern design have not taken root. This is not a situation that is easily resolved with a single word, but rather a problem that leads to the essential question of what graphic design really is. At the moment, we have yet to find the answer to this question, but at least in the context of the small magazine medium, we remain free to take up and communicate mean-

ingful design practices, whether real, imaginary, or il-
lusory. With the complicity of designers from around
the world, we hope to continue to create a magazine
that challenges the existing design paradigms with a
sense of optimism.

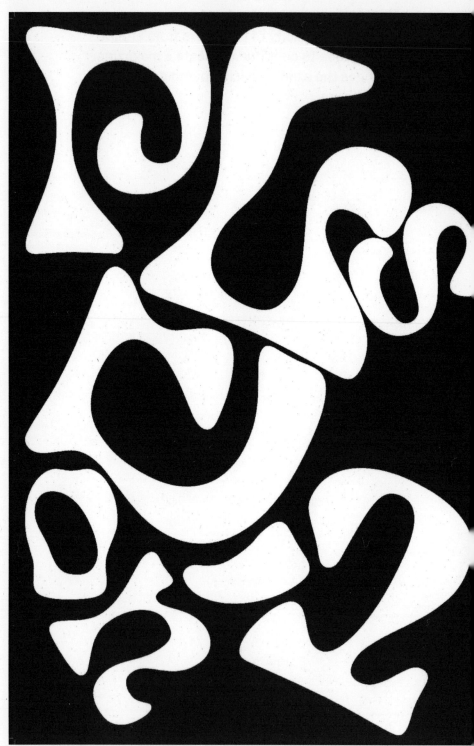

Graphic interlude by Manon Lambeens

We've Never Been Homogenized

Prologue

This essay starts with me looking back upon my childhood experience. Admittedly, it may be somewhat disconcerting to share my personal stories dating back to about three decades ago in a text that is supposed to touch upon graphic design. But I strongly felt that I needed to point out one thing – I realized many years later, after reaching adulthood that there are a few things overlapping between the experience during my childhood years and the graphic design scene that I am currently researching. In these times of pandemic, past experiences may easily be regarded as nostalgic images, but the part of my childhood I seek to recall here may be helpful in understanding the current circumstances.

What Western Europe Once Taught Me

The memories from my childhood in the distant past are penetrating my everyday life. As I grow older, the graphic images from my childhood persistently crop up. The images of childhood overlapping with what I see and feel now bear some similarities with double exposure photo images with blurred outlines. There has always been something I experience every time: something that I had not been aware of in my childhood years but have come to know now. What I perceived as a random event revealed to have been a consequence of the ideology of a certain society. In fact, whereas things that I witnessed in my childhood years were mere effects, the images and scenes of the earlier years that I recall now had their own causes.

My childhood dates back to the 1980s. Back then I was a Korean teenager with black hair who was living in Europe. Because of my father's promotion at work, I had to relocate myself to Vienna, Dusseldorf, and then Zurich. Before I finally ended a decade-long life in Europe in the beginning of 1993, I had been moving back and forth between the two different cultures of Europe and Korea. The experience had been so impactful that I ended up having a keyword engraved in my ego and mind like a set of scarlet letters: hierarchy. And the word, indeed, played a crucial part in building my identity.

I was born into a middle-class family in Seoul. Before my second relocation to Europe in 1985, I was one of so-called 'good students' who did well at school and listened to the teachers. I purposefully disclose this piece of my past, because I assume that if I had not moved to Europe, I would have taken a path that the majority of people of my age took in those days. In short, I was one of those unlikely children who could have been marginalized in the society, and thus, the vocabularies such as hierarchy would have only been a conceptual word that I might have encountered in a dictionary. The years in Europe, however, turned my stable position upside down.

I remember it was when I went to a Gymnasium in Dusseldorf, Germany. One of the teachers teaching politics referred to me as "a student from a small country in Asia." To me, the reason why the teacher chose such words remains a mystery, yet I can recall that I felt intimidated by the words, "a small country in Asia." I found myself being starkly set apart from the rest of my classmates, while I already stood out because of my looks. Moreover, one of the classmates mentioned one day, "it would be boring back in Korea, because everybody has the same black hair."

My German was too limited back then to make some proper counterargument, but the notion to equate 'black-colored hair' with 'boredom' has been a dismay to me even to this day. In this logic, all monochromatic painting is nothing but a tedious visual world. Indeed, the gap between Korea and Western European countries was vast in culture and economy in the 1980s. Back then, so many conditions in Western Europe—for example, nicely designed textbooks, well-furnished public swimming pools that were accessible at affordable cost, and unparalleled awareness for the environment—would ceaselessly remind me of the hierarchy among countries.

In the meantime, discriminatory remarks from around me kept dampening me, and being keenly aware of the hierarchy further led to psychological isolation. Even though I may have looked like a bright child, I set myself a psychological defense line that I would not be able to make my foothold at the center of the Western European culture. Moreover, it was not a matter that could have been converged simply into racial or national hierarchy as it coincided with the time of utmost sensitivity in one's life: teenage years.

At least twice a day, crossing the threshold of my home, I was compelled to shift from one culture to the other. This was not a simple shift from liberal and individualistic values of Europe to the Korean traditional values, because it also signaled a time shift. In layers of time zones, a hierarchy of times was formed. To me, back then, the time of Western Europe tilted towards progressiveness, whereas my home inclined closer to conservativeness. As layers of time collide and coexist, and then at the same time, form borderlines, I found myself being urged to find some guidelines that would help me with clarity in being myself. Figuratively, I wanted to know where I was, standing on the contour line. But in reality, there wasn't one. Sometimes, I was pushed to the periphery, at other times, I would receive warm welcome thanks to the kindness of my friends, while at still other times, I would be jeered at by strangers on streets yelling at me "Chinese" or I was sexually harassed with flirting remarks like, "Ciao, Bella!" Every time I headed back home, leaving parties at friends' houses where by the then Korean standards unimaginable intimacy was displayed amongst couples, I had to leave aside some of the value outside the door, like a mask I would take off. I might have to label myself back then with 'multiple consciousness,' superseding well beyond what Du Bois referred to as "double consciousness." Hovering on borderlines so many times within a single day, I would gain experiencing in acting in multiple worlds.

Hierarchy, in and of itself, was hierarchical. Whereas lower ranks would endlessly continue below higher ranks, still lower ranks would ceaselessly do so below such lower ranks. Only the relative relationship and the keen sense accompanying it could be helpful in discerning the difference.

The Sub-empire Called Seoul
Graphic Design

When I went back to Korea in the beginning of the 1990s, I could feel that my home welcomed me with warmth. Psychologically and emotionally, I could finally retrieve stability. But then I found something strange. Everybody around me envied me endlessly. And it did not take me long to realize that a person like me who spent years in Europe would 'unconditionally' become a subject of attention and envy in a then developing country like Korea. The discrimination that I experienced due to hierarchy transformed into a basis and prerequisite for a brilliant personal record. Having spent years living outside of Korea and being able to speak a few foreign languages, I found myself placed in a 'position' that deserved special treatment. This obviously made me feel tremendously uncomfortable, yet thanks to what I earned from the discrimination that I had experienced, I was able to stay active in Korean society after overcoming challenges in blending myself back home in Korea for the first few years. And quite unexpectedly, I once again encountered the word 'hierarchy' in the very unlikely graphic design scene.

I currently live in Daegu. Daegu is a medium-sized city in Korea with a population of two point five million, and can be reached from Seoul in less than two hours by high-speed train. Admittedly, the city is small compared to the metropolis Seoul with a population of 10 million, but it boasts of its own pros: the city does not have issues of horrific traffic jams; any place is accessible in less than half an hour; and most places are accessible on foot or bicycle. However, for its political conservativeness, Daegu has historically earned such notoriety that some Koreans express their disgust about the city. In fact, Daegu is one of the conservative cities, just like most other regions in Korea. Rather than being open to influence and influx from outside, the city is closed. Because there are a limited number of adequate jobs, the younger-aged population that seeks changes naturally leave their home for Seoul or the metropolitan area. For a person like me who runs a studio making photobooks, I am less than satisfied with the fact that the majority of great exhibitions are held in Seoul. Local galleries and museums promote local artists, but what they highlight is locality, not artistic value. This is quite a pity from my perspective.

Based in regions outside of the Seoul metropolitan area, such as Daegu, what I felt acutely is that Korea runs a tremendously centralized system pivoting around Seoul. So much so that some refer to the country as the 'Republic of Seoul.' Even in the digital era with hyper-connectivity like today, the cultural and emotional gap between Seoul and 'non-Seoul' areas is wide. Whereas graphic design thrives on cultural capital and resources, such assets and resources are so much concentrated in Seoul that graphic design scenes outside of the Seoul area can barely grasp the opportunity for growth. I opened my eyes to this, because I became part of the minority as a 'non-Seoulite', and was placed on a periphery.

When graphic design in Seoul claims relative advantage over that of Daegu, then it is logical to question the significance and position of graphic design in Seoul. Before rushing to find answers, it would be helpful to take a closer look at how the term 'design' was first coined and spread throughout Korea nationwide. First, I personally figured, while studying graphic design in Seoul, that industrial design was placed on an upper area that dominated the graphic design scene in Korea. One of the recent publications, *Design Korea* (2020) illustrates how design evolved along the path of nationalism. After the Japanese colonization in the beginning of the twentieth century and the Korean War in 1950, South Korea could not recover without aid from the United States. Against such a backdrop, the dictator regime in the country back then strongly pushed ahead with industrialization, in parallel with pro-American policy. The entire country operated like a factory at full throttle, and the only goal was modernization to escape from poverty. Design was one of the tools to foster industries in the name of 'exporting art.' State-led promotion of design continued in the 1980s, reaching the zenith in the Seoul Summer Olympic Games of 1988. Indeed, the modern design of Korea is deeply rooted in the idea that design should be part of public offering for national reconstruction.

The origin of the Korean design later left an enormous impact on the perception of design and placed graphic design, which deals with visual communication revolving around texts and images, outside of the visibility range. One of the Korean design critics, Choi Bum, commented that "graphic design in Korea is a colony to the Korean industrial design." Within the criteria of what is called 'design,' graphic design barely receives spotlight within the sub-category of design. Publications on 'design in Korea' have been released, yet most of them touch on industrial design, while graphic design is often only featured in a limited number of pages despite its vastness in themes and categories ranging from Hangul and typography to posters. I am currently working on the Korean graphic design in the 1980s, and face some difficult challenges. Believe it or not, no research or publication on the Korean graphic design in the 1980s has been done thus far. A handful of publications may have featured it, yet the focus was mostly on heroic narratives or one-off events such as the Seoul 1988 Summer Olympic Games.

For those who have seen and experienced the contemporary Korean graphic design may see some oddity in such an imbalance. Some contemporary graphic design in Seoul, which is featured in numerous publications in Europe and the United States including *It's Nice That* (www.itsnicethat.com), exude outstanding capabilities of designers. Indeed, the graphic design in Seoul has reached its peak today. And the scene is led by young and promising designers in their twenties and thirties. Unlike older generations, they don't have any cultural inferiority complex toward Japan or the West. For them, the design language of Western graphic design is one of the contemporary visual languages that they can accept and choose any time, before labeling it 'Western.' For instance, the quirky scene of multilingual typography is an outcome of fascinating graphics that would stimulate retina, as well as a part of phenomena. To make a critical review of the scene in 2020, however, there are few historical documents available.

Whereas the past can be a good reference to understand the present, the graphic design scene in Korea is facing the absence of its past, as the past has not been documented. The absence of history as a rich resource has thus led to a sluggish pace in understanding and keeping up with the design scene today. In turn, the graphic design scene in Seoul is the most glamorous yet empty at the same time. Most of all, the opportunity was limited to discuss the history of graphic design in Seoul. Today, the graphic design in Seoul is dominating the local graphic design scenes in Korea. But interestingly, from what was once one of the 'lower-ranked empires' within the hierarchical context dominated by Europe, Japan and the United States, Seoul has grown and evolved into a 'global city' and maintains an equal relationship with other metropolitan cities around the world. Indeed, just like the critic Seo Dongjin quoted Saskia Sassen's notion on 'global city,' Seoul assimilates more with New York in the United States or Tokyo in Japan, than with Daegu in Korea.[1] This becomes clear in the graphic design scene, and Daegu keeps being marginalized in the hierarchical structure. However, when compared with the industrial design scenes that systematically respond to the national policies, the graphic design in Seoul is placed in a status of less significance and importance. Johanna Drucker once asked, "How are we to conceptualize what is graphic about graphic design?" In Korea, a multi-layered hierarchy makes the Korean graphic design into 'graphic.' And all surrounding circumstances makes the Korean graphic design technique difficult with so-called 'multi-layers.'

We've Never Been Homogenized

Many design writers of today, ranging from Philip B. Meggs or Victor Margolin to Alexandra Midal, have indicated that design history has been heavily dependent on art history or the history of architecture. Turning pages of related literature, I came to look back upon the writing environment in the design scene in which hierarchy has inevitably been established. And then I find myself being urged to ask once again, whether the Korean graphic design, which is subordinate to the discourse gravitating around industrial design, can

1   Introducing Saskia Sassen's book, Seo Dongjin described: "because cities now have flow of financial capital as the main axis and are placed in the circuit of information as the key route of movement, she made it clear that the cities assimilating with Seoul are New York, London, Singapore and Shanghai, rather than Incheon or Suwon in Korea." Seo Dongjin, 'Texts on City', in *xyZ City* (Seoul, 2010), p. 194.

ever be depicted, given that the design scene in the Western world has not entirely been free from such hierarchy. Ruben Pater described in his book, *The Politics of Design* (2017) that graphic design shall never be fair in the context of global capitalism. Hyper-connectivity promotes itself saying that any communication will be possible, yet communication issues are still lingering at local level. Moreover, there are still regions and groups that are marginalized from communication. So many declare habitually that the world has been homogenized, whereas it is still full of bumps.

While the graphic design in Seoul is relatively inferior in terms of discourse of the industrial design, it is claiming relative advantage over the graphic design in non-Seoul areas. And at the same time, the graphic design in Seoul is sharing the visual languages of the time with the global cities. Without awareness for the topology of this hierarchy, some graphic design activities will inevitably be volatilized or nullified, and many of us could be misled in thinking that graphic design has captured the global language of today. This is the motivation behind maintaining a conservative stance, and adhering to the term 'graphic' design in the research and studies, despite what many would refer today as 'the era of convergence.' Hierarchy is steady and omnipresent. We have never been homogenized. I suppose now I have seen a glimpse of the reason why my childhood in the 1980s is still lingering in my present.

EVERYTHING IS A

COPY OF A COPY OF A COPY
OF A COPY OF A COPY OF A
COPY OF A COPY OF A COPY
OF A COPY OF A COPY OF A
COPY OF A COPY OF A COPY
OF A COPY OF A COPY OF A
COPY OF A COPY OF A COPY
OF A COPY OF A COPY OF A
COPY OF A COPY OF A COPY
OF A COPY OF A COPY OF A
COPY OF A COPY OF A COPY
OF A COPY OF A COPY OF A
COPY OF A COPY OF A COPY
OF A COPY OF A COPY OF A
COPY OF A COPY OF A COPY
OF A COPY OF A COPY OF A
COPY OF A COPY OF A COPY

Graphic interlude by Lisa-Marie Fechteler

To Change and Not to Change
From Graphic Design to Visual Communication Design

When I was in college my major was called Graphic Design. Today, I teach the same major at the same university but the name has been changed to Visual Communication Design. I'm not surprised by this change, for I know universities worldwide have been doing the same. Whereas in Europe, where tradition remains intact, universities choose a less radical path. They combine the two terms, and it becomes 'Graphic Design/Visual Communication Design.' But renaming of a major is more than keeping up with the 'trend'. It has a deeper and wider connotation, which a change of name cannot express sufficiently by itself, i.e., whether the decision is made merrily or reluctantly. We need to think about what's behind the change and try to make sense of it. That's how we know where we're going next. Here I would like to share some of my personal observations and thoughts.

Similar to 'product design' and 'interior design,' 'graphic design' is also a product of labor division in modern society. But the difference with the first two is that the word 'graphic' does not refer to an entity or carrier but to a pure visual form. Reality gives birth to it but is not always truthfully reflected by it. Graphic design is people's understanding of reality, or the reflection or imagination of it. From the perspective of social production, graphic design is the bridge of the front-end message or content, which is non-visual, and the back-end carrier, which is visual, such as posters or books. In other words, 'graphic design' plays the role of a 'visual translator,' the necessity of which is obvious because our eyes are the main access to the information we acquire. However, if the social function of graphic design is only that of visually translating or transforming a message, it should be a major in schools of journalism, communication or humanities. Yet, it is a major for art or design students at most of the universities in the world. Some attribute this to history, for practical disciplines are doomed to be constrained by technologies. Of course, graphic design should be in schools of art and design since its knowledge and skills are closer to what is taught in these schools. But I don't think this explanation is sound enough, because if it is more reasonable to craft graphic design in the academic system of social communication, undoubtedly a more rational and scientific repertoire of knowledge and skills can be established based on this. In the old days, drawing skills were restricted by knowledge and techniques. However, today's practitioners are able to leverage all kinds of tools, from the ever-maturing computer-aided drawing to image processing software and even big data and artificial intelligence. Are drawing skills still an insurmountable barrier in front of us? Why is graphic design still a major in art or design institutes in most countries? In China, graphic design is no longer the specialty of art schools but exists not only in communication and medical schools but also in mining, agricultural, or geosciences universities. However, nearly none of this large number of bold attempts can prove the success of a graphic design major when it is separated from the soil of art and creation.

Hence, like I said, the social function of this discipline is not as simple as visually translating information. Otherwise, personal expression would give way to standardization, artistic imagination to rationalism and logicism, free exploration and wild attempts to dogmas and repetition. But the truth speaks exactly the opposite. Graphic design can be one of the freest and most personalized field even in art and design schools. Moreover, many graphic designers share similar bearing and ways of doing things with artists. They like to call themselves 'artists' too, instead of 'design workers.' (Poster designers in Europe like the 'artist' tag very much.)

You could say it's only a matter of choosing one's preferred working title, just like a preference for formal or casual clothes. But if we take a closer look at it, we will find that choosing between 'designer' and 'artist' is not only a choice of identity, but also of value. The former emphasizes the designer's function of serving society while the latter stresses an artist's creativity and personality. Practitioners may easily find either one relatable, but the social value of graphic design as a whole is co-generated by both of them. In this sense, visual communication has become an act that integrates cultural thinking and artistic expression. Graphic design has become, naturally, the most popular and largest creation of public art.

Before the time of electronic media and the internet, print media dominated the social visual communication system. The knowledge framework of graphic design was essentially established on the basis of characteristics of printing technology and media. The framework has gone through the industrial age of handicrafts, machinery, and electronics. It remains stable and continues to mature. In the second half of the twentieth century, graphic design reached its peak in the entire Western world in terms of artistic achievement, contribution to business ecosystems, and social influence. Many universities provided graphic design majors with a complete teaching system from basic training and experimental workshops to theory study and field applications. Numerous excellent art pieces emerged. Successful creators were also praised as art masters. Various industry associations and organizations were founded where academic and public cultural activities were held. Brilliant works were welcomed by museums and galleries as art masterpieces. At the same time, it also flourished in developing countries. (For example, graphic design has become the fastest-growing design major in China, provided at over 2000 universities, according to statistics.) However, all of this is built on the dominance of print media in the social visual communication system. When electronic media and the internet began to wield their advantages, print media collapsed almost in the blink of an eye. The seemingly solid knowledge framework started to crack from the inside out.

Although electronic media and the internet use graphics as the visual carrier and so do print media, there are huge differences. Therefore, the old knowledge and skill framework of graphic design, which was deeply rooted in print media, are difficult to implement through electronic media and the internet. The biggest obstacle is that the techniques of screen display are completely different from those of paper printing, and it requires different ways of watching or reading. Hence, much knowledge or many fine skills in print media area will be useless on the screen. Another problem is that screen media is born for dynamic content as dynamics are one of the most essential elements in the entire picture. Whereas print media depends on static content to form the basic format or even the boundary of the entire piece. Although both of them create and rely on images, the format and system are completely different. The final and most essential difference lies in the information logic behind the two. Screen media (especially on the internet) share the logic of 'growth and interaction'; print media that of 'stable dissemination.' Without doubt, the former adapts better to the internet landscape where the information flow is literally among everyone. Although the change of media does not necessarily mean that the original knowledge and skills will fail completely, the reconstruction of the entire knowledge system is inevitable.

Technological advances have no limit at all. Today, the impact on graphic design is far more than screen media and the Internet. For instance, AI has involved in daily creation. Big data and machine learning enable AI to design a poster or a logo that meets functional requirements and aesthetic standards with the greatest ease, the efficiency of which is far higher than that of manual work. Some graphic designers scorn at AI and believe it will never replace personalized creation and the brilliance of the human brain. Although no definite and convincing answer is available at present, it is obvious that, like in many other industries, the service provided by AI can already meet the most basic demands in society, and perhaps even better than the creations of human practitioners who are less capable.

With the argument above, I believe the true intention behind the renaming is now clear. Abandoning the word 'graphic' is transcending the stale knowledge framework based on print media and returning to its most original and fundamental function of communication. In a word, the new name demonstrates the state of not being confined in or defined by any specific media or technologies and represents the attempt to communicate with society through visual channels. Of course, it is only a starting point from which a new academic framework that keeps up with social development should be established. In this reshaping process, changing our concepts should be the 'primary productive force.'

First of all, we should keep an open mind with regard to the concept of 'media.' This does not refer to the renewal of media but that we should recognize that in the changed time we now live in nearly everything can be a medium for visual communication. (In fact, the development of media is not about replacing the old with new ones but to provide more options. Besides, print media have some advantages that screen media cannot have.) Thanks to the development of electronic technologies and the internet, screen media have reigned the world of graphic design for the past twenty to thirty years. But society never ceases to move forward. Today, scholars and industry leaders in many fields agree that online and offline will be increasingly integrated in the future. In this sense, at least two messages are clear. One is that the connection and integration of screen and offline media will be an important subject in the near future. The other is that people need to reconsider the value of the offline world, which suffered from erosion over the past few decades. However, it will again become the main scene on which media can be applied. Or even the scene itself can serve as the medium. Thus, how to design within a cross-media structure will be a significant question in the new knowledge framework of Visual Communication Design. Also, 'open' media involves the shift from a static pictorial art to a comprehensive one that includes static, dynamic. and synthetic scenes.

Secondly, we must face up to the impact of technological innovations and embrace the change they bring, be it a helping hand or a menacing threat. Both technologies are closely related to graphic design and may not deserve our attention. Because today's technologies tend to intertwine with each other and cross disciplines very easily. As I mentioned before, we have failed to react and adjust to the rise of screen media and the internet. Now we don't want to repeat the same mistake when facing the presence of new technologies in design such as AI, although to some extent, adequate discussion has already lacked. But as I insist, an open mind is essential. Only then will we realize that technologies that used to 'threaten' us now hold huge opportunities. They are the boost for the reshaping of a new knowledge framework and for future development of the major. I'm not denying the attention paid to technological innovations in the past. As a matter of fact, the continuous improvement of printing techniques by generations of practitioners contributed much to the golden days of graphic design in the last century. But what is different from then is that we need to keep a watchful eye on far more technologies and respond faster and better to any new changes. After all, we, as individuals, are destined to adapt to a future with fast-changing technologies. How can graphic design survive without doing so? If the discipline belonged to liberal arts in the past, 'Visual Communication Design' is undoubtedly to be interdisciplinary, fusing liberal arts, science, and engineering.

Thirdly, the new knowledge system should transcend the single channel of expression, like the new name suggests. Of course, from the perspective of study, focusing on the visual channel brings deeper understanding of know-how. But in the real world, people get their information and communicate with each other not only through the visual channel. As a matter of fact, in social life, vision is integrated with other sensory channels in most cases. Before the electronic age, almost all visual art pieces were created following the rule of 'watching silently,' and graphic design is no exception. Technological advances have given us the opportunity to welcome collaboration between vision and other senses, an opportunity that was not available to past generations. Practitioners today should cherish this and exploit it. Cross-discipline has become reality and an important tool to inspire creativity. This is why Visual Communication Design, as a practical field of study, should not only be about knowledge in the coterie, but also about new capabilities and opportunities brought by 'visual plus non-visual' ways of thinking. Only by being open and connecting to other knowledge systems can we create a greater synergy. In this way the new knowledge system can stay vigorous and sustainable.

Readers probably noticed that the three conceptual changes listed above are all related to technological progress and innovations. In fact, the crisis graphic design's knowledge system has encountered in recent years is largely due to a reluctant attitude. Apart from learning through bitter experience, we also need bold changes. But while looking out, we should also revisit the road this discipline has walked down and think about the core social value of it. There must be something that is worth holding onto, without overdoing it. Because if an open attitude to media, technologies, or social function means deserting the value of graphic creation, losing the human touch in it, or compromising the splendor of personal creation, the innovation might as well not take place. Of course, with all of this being said, reconstructing a knowledge system is a huge project that will take a long time and efforts by numerous individuals and organizations to accomplish. But as educators and researchers, each of us should pitch in and make due contributions.

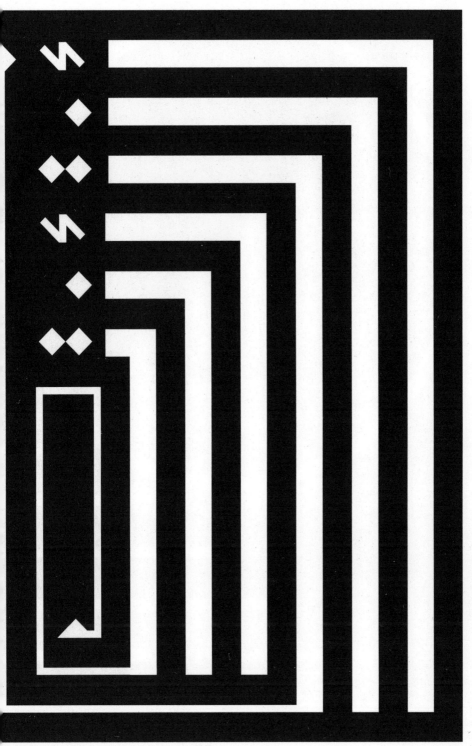

Graphic interlude by Yaman Albaker. *You are you*, 2022

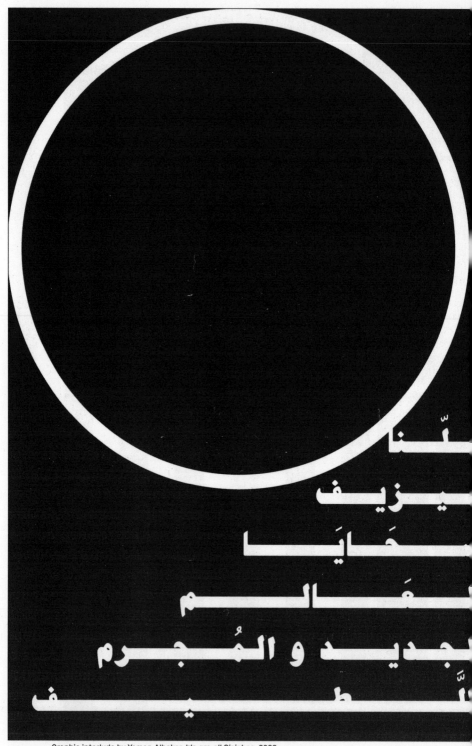

ـلنا

يزيف

ـحَايَا

ـعَالــم

لجديد و الـمُجرم

ــط ي ف

Graphic interlude by Yaman Albaker. *We are all Sisiphos*, 2022

Graphic Design as a Narrative Tool

In the early 1820s, investments in South American countries were booming. Especially the London stock market merchants were trading bonds of Peru, Colombia, and Chile like hot cake. Among those who smelled blood and profit, was also Gregor MacGregor, a Scottish soldier and adventurer, who bought land in an area of what is today known as Honduras. His only problem: the land was mainly swamp, bombastically unattractive to invest in.

So, what was not there, had to be faked. MacGregor created the imaginary country of Poyais, which he promoted through leaflets, ads, and a 355-page book in which he praised the fertility and beauty of the land. As a central component of his fake he distributed a map of Poyais, which made investors and emigrants trust him. Tricked by MacGregor, hundreds of settlers bought land and sailed towards their new home country, full of hope, only to find a mosquito-infested moor. Most of them died, only a few were saved by a British rescue mission.

Thankfully, maps haven't always had such deadly consequences. But nevertheless, they have been used throughout history to disguise, manipulate, and lie. Maps are an effective narrative tool for

A   Gregor MacGregor, *The Imaginary Country of Poyais*, c. 1820.

storytellers of all sorts, because people hardly question what they depict. Their aura of objectivity, science, and neutrality make them particular trustworthy. This powerful aura emerges first and foremost from the way maps are looking at the world—the bird's-eye view. A physical place, seen from above, is associated with a god-like, all-seeing, all-knowing perspective. It is a perspective of control and power, of wholeness and truth. What's on the map is alive and what's not, is dead. And exactly this is why maps have the power to give a physicality to places that do not exist, like Poyais.

This creation of physicality through maps is essential for the modern nation state and its political imagination. For example, China unveiled a new official map of the country in 2014, making the disputed waters of the South China Sea more clearly seem like Chinese territory by drawing a heavy dashed line around it. Obviously, this map represents hunger for territory and resources. It is a dream about a new geopolitical physicality, dreamed from the bird's-eye view. But at the same time, this map is much more. It is the graphic evidence of an agenda that wants to, as the Indian essayist Apoorva Tadepalli puts it, "root people to entities to which they would have to be loyal, but could not see." This way maps manufacture a sense of collective identity by telling stories about the spaces we live in, by narrativizing us and our physical environment.

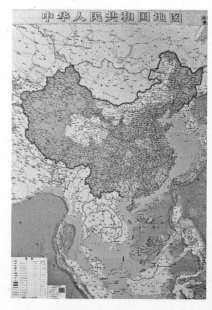

Different maps of the South China Sea, created by its surrounding countries, tell different stories about its territory because the narrativization of space is always subjective and ideological. Not least because maps are at heart a collage of distorted information. The process of

collecting, selecting, editing, visualizing, and producing this information is determined by various precon-
ditions, biases, and technologies, all of which can be
affected, or manipulated in one way or another, consciously or not. In the end, all maps are inherently
distorted views of the world. But where do these distortions exactly happen and who is in control of this
process?

Let's look at this example. Maps are made of
raw basic data, called primary data, gathered through
different methods. Firstly, it can be collected by people working in the field, measuring roads and buildings. Their results will depend on endless variables,
such as their tools, experience, skill, the agenda of
their bosses, and maybe even also on the fact whether they are hungry or not. Secondly, the data is produced by photogrammetry, a method used to analyze
aerial images. These images are taken from planes or
satellites with cameras that will always distort what
they see. Resolution, lenses, weather, altitude, manipulation, and so on can all affect this process. And at
the end, the quantity and quality of this primary data
will influence the map, its possible scale and amount
of detail entirely.

But now it becomes even
more tricky: in order to create a map
as we know it, mapmakers have to
translate this primary data from the
real world onto a flat surface, a process called 'projection.' Projecting
in a neutral way is truly impossible,

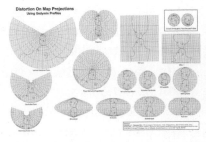

since each projection distorts the global sphere in
one way or another. Mapmakers are doomed to fail.

Today the most common and popular projection is the Mercator projection. It was drawn in 1569
and optimized for navigation at sea, using compass
directions as straight lines. This has dramatic consequences: the northern and southern poles are
stretched upwards, making some areas of the world

B   China map, 2014.
C   Distortion On
Map Projections, Using
Gedymin Profiles,
PB Anderson, 2009.

appear too small. For example, although Greenland and Africa look the same size on the Mercator map, Africa is actually fourteen times bigger. Also, South America appears the same size as Europe, when in fact it is almost twice as large. These inherent distortions of the Mercator projection are not merely a cartographer's problem, they are a political one, because they correspond to a sixteenth-century world view, when colonial powers were dominating the world. Europe is at the center, Western empires are bigger and situated on top of the map, whereas the suppressed others are smaller and at the bottom. But you will be surprised, despite its difficult socio-political connotations, that the Mercator projection is used almost everywhere today. Google maps, Apple maps and Bing maps are all using it, and probably you have used it at school too.

Although there is no neutral and correct way of projecting the world, we have to be aware of the fact that each projection tells a different story about the world we live in. For instance, the Gall-Peters projection tells us mostly a story of political correctness, because it represents the areas and surfaces of the world equally. Not surprisingly, this makes it look distorted to the eye that's used to the Mercator projection. It is promoted by the United Nations, used in British schools and was introduced in some Boston schools recently. There, most children seeing it for the first time, were astonished, asking emphatically, as if they were betrayed for years: "What, Africa is this big, really?!"

But if you think that primary data, scale, and different projections cover all of the inherent biases that can be found in maps, I have to disappoint you. It's really just the beginning. Because on top of this, maps show their actual content through graphic symbolism. Roads, bridges, buildings, harbors or process-

D   Distortion on map projection, Greenland in real comparison to Africa.

es of trade and politics are represented through colors, shapes, thickness, contrast, sizes, patterns, and a million more things, which tell you what is important, dense, long, or short; they are graphic codes that create stories about the world.

Like the map of the oil and fuel company Esso from the early 1970s. Conveniently, it showed a visual difference between fast and slow roads. Fast was bright yellow, slow was less saturated. But this turned out to be wrong if you looked closely—because the bright yellow lines actually highlighted not the expressways, but the ones that contained Esso gas stations.

As we see maps are, as map theorist Denis Wood describes it, not *naturalized windows* on the world at all, but *arguments about* the world. Maps are not neutral, they are narrativized space, stories written in the language of graphic design. And if we consider—pointed out by journalists, sociologists, and writers again and again—that we will eventually become the stories that we *tell* ourselves, we start to understand the delicate terrain we are in when we draw a map or look at one.

But now the question is, how do we deal with these issues of bias and manipulation as authors and graphic designers? Especially in a world that is full of maps and infographics, generated by the media, states, companies, individuals, and algorithms alike. How do we design maps in an age of democratized and automated map making tools, where maps are travelling fast as light, creating evermore what Walter Lippmann has described as "pseudo-realities" of our information bubbles? The bad news: we don't have final answers to these questions. The good news: here are some ideas.

For sure, you could do it like Google maps and pretend that everything is fine. For instance, during the height of the Russia-Ukraine conflict Google decided to show the Russian version of the border line if you accessed Google from Russia, and the Ukraine version if you accessed it from the Ukraine. So, if you want to run away from political problems of our time and please everybody in the name of slick usability and its related profits, you should go for this option.

Or you could do the opposite and face the contradictions our world has to offer. Like Herbert Bayer, a Bauhaus-trained, Austro-American graphic designer, artist, and architect. When approached by the Container Corperation of America to design an update of their *Atlas of the World* in 1953, he decided to create a publication that shows a "new graphical narrative of humans and geography." In order to achieve this, he collected most of the data himself, travelling and researching for five years throughout Europe, because "a scientist would not think in terms in which I worked." Bayer called it "a good adult education"—and indeed, his approach represents the idea that a graphic designer could also become a much more active and educated actor, an author and editor of content who doesn't accept the pre-

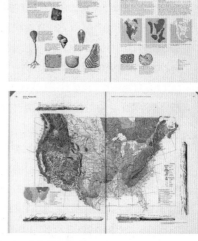

fabricated data and shapes of his time and looks for new ways of collecting and visualizing information.

The American conceptual artist Mark Lombardi pushed this research-driven, investigative approach even further. He spent months in libraries, browsing public sources for new entries into his extensive archival system of more than 12,000 index cards about politics and economics. This research was so elaborate that journalists and supposedly even the FBI used it. In a following step he tried to carve out otherwise invisible connections by extracting interlinked peo-

E   Herbert Bayer, *World Geo-Graphic Atlas: A Composite of Man's Environment*, The Container Corporation of America, 1953.

ple and processes from these cards, creating huge paintings, which he called *narrative structures*. Although he didn't make use of cartographic elements, Lombardi's structures are mapping information almost like maps do, showing us that there are no easy answers in a world full of complex interdependencies.

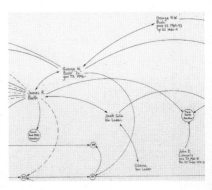

Another way of making people aware of map-inherent distortions is to confront different kind of maps, projections, and views with each other. For example, in our practice with *Migrant Journal*—a publication about the movement of people, goods, information, capital, flora, and fauna—we try to use different projections of the world depending on the context of the story. This relates to the approach of the journal, where we try to disrupt and challenge existing notions and stereotypes about migration, and challenge our readers. If design, as Tony Fry argues "either serves or subverts the status quo," we definitely try to be on the more subversive side with the way we draw our maps and infographics in *Migrant Journal*.

Last but not least, both in *Migrant Journal* and also in our involvement with *Colors Magazine*, we've tried to escape the inherent traps of maps by balancing them with other narrative elements, like journalism, photo-journalism, illustrations, or infographics, a practice that you

could call 'visual storytelling.' For example, *Colors Magazine* takes a global outlook on issues of our time by telling stories in an engaging, multi-layered, and narrative fashion. Very different visual and textual components come together for a rich reader experience—the single elements provide different entry points, create rhythm, intertwine with each other, and unfold eclectic narratives that are more than

F   Mark Lombardi,
*Narrative Structures
and Other Mapping of
Power Relations*, 1990s.
G   *Colors Magazine*.

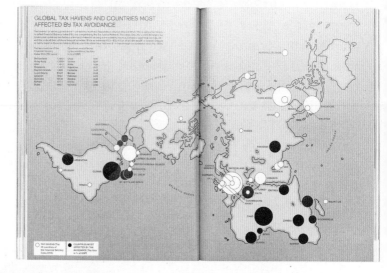

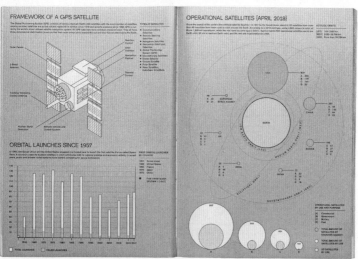

Magazine design *Migrant Journal #2 – Wired Capital* by Offshore, 2017.

the sum of their parts. This allows us to use maps where it's appropriate, but also to compensate for their weaknesses with other visual and conceptual approaches. Quite often, this creates more balanced and nuanced, but also stronger, more engaging narratives.

Interestingly enough, *Colors Magazine* and *Migrant Journal* were encouraging designers to realize this potential by questioning what a graphic designer should and can do. Both magazines pushed designers to investigate, research and dig

really deep into the content; they could even suggest and create stories by collaborating with journalists, researchers, photographers, and illustrators. This way graphic designers and everybody else involved becomes an active part in reading, negotiating, redefining, and telling more critical and nuanced stories about the world we live in.

But in order to use graphic design as a narrative tool that doesn't make simplistic and biased judgments about the world, we need to realize first that no graphic shape is innocent, nothing is neutral, nothing is objective. Every visual expression comes with its politics and it's up to us whether we want to use these inherent politics blindly or want to accept our responsibility in questioning and challenging them. Because, as Jerry Brotton puts it: "We always get the map that our age deserves"—and probably we want to make sure that the map of our age is not a seaman's map from 1569.

WHAT DO YOU SEE? *

*A CRYSTAL GOBLET OR TWO THOUGHTFUL GRAPHIC DESIGNERS?

Graphic interlude by Lea Sievertsen

Designing Feminist Tools

The internet has become inseparable from culture. Its networks and technologies are interwoven with the very fabric of our daily lives. Their presence can be felt at almost every moment of the day, from the devices in our pockets, the watches tracking our fitness and the digital assistants in our homes controlling the lights and ordering our shopping. However, the internet is much more than just a service or tool. At Feminist Internet we believe the internet is imbued with radical potential. We saw this in 2020, as the dissemination of a video depicting the death of George Floyd in the United States at the hands of the police, first shared on Twitter, led to a global civil rights movement. In the weeks that followed his death, social media platforms became a space where resources were freely distributed and necessary critical discussions were held.

While the internet does hold the potential to enact change, so often we see its spaces and technologies co-opted by systems of power, with capital gain given paramount importance, leaving women and minority groups disproportionately vulnerable to violence. Violence is coded into many guises on the internet, such as the racial biases found embedded within facial recognition software[1] or the discovery that Facebook's algorithm was actively promoting Holocaust denial content.[2] In a society where profit margins are the ultimate goal, we want to question the re-

1   Joy Buolamwini, *Gender Shades: Intersectional Accuracy Disparities in Commercial Gender Classification* (Cambridge US, 2018).
2   Mark Townsend, 'Facebook Algorithm Found to "Actively Promote" Holocaust Denial' (*The Guardian*, 2020).

Designing Feminist Tools

lentless commodification of bodies that leads to such violence, recognizing value as something that should be defined by more than capitalist motives.

Formed in 2017 as part of a workshop at University of the Arts London, Feminist Internet is comprised of a group of individuals of varying gender identities and backgrounds. We place collaboration not competition at the heart of how we operate, working as a collective without a hierarchical structure. Feminist Internet seeks to harness the internet as a tool, tackling a range of internet-based inequalities, using the online to affect change offline and the offline to affect change online. Our goal is to create a more equal and fairer internet for all.

A key framework for how we operate is found in our 'Feminist Design Tool'. Developed as a continuation of AI researcher Josie Young's 'Feminist Chatbot Design Process' the tool is a framework of defensible decision making for interaction design and AI. So often technologies and AI have societal biases and inequalities encoded within them. An example of this being in summer 2020 when an algorithm used to predict exam grades in British schools (following their cancellation due to the coronavirus pandemic) was found to be disproportionality downgrading grades of pupils from lower socioeconomic backgrounds.[3] The problem isn't that the technologies are biased, it's that the biases of their creators and the selective data fed into them are.

'The Feminist Design Tool' seeks to challenge this by asking designers questions such as "Does your design meet a meaningful human need or address an injustice? Do you have a good understanding of the context your design will be part of and the power dynamics at play within it? Have you reflected on how your values and position might lead you to choose one option over another or hold a specific perspective on the world?" The tool allows developers to deepen their understanding of the values they are embedding with-

3   Richard Adams, Niamh McIntyre, 'England A-level Downgrades Hit Pupils from Disadvantaged Areas Hardest' (*The Guardian*, 2020).

in their design as it is created. The questions laid out in the tool are crafted to help make the design process more reflexive, aiding designers in being critical about their own biases, creating a framework for design to ensure that what is being developed doesn't knowingly or unknowingly perpetuate stereotypes or inequalities.

'The Feminist Design Tool' was initially created as part of our 'Designing a Feminist Alexa' project. Beginning as a talk at IAM Weekend in Barcelona in 2018, the project grew into a series of workshops in which participants were tasked with thinking about how we could create a personal intelligence assistant that meets a meaningful human need. The need for such a technology arose out of criticisms of devices such as Amazon's Alexa or Apple's Siri, in that they were reinforcing negative gender stereotypes, placing women in a subservient position. Simultaneously they were inadequately responding to misogynistic language and abuse.[4] For example, Siri was found to say "I'd blush if I could" when told an expletive comment.

We put our design tool to use in the creation of F'xa, a chatbot that provides users with a feminist guide to AI bias. Created in collaboration with design studio Comuzi, F'xa is designed to teach people about AI bias and point them towards actions that can help reduce it. F'xa has not been assigned a gender and in the conversation design it was important for us that the bot never says "I". This was in recognition of the complex emotional relationships people can develop with chatbots that are designed to feel human. Not saying "I" keeps the user aware that they're not talking to someone or something with a consciousness of its own. This was reinforced through the user interface design as F'xa is depicted as a simple blinking eye. We would not describe F'xa as a feminist because F'xa is a chatbot and is not able to self-identify. Rather, we would define it as a feminist technology because it has been designed using our stan-

4   Unesco, 'I'd Blush if I could' (Unesco: Equal Skills Coalition, 2019).

dards with feminist principles embedded within its architecture.

Since the creation of the design tools in 2017, we have developed them further as part of our exploration of Eco-Feminism. 'Designing an Ecological Alexa', first presented at Impact Festival in Utrecht in 2019, asked participants to consider how we can reduce the environmental impact of technologies. The design standards were adapted to become the 'Eco-Feminist Design Standards' expanding on the original standards by asking questions such as "Does your design meet an environmental need or address a climate injustice? Does your design encourage people to spend excessive amounts of time online? And how could your design minimize the consumption of large/high-quality images/videos et cetera to reduce energy use?"

The creation of the ecological standards became a poignant moment for us to question how our own designs met an environmental need. In designing the branding and promotional material for 'Designing an Ecological Alexa' we wanted to create assets that were as digitally weightless as possible. This meant creating bit-mapped low-resolution imagery using minimal colors to create file sizes much smaller than what is normally found on the internet. We have come to understand that as the demand for higher-quality content continues to grow we must question the consequences of big data on the environment. Recent studies have shown that data centers account for around three percent of the global energy supply and two percent of greenhouse gas emissions, with the global tech industry having the same carbon footprint as the aviation industry.[5] With only around half the world connected to the internet, it's important to understand the impact that our always-online culture and its continued growth is having on the global environment.

As Feminist Internet we feel it is important for us to highlight and tackle the breadth of inequalities

5   Adam Vaughan, 'How Viral Cat Videos are Warming the Planet' (The Guardian, 2015).

and issues embedded within the internet and its technologies. The consequences of an always-online world have lasting effects offline and we believe that education is the key to eradicating ignorance and prejudice. We want to cultivate spaces where  we can begin to creatively and critically solve these problems using an intersectional framework. We recognize that many overlapping systems of oppression create the very inequalities we are trying to tackle, including racism, sexism, transphobia, xenophobia, anti-Semitism and ableism. For us, it's about building towards concrete actions and creating solutions to bring about real change so that the internet can be a more equal space for all.

A   Alexa Halftone.

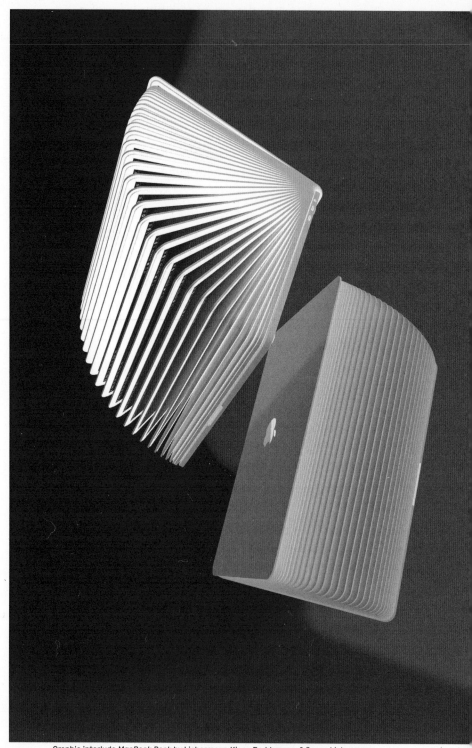

Graphic interlude *MacBook Book* by Liebermann Kiepe Reddemann & Jonas Liebermann

Konrad Renner (Knoth & Renner)

Resistant Web

The Web is standardized. In the thirty years of its existence, it has been increasingly conditioned and adapted to the primarily economic needs of its protagonists. Today, corporations and autocratic governments stand in the way of the loose and anti-authoritarian network of scientists of the late 1980s, based on the idea of decentralized organization of knowledge, freedom of speech, and the unhindered exchange of information. When Tim Berners-Lee published the world's first website at CERN in Switzerland on 6 August 1991, it read: "Hypertext and HyperMedia are concepts, not products."[1] Almost twenty-eight years later, it must be said that his hope has not been fulfilled.

Driven by constantly developing technology, the expansion of infrastructures, and the economic power of the new marketplace, standards have been agreed on over the years—recurring patterns, a visual language that determines digital surfaces. On the technical side, the World Wide Web Consortium (W3C) has been deciding on technical standards such as CSS attributes[2] and HTML elements[3] in a complex coordination process since 1992. The consortium currently consists of 481 members, mainly from companies and foundations with close ties to government, such as Amazon, Volkswagen, and the Sovrin Foundation.[4] In other regards as well, the consortium is not very diverse and is a frequent focus of criticism. The decision-making processes are not transparent.

1 info.cern.ch/hypertext/WWW/WhatIs. html (accessed on 11 September 2019).
2 Cascading Style Sheets (CSS) determine the appearance of a webpage with specified formatting.
3 Hypertext Markup Language (HTML) structures websites into defined areas.
4 The Sovrin Foundation is developing a network for digital identities for banks, social media, and registration offices.

Resistant Web

For a long time, the premise was that new standards must be made available to the general public free of ownership claims. In 2017, with EME (Encrypted Media Extensions), a non-free Web standard was introduced for the first time—at the request of Google, Microsoft, and Netflix—and the old guiding principle of maximum transparency and accessibility was broken for the first time.

On the other hand, when it comes to visual standards, mainly the same gatekeepers have a significant impact on the appearance of the Web. To this end, they use design templates that they force into the collective perception. The digital templates can be arranged independently of specific content and allow users to easily publish on and through a website. Users are not required to have a knowledge of programming, nor must they make more complex visual decisions: the template ensures a suitable result within a programmed and defined radius. Thus, it is the visual connection between the back end and the front end,[5] between transmitters and receivers, and ensures a radical visual non-directionality, a maximum spectrum of possible uses. The digital templates are then offered as downloads for sale on platforms such as ThemeForest, where they can be found using technical parameters or categories such as 'Education,' 'Wedding,' or 'Political.'

In the 2016 United States presidential election campaign, a whole series of political templates for the different parties and positions emerged. From local sheriffs to candidates for the United States Senate, the political tools could be obtained from the same online marketplaces. The prices range from $30 to $59. Most of them are made available for download from companies based in Indonesia and Bangladesh. The providers are by no means specialized in political tools, but offer templates and themes for all online needs. They create generic visual interfaces that consist of the same modules, such as slideshows, feeds, and

5   The front end presents the website to visitors in a web browser. The back end is the administrative area of a website for editors to change its contents.

Konrad Renner (Knoth & Renner)

Website design *k-komma.de* by Knoth/Renner, 2018.

Magazine design by Knoth/Renner, 2017.

Website design *Schiiwerfer* by Knoth/Renner, 2016.

Poster design by Knoth/Renner, 2017.

combinations of text and images. In this case, templates consist of many templates—and thus the principle of convertibility and reuse extends even to the smallest building blocks.

It is easy to see that these templates are not only used in American politics. The 'Campaign' design template for $49 enjoys international popularity. For example, 'Campaign' is used by the German AFD politician Beatrix von Storch for her personal website without many adjustments: only the logo and the likeness were replaced. But there are more providers of design templates for the Web. Since 2014, Google has invested a great deal in its design department and launched the 'Material Design' development program. It is an attempt to use materiality as a metaphor for the physical, real world and to transfer it to digital surfaces in textures, light, and shadows. The element of materiality not only serves as a visual derivation for the designs; it is also an integral narrative of the accompanying campaign and an attempt to make the Internet giant seem more human, natural, and accessible. To this end, Google has assembled a professional team of designers and, with its own design conference and specific publications, ensures closer integration with those involved. Defined color schemes, coordinated animations, and the exclusively designed 'Google Fonts' ensure a coherent visual world that is gladly accepted by designers and developers. This certainly makes for a successful branding and at the same time a visual appropriation of space.

And now I will address a final example of design templates for the Web. Since 2015, the United States government has published the US Web Design System,[6] an open-source style set for the country's institutions. The design principles declare flexibility, speed, and ease of use as their maxims. In addition to ready-made solutions for the layout of websites, navigation elements, and typography, the framework also includes its own analysis tool,[7] which stores the col-

6   designsystem.
digital.gov.
7   analytics.usa.gov.

lected data on US government servers. Here strategies such as those taught in seminars on modern corporate communications and customer loyalty are used and further mix the realities of politics and design.

The use of templates and design frameworks results in vagueness. Clear connotations are avoided. Otherwise, the templates cannot be universally applied, and the additional effort reduces profitability. The generic forms of typography, aspect ratios, color spaces, and visuals are a principle on the part of the authors, because they are inherent to the utilization chain of design templates. Generic graphic design denies the possibility of making things distinguishable. It reproduces the same formal solution and entices with economic profit. However, since graphic design is always a time-based medium and should be linked to current social discourses, repetitive approaches are dangerous. Radical positions disguise themselves as the 'normal Web.' At first glance, they can hardly be visually distinguished from other positions or the next innovative IT startup.

Furthermore, design templates contribute to the widespread notion that we associate supposed smoothness with the Web. It is always around us, always at our side, only visible when we need it, and even then hardly noticeable and always trying to make things as comfortable as possible for users. Noiseless strolling through live data, imperceptible browsing through responsive cookies, and dark patterns of like buttons—the Web in its ideal state offers no resistance.

For graphic design on the Web, this once again leads to the task of making significant differences visible. Contrasts must be tangible, legible, and made accessible to as large an audience as possible. Dysfunctional navigation elements and stubborn search fields are obligatory methods to increase engagement with specific content. After thirty years of visual harmonization, the Web now deserves more friction.

GRAPHIC DESIGN
IS
A

NON – Neutral
NON – Individual
NON – Independent
NON – Bystander
VERY – Social
          Endeavour

MAKE SPACE
OR THE OTHER

Graphic interlude by Felix Egle

Smash the symbols of the Empire in the name of nothing but the heart's longing for grace.

Hakim Bey – Art Sabotage
Autonomedia, 1985

Graphic interlude by Felix Egle

Always Say "Graphic Design"

Always type aoufhdlkvjblifbvl49 67cnvlkdfjbh9xi seughcnlkxhgfklxh jfclnskghlakejfh.

I'd like to present a few ideas, maybe more thoughts, about graphic design discourse and criticism in general, illustrated with some examples. I started to type this text in the 'Notes' app on my phone. Since Monday it was moved to Adobe Indesign to be finished, and typeset in a font called 'Brazil'.

I would like to begin with the word, or term, that has been most important, or useful, to me in relation to my work of the last years. Especially the work I describe as 'research work.' For me research works are the published outcomes of various investigations into graphic design—it could be a book, a poster, a web page, an exhibition, essay, or a free font; it is always something transformed through the tools and devices of graphic design, the discipline to which I feel most close. The word I want to share is 'contingent'. Both as an adjective and a noun it is a word that helps me connect the many processes inherent in the production of a piece of graphic design (that leads to an output), and also a powerful starting point from which to begin to study a piece of graphic design in particular (that leads to a research). The origin of the word 'contingent' is basically a combination of the words 'happen to' and 'touch.' This word combination helps me to feel engaged as a person in the making of graphic design. A contingent graphic design, to me, is something that is chance dependent, true by process, yet not necessarily logical. Because of this its outcome is a product of how things went (and perhaps are). 'Contingency' helps me believe in a graphic design as being intentional and through that I can acknowledge the responsibility toward how I want to work within it. A contingent graphic design connects me to a history, present, and future of graphic design, but more importantly it connects me to the people and things involved in the production of it. 'Contingency' can be a way to produce criticality, it can be a method of working from a piece, or pieces, of graphic design outward, exploring its commission, its historical, formal, material, ideological, and maybe even social impact. This word, or idea, of contingency is present in many of the theoretical and designed works that I've found influential over the passing years. To name a few: Lisa Gitelman's Paper Knowledge, the work of Joseph Churchward and Karel Martens, Marie Dabbadie's transgender skateboarding fanzine XEM Skaters, and so on...

But.
As a Bachelor's level teacher and head of a department of graphic design at an art school, I realize that this word, its suggestion, or conclusion, that I have come to—through and with the help and work of, others —cannot be enough to pass on as any certainty to our students, but it can be discussed. In the last few years, I have noticed students willing and enthusiastic to redefine what graphic design is through shared, and even new, discourse. This can be read in some-

thing like See Also—an alternative graphic design Lex-
icon, whose definitions were the results of a writing
class that our department published in 2017. As practitioners and students we are all trying to find a connection to what we do and at school there is the time
to explore this connection outside of, I quote, "the
logic of standardized work processes." I type this as
not to suggest the school as being outside of reality, the 'real world,' or even standards, or work, or processes. As far as I can see school is very much a part
of the real world. (Perhaps we have to take the often stated, and conservative, suggestion that it isn't
more literally, and into our OWN hands). At school I
see and hear the students talking a lot among themselves and sharing their work. As a generation where
the distinction between physical and digital is much
more blurred, even collapsing, through their daily lives—
their study, agency and desire—there are some words
that have to change and take on a new meaning within this collapsing. Words such as Wildness, Body, Pressure, Touch, Feel, Spirit, Message, and even Communicate (among many others). These words we know (or
knew?), and the ideas surrounding them, are questioned and worked on by students; they can be reformulated. These words are part of our contemporary
condition, and their meaning spans all disciplines that
work with text, image and in the visual realm. I begin to
wonder if the true capability of graphic design is not
to create discourse and criticism, but to multiply it;
this paradigm, although more fragile, and more dangerous, seems closer to what graphic design is, and
does, as a discipline, to me.

　　To look at this idea of multiplication in another way I have to think of all the particular 'designer as'
prepositions of the passing years: graphic designer
as service provider, graphic designer as crafts-per-
son, graphic designer as author, graphic designer as
publisher, graphic designer as researcher, modernist graphic designer, postmodernist graphic design-

er, (post)internet graphic designer, [graphic designer about graphic design]? If we look at these things
as left behind—'as graphic designed'—then, are these
the things that can help us define what graphic design really is? An incredibly fast and efficient multi-
plier of information, of communication? A discipline
that is comfortable to shed its proverbial discourse
skin every few years? The wringing out of an enthusiastic sponge? Does it matter if we can't keep up?

 In 2007—after graduating from a Master's
course in Typographic Design—I put my website online. At the same time—because of the facility on the
web to type and publish text quite easily—I started
to type notes that have come to be called 'notes on
graphic design', on a webpage linked to my site. 'Notes
on graphic design' are exercises and reflections for
myself to practice ways of writing about graphic design in a freer way. On the one hand I started it as
a place to collect all the notes I made (we all make
notes), but, on the other, they are mostly to try to
write about graphic design in another way than I was/
am used to talk about it: to basically look for an alternative discourse or method of critique that I could
use within, or influence, my work. I'm not necessarily interested in them having an audience (to access
them you need to click on a bullet point near the bottom of the homepage), but writing them, publishing
them, and refining them has sometimes led me to new
formal ideas. I still update them periodically. Thinking
about them today, I guess they have been more helpful as 'sketches' of (a desired) discourse and critique,
as they are perhaps more formal than textual. Writing them feels closer to doing graphic design, more
than actually writing.

It's like the closer I get to being precise the more complicated the thing becomes. I'm O.K. with this now.
Precision is a somewhat desirable, and perhaps rightly celebrated, quality in graphic design practice. Yet it

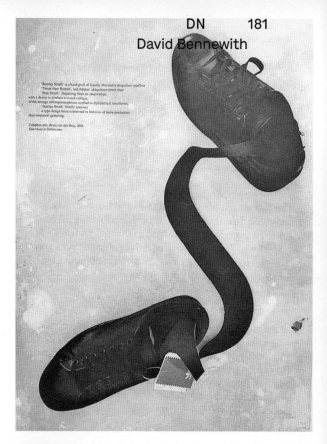

'Stanley Smith' is a hard-graft of Stanley Morison's ubiquitous typeface
'Times New Roman', and Adidas' ubiquitous tennis shoe
'Stan Smith'. Departing from an observation,
with a desire to produce a visual critique,
of the strange anthropomorphisms applied to alphabetical letterforms,
'Stanley Smith' bluntly assumes
a type design more connected to histories of mass-production
than corporeal gesturing.

Colophon info, Bram van den Berg, 2016
Download at Dafont.com

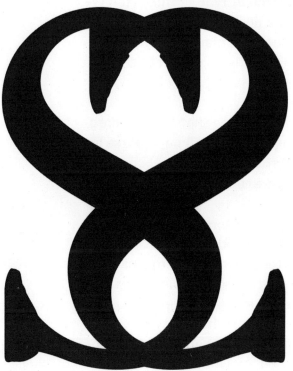

Experimental type design *Stanley Smith* by David Bennewith

is also a form of power that can shut things out rather than open them up. Is precision anti-contingent?

Finally, I've become more interested in discourse through others. And I can't somewhat help feeling even more free and inspired by other definitions or imaginations of graphic design. In particular the discipline of type design, where—since 2013—I've been using a Twitter account to retweet other people's (and even some bot's) comments and views on type design and its ever near product: fonts. This includes professionals, newcomers to the discipline, or people that are noticing their font for the first time and need to type something about it.

Within a typographic discourse these retweets are connected to a piece of text I've been fascinated with for a long time. It might have even been the impetus to start the Twitter account in the first place. I quote from a letter written in 1956 to the Dutch typographer, book and type designer Jan van Krimpen, from British typographer, type historian and executive at Monotype Stanley Morison, who in this letter questions Van Krimpen:

Do you stand with me in believing that four hundred years of such engraving {of Roman Type} creates in the image printed from these castings a second nature which is so strong as to be unchangeable?

Maybe the image of a letter is somewhat unchangeable (although they have been pushed to their limits), and we all know that letter forms are far from natural. But the retweets that I like the most provide a strange and often far out relation to Morison's question to Van Krimpen through the notion of their images having a 'second nature': that which is characteristic or instinctive to the thing itself. So, whether it be the use of brow-liner make-up being compared to 36pt Times New Roman Bold, a popular U.K. grime M.C. commenting about the design of the last few letters of the alphabet, the embodiment of a political ideology in a font, a lament in a broken relationship that could be fixed by an even better one, or the complete collapse of speaking and typography, these retweets suggest how deeply, and weirdly, visible language and graphic design are embedded in us, since birth.[1]

1   Since writing this text (in 2019) my idea of—or desire for—contingency also needs to be updated. While contingency does involve and require the discourse, skills, participation and labor of many, it also must be acknowledged that this process is not all-inclusive, and that contingency cannot exist without a process of exclusion. While this idea might demonstrate a way of working, it doesn't make it infallible.

Semester presentations. It must have been 2016/17
in Klasse Grafik brings recent work for discussion.
alongside Ingo Offermanns, add an outside, while
perspective to sketches, projects for artists from wi
university, or other projects.

Julian Mader, Max Prediger, and David Lie
speak about having free capacity from a project the
in China. So they decided to print business cards f
David asked Max to do his.

Max settles in front of the class and opens
Ahah? He begins a new document 85 by 55 mm ai
margins, and columns set to default, untouched. U
spreads. What is he doing? He selects the text fran
the area to the margins (12.7 mm). With Minion F
12/14.4 pt auto-selected he types David Liebermar
No telephone number, no address, no frills.

This act, fostering some permanently critic
infects everything. It seems like a ridiculous detail
graphic design is all about considering ridiculous
Bertolotti-Bailey paraphrase).

Max's card had a gold embossed pictorial t
every letter depicting an animal. I remember the N

David Liebermann

Anna Lena von Helldorff

Scripting (of a) Statement

Scripting [of a] 👁 visual statement
Hamburg 2019, January 21, 👍 point of no return
🐂 revised, transcripted, translated and transferred into this layout 2022
standing point: here.
What's it about? 👆 Graphic design*

*Gestaltung

👁 pulsing emoji 35 sec
So it's about design.
Are we gonna talk about the occupation
or the praxis?
If design is an occupation,
what are you occupied with?
If design is a praxis,
which discipline does it refer to?
How good is design in lying?

Design is relative to the context of text and image,
languages, people, mankind, institutions,
lone wolves, groups, sidekicks, sub-workers,
manufacturers, authors, machines, techniques
and systems.
If design visualizes context, why is it
that everything seems so fragmented?
Is everything readable?
When are the good times over?
Why are we not afraid of emoticons?

Anna Lena von Helldorff

👁 Screenshots of the iPhone display in iMessage mode
[a sequence of one month displaying often used emojis, the 💜
being on top position over the first slides; followed by the tennis ball 🎾,
a waving hand 👋 and a water drop 💧.
In the end the heart 💜 is showing again on top position of *often used.*]

I can see something that is seen by anybody else.
The only question is: under what criteria?

〰️ **audio**
   male apple voice reading the programmed meaning of the emojis.

"on display, often used:

[emoji sequence] and so on."

✏️ [transcript]

"on display, often used: red heart, ok hand with dark
skin tone, chart with downward trend, ram, tiger,
kiss mark, up-poiting index, hot pepper, smiling face
with squinting eyes, four-leave clover, rocket, owl,
mermaid with trident, alien monster, thumbs up,
rose, dragon, mushroom, balloon, crocodile, key cap
ten, gust of wind, waving hand with dark skin tone,
and so on."

☝️ **comment**
   while transferring the script into this layout and copying the emojis
from text edit to pages, the black featured hands and fingers turn white again—
in their 'basic character setting', of which the 'skin tone' has later become a
variation for political reasons.

〰️ **audio**
   male apple voice reading the programmed meaning of the emojis,
   concluded by inserted language and grammatical joints.

"on display, often used, one month later. At the
beginning there is the 💜 again, followed by a 🎾.
Then the 👋 hits in, almost run over by the 🚗 next
to the 🌲. The form of ◆ seems to be the opposite
to the 🌷 which cannot survive without 💧, while a
☁ from an 🍒 to an 🍐 can be simply drawn with a ✏️.
That deserves a 👍 and finally by now also politically
correct an 👌. I am not sure if 🍄 are appreciated by
an 🐘, he might prefer the 🍎. A 🐒 swings in the 🍃,
that will even make the 💜 beat stronger. Now a break
with 🍵 and 🍂. Or would you prefer a 🔍? Actually,
can the 🏐 express the same as a 🌹? And how about
👋 and 〰️? What this 🌍 is trying to say, I don't know
actually, however, it does stand next to 🔝. Sorry, but

Scripting (of a) Statement

this is hard to articulate now. But then, in the end,
we have the . There must be a deeper meaning."

 the letter 'I' and a 'red heart' emoji, as *often used* expression.

I
Form follows function?
Or fiction follows form?
The question is: what do you see?
What do you think about it?
And what do you do with it?
And how long can you cope with that?

Can a gust of wind be a stronger expression
than a red heart as exclamation mark?
What if everybody would say what they see?
If you see something, say something.

 **action**
changing garment: taking off gray sweater with letter 'I' and 'red heart';
the 'red heart' emoji on screen, animated to pulse again.

How can one gain back attention?
Why do certain things never change?
Can we design empathy?

action
changing of sweater completed, now wearing a white one with black
eyes.

context
When everybody is speaking at the same time,
who has the word in the end?
Which role inside the praxis of design is
mostly overestimated?
Eyes wide shut or cancel?
Which aspects of visual culture are not
visually configured, designed?

reading Mexico City, September 2018. Temple with Sun- and Moon-Pyramid.

video of two men in front of the pyramid; the hands of the guide translating
the verbal description into gestures and movement: 'the long long snake'.

Anna Lena von Helldorff

 [transcript]
"... we know that there were seven platforms here.
We have carvings of conshells and seashells an at
the bottom part we have a long snake. One long long
snake on this land"—the man's hand illustrating
by gesture the length of the snake which simulates
the visible stone structure in the background—
adding: "and that is a river, flowing water.
A long snake, one long long snake—and that is a river
flowing waters, long flowing waters."

Do you see the long long snake
like the long long river?
Is communication now a value within the market?
What is the biggest foul in the penalty box of design?
Which part or role does the gesture play
in the grammar of visual language?
What's up with the language anyway?
👁 🖤 reference

👁 'speaking tongues', image taken at same site, Mexico.
If design is a service delivery, what does it
deliver to the service / cause?
If there was a god on the Olympus of Design
what insignia would characterise his or her figure?
Does this look like communication now?

👁 🖤 language
And who actually takes care of the continuity?
We know what we have—so we can
read what we see?
Which are the facts that are not spoken about?
What exactly gives good reason for critique?
If there was a god on the Olympus of Design
which sins would he or she be charged for?

Why doesn't anybody look closely enough?
If design visualizes context, why is it that
everything seems so fragmented?
Is everything readable?
Form follows fiction.
Or function follows form?
Do I really need to read all the messages?
When everybody is speaking at the same time,
who has the word in the end?
How many aspects can we keep in a perspective of
continuous standardization?

Eight posters announcing the Oktoberfest are animated to 'fall down'
into the slide, with a slight bumpy effect; (it's a keynote feature, maybe often used.)
All publicly and online displayed posters must contain the three icons of
Oktoberfest: Pretzel, Heart and Beer.
Note: The poster competition for the Oktoberfest used to be one of those traditional
features of excellence in graphic design, at least in the local scene in Munich.
By accident I came across the online competition in 2019, where the public is asked
to vote for 'the best'—most of the posters at choice online, display next to the
compulsory stereotypical elements—the beer mug, the 'Pretzel' and the decorated
gingerbread heart—a heteronormative setting of male and female-female curves
in 'Dirndl' and strong males in 'Lederhosen'.

Who is actually still taking part?
If diversity of opinion is not en vogue and
presentable anymore, can design help out by
empowering freedom of interpretation?
Response?

reading mail written just before symposium on January 22nd, 2019.
Mail to oktoberfest-plakatwettbewerb @ muenchen.de

"Hello and good day, the public voting process about
the poster contest is not the only reason to actually
approach you here. What is of actual concern to
me—and it should be to anyone—are the kind of
drafts and designs of the posters published
themselves! Their stereotypical and hetero-normative
configuration sometimes even dumb-sexistic
illustration must be a reminder that it is absolutely
necessary to oppose—publicly!—this constant
reproduction and irresponsible affirmation of the
same normatives in public!

Anna Lena von Helldorff

I very much hope, that in 2019 there will be no
boy & girl—no 'Dirndl-Blondie' in *Disney* style—as
none of the other normative clichés—announcing
the Oktoberfest as a public and world-open
spectacle. Rather, I would hope to see the choice
of a configuration that actually shows the diversity,
heterotopian and even utopian atmosphere of the
Oktoberfest.

👁 the posters are starting to disappear, the effect is called 'verfliegen'
(flying away). Only for one poster the effect 'Flamme' (flame) is applied, burning the
'sheet' with a blond, barbie-like female figure, swinging her hips and holding up a
beer mug as if inviting to shake her up.

📖 continue reading the mail

"I would greatly appreciate if the city of Munich keeps
the level and impact of such a public tradition and
event also and especially through the means of visual
representation and communication. This level and
therefore responsibility should be part of the briefing
in the open call for the poster competition! With high
regards, … "

📖 reading response by mail, January 23rd 2019.

"Dear Miss von Helldorff, Your voting at the
competition was successful. Thank you for your
participation. […] However, you can adapt your
choice and change your vote as often as you wish.
[…] Thank you for your remarkable comment on the
poster designs. I will forward them to the responsible
department! We are always very grateful receiving
constructive feedback. With high regards, ▓▓▓▓▓▓"

👁 🖤 responsibility

Who is actually still taking part?
What is the moment to realize
that there are too many players on the field?
Who has the means?

👁 image of a poster by the christian conservative party CSU; cyan background,
'dynamic type': a big 'JA' dominates the top and is followed by a crossed circle,
announcing yes to political resistance. the further reading is a 'Nein' to the term
#ausgehetzt*, which itself is crossed out in red marker; the bottom line claims:
Bavaria will not be incited.
*hashtag *ausgehetzt* meaning 'un-incited'

And who has the money?
And what exactly does it mean: public?

📖 reading extract of an article, *Süddeutsche Zeitung*, Munich, July 2018.

"With the slogan '#ausgehetzt*—united against a
politics of fear' people in Munich are demonstrating
against a shift to the right in politics and society—
especially against the refugee policy of the CSU.
The parliamentary group of the CSU had tried to
prevent the demonstration beforehand.
In the night from Saturday to Sunday, they installed
numerous posters overnight claiming the following
message: 'Ja zum politischen Anstand—Nein
zu hashtag ausgehetzt—Bayern lässt sich nicht
verhetzen'. Meaning: 'Yes to political integrity—
No to hashtag un-incited—Bavaria will not let itself
be incited.'"
Why does the reproduction of visual stereotypes
continue without being interrupted?
Why doesn't anybody read what is actually seen?
Which role in design is taken on essentially?

👁 Sunday morning, July 2018, morning of demonstration,
posting digital response on social media.

Who has the means again?
Who has the money again?
Who's talking?
Why do people not rely on each other?
What is in progress?

Anna Lena von Helldorff

Can repetition be of capital?
How come anyone can see, but nobody is
watching out?
Who has the right to publish?
Are we talking the same language?
(And why do we keep asking that question about
the difference between design and art?)
👁 🤍 ambivalence!
Who holds the power in the ambivalence of images?
Does everything have to be unambiguous?

〜 audio
Extract from Robert Musil: *Der Mann ohne Eigenschaften*. Remix*
A Production of Bayerischer Rundfunk / Hörspiel und Medienkunst 2004.
*The Man Without Qualities

👁 Screenshots of iPhone display typing message in iMessage

Have I seen this before?
Can repetition as a method survive within capitalism?
How am I supposed to make a decision now?
Can you repeat everything?
Is translation a method or a skill?
Can polyphony mean collective authorship?

✎ [transcript]

"Da sagen die Leute hier zu einem Eichhörnchen Eichkatze fiel ihm ein. Aber es sollte
bloss einmal einer versuchen, mit dem richtigen Ernst auf der Zunge und im
Gesicht die 'Eichenkatze' zu sagen. [...] In Hessen sagen sie dagegen Baumfuchs.
Ein weit gewanderter Mensch weiß so etwas. Und da taten die Psychiater wunder
wie neugierig wenn sie mossbrugger das Bild eines gemalten Eichhörnchens zeigten
und er darauf antwortete: Das ist halt ein Fuchs oder vielleicht ist es ein Hase.
Es kann auch eine Katz' sein oder so. [...] "

☞ [translation]

"People here (Bavaria) call an 'Eichhörnchen'
(squirrel; *Eich* = oak, *Hörnchen* = small horn)
'Eichkatze' (oak-cat) came to his mind. But someone
should just try saying 'oak cat' with the right
seriousness on his tongue and face. [...] In Hessen,
on the other hand, they say 'Baumfuchs' (tree-fox).
A man who has wandered far knows such a thing."
And so the psychiatrists were surprised and curious
when they showed Mossbrugger the picture of a
painted squirrel and he replied: "That's a fox or maybe it's a rabbit. It could also be a cat or something."

Und wenn ein
Eichkatzerl keine 🐈 ist
und kein 🦊 und statt
eines Horns Zähne hat,
wie der 🐰

Und wenn ein
Eichkatzerl keine 🐈 ist
und kein 🦊 und statt
eines Horns Zähne hat,
wie der 🐇, den der 🦊
frißt, so braucht man
die Sache nicht so
genau nehmen.

👁 "Und wenn ein Eichkatzerl keine Katze ist und kein Fuchs und statt eines Horns Zähne hat wie der Hase, den der Fuchs frißt, so braucht man die Sache nicht so genau nehmen." [...]

"Aber: sie ist auf irgendeine Weise aus alledem zusammen genäht und läuft über die Bäume. Nach meiner Erfahrung und Überzeugung kann man kein Ding für sich herausgreifen weil eins am andern hängt!"

♉ [translation]

"So if an 'Eichkatzerl' (Bavarian slang for squirrel, *Katzerl* = small cat) is not a cat and not a fox and has teeth instead of a horn like the rabbit, which the fox eats, you don't have to be so precise.
However: it is somehow sewn together from all this and is running over the trees. In my experience and conviction, you can't pick out one thing individually only because it is attached to another!"

👁 🖤 together
Cohesion?
Solidarity?
Why is it so hard?
When the scope of debate is shrinking, how do we expand it?
What kind of principles can be displayed through collaboration?
Is collaboration a mean to flirt?
Which truth can not be designed?
Wich resources does design need?
How can we defend the potential of participation?
Who has the power over the images?
Does it really all have to be explicit?

Anna Lena von Helldorff

Screenshot of first draft DVD cover layout for memorial concert 9/11 by the
NY Philharmonics, first draft, silver background,
typographical setting: the 9/11 is partially covered with a white bar, as if 'whitened'

reading [response by label manager].

"Dear Anna Lena, thank you for the cover!
I am absolutely convinced—but xxx is not yet.
I immediately read the 'branding' 9/11 as
recognizable, even though only a third is actually
visible. So one does see the relation, without
explicitly being a mere mourning ceremony but
instead it can be read as an almost encouraging
reaction to leave the grief behind… well, but… in
Pauls words: it is too European intellectual. Sounds
like a compliment, it is actually, but it does not help
in this case… the result of our brainstorming is: the
cover needs to become more explicit, sorry to say
but more illustrative—as for the American market.
Paul suggests a visual link to the Twin Towers …"

Have I seen this before?
Can repetition as a method survive within capitalism?
How am I supposed to make a decision now?
Can you repeat everything?
Is translation a method or a skill?

reading forwarded mail by NY Philharmonics to label manager.
Concerning: Draft Agreement

"Here the comments of our American friends:
1. First of all, we prefer the version with the vertical
beam of light. 2. We are seeing some funny white
blocks behind the text, which we are not sure are
a flaw in the file or if they are purposeful. For
instance, the white bar running behind '9/11'–
we think that looks a bit off, but 3. We think that
the title 'A CONCERT FOR NEW YORK' needs to
be connected to 9/11, and there are key elements
of the messaging that are missing. Please see our
suggestions below for text changes. 4. There are
some typographical problems in the listings of the

soloists—the Umlaut over the soprano's last name is colliding with the line above it, and the e in DeYoung needs to be in a smaller font, like a small. 5. The New York Philharmonic logo feels a bit like it is floating on the right, not anchored anywhere. Might it make more sense to have it on the bottom right corner? Also, could you use the version with ██████████ 6. We would like some changes in the bolding of the text. First, ██████████'s name should be bold along with 'New York Philharmonic,' so that the emphasis is the same. Please see below."

9/11

⊙ Screenshot final version DVD Cover,
typographical setting: the 9/11 is sitting on the white bar

📖   reading mail Label Manager to NY Philharmonics

"thank you so much for all your comments—which of course make a lot of sense! I'm glad to hear that—just like we do—you prefer version #2 with the vertical beam. I'm happy to make a few first comments on the different points listed below. But Ulrike together with our graphic designer will get back to you tomorrow in a more detailed way— changes in the design will then be made right away. [...] 2) the white blocks are purposeful—please take into consideration that the color is not supposed to be gray as it looks like on the pdf but silver—the white behind will work very well in that combination and make the writing very clear and strong.

📖   reading mail, some time later.
Concerning: Gramophone Magazine about the 9/11 DVD

"... this DVD release is not designed solely for those focused on music-making. Presentation and packaging signify a ritual of remembrance."

Does it really all have to be explicit?
How many aspects can we keep in a perspective of continuous standardization?
Are you still there?

Anna Lena von Helldorff

How do you calculate the value of expression?
The show must go on. Really?
Do we speak the same language?
How can we design the means of participation?
Can diversity of opinion become collective
authorship?
Once upon a time?
Solidarity?
What's so hard?
Who does the world belong to?
When the scope of debate is shrinking,
why don't we expand it?
What kind of coherence appears through
collaboration?
Is the collaboration congenial, a hot flirt
or a passage passing by?

mani bucate money fest—a sheet containing 24 (bank)notes.
A collaboration with Heike Geissler in 2017.
[The image of a toad repeats as an icon on all the notes. The 'toad'—'Kröte' in
German—is a term used as metaphor for money—'bugs'. And it's all about money.
money for everybody, for free; a fairy tale, a manifest in fragments.
"This money has more values than just one. This money is distributed only in person.
'Power is usually not given willingly, but taken.'"]

What kind of story telling would you prefer?

reading [the text on the money]

The manifest says:
This money has no fear.
This money does not pick a quarrel,
it would though—in case of emergency
find rather good arguments to do so.
The fairy tale says:
Once upon the time there was a piece of paper.
The facts are raising the question:
Which epoch does this story belong to?

banknotes

This money acts in the case of surplus value.
Can one keep up the demand about surplus value
through design?
Why good and cheap?

Scripting (of a) Statement

How can one avoid the idea of merchandise?
If design was a territory,
where would be its borders?
What do we really want to do?
How often can you turn the page?
How often can you change allegiance?

👁 videos of the opening day, Festa dell'Estate 2017, Villa Massimo Rome.
[hands touching, counting and exchanging the 'money', Rome]

Is what you see what you get?
Do we need to talk about money?
If design would also be meaning
redistribution of attention would that be
a contribution to fairness concerning
single positions and the ones on the fringes?
What is it that we can agree on to then
make a difference?
Is the action deriving from design
a result of design or collaboration?
Is the value of collaboration congenial,
social or economical?
Let's talk about money?

📖 reading mail by the event manager to the author and former stipend, 2017
Concerning: presentation at the event, Berlin.

"Dear Miss ███████, I hope your family is well. I am
writing to you concerning your request on the budget
that will be available for you at the final presentation.
Unfortunately we can not afford any further costs
beyond the calculated budget."

📖 reading mail by author to event manager. Nov., 2017.
Concerning: presentation at the event, Berlin.

"Dear Mr. ██████, Every budget is limited, of course.
Only I would like to point out one more time that the
work that I want to show is a collaborative work. Just
as it was performed at the Sommer-festival in Rome:
A. L. v. H., T. L. and H. G.. The 'money' is the result of

Anna Lena von Helldorff

this collaboration, thus I would like to ask you once more for a budget including payment and travel costs. If in this case, the budget for the final presentation is being distributed by the principle of 'first come, first served'—I need you to reconsider as I have not been informed beforehand that I need to apply for a budget."

📖 reading response by event manager. November, 2017.

"We have actually discussed and calculated the budget one more time. Without going too much into details—it will be tight, we might have to transfer the payment into next year's budget—I would like to offer you a compromise: your collaborators will receive the same amount as the other participants of the stipends."

👁 [videos of handling, counting money in Berlin]

Is what you see what you get?
If critique would mean the re-distribution of attention would that be a contribution to fairness concerning minor positions and the ones oppressed?
How can we design participation?
Can we rethink the architecture of information?
Is collaboration an option or a necessity?
Can you still follow me ?
Do we have to think about the following questions?
What is my individual experience?
How do I construct myself?
Who am I (in this context)?
What is the perspective I am speaking from?
How do I think about my privileges?
Do you speak up whenever you have the option?
If design is relative to the context of text and image, languages, people, mankind, institutions, lone warriors, groups, sidekicks, sub-workers, manufacturers, authors, machines, techniques and systems—how can we know about the context when looking at the result?

📖 reading Ad popping up on instagram at nine o'clock in the morning, 2019

"Create a beautiful design. You have an upcoming
holiday or design project but no design skills—don't
worry! xxx got you covered. xxx has an astounding
library of templates to choose besides the templated
sizes you can also make your own size to fit any of
your needs … Just type in what you are feeling in the
search box because the search function is powerful
and flexible"
Do I know this?
Does this feel familiar even?
Do we have enough future to kill?

👁 poster and display, x on display, window setting, Munich 2019

Can we design the climate change?
Will climate change affect the progress of wdesign?
Do you like comments?

What are the facts that are never spoken about?
Who is taking on visual responsibility?
How dangerous is the 'right' shift to visual culture?
Which forms of visual narration can we differentiate?
What kind of design can speak critique?
When everybody is speaking at the same time,
who has the word in the end again?
What would be the biggest conflict
in the context of design?
Who is being served by the difference of culture
and design?
What can design oppose to the automatization
of coherences?

And what happens when there is a power blackout?

Graphic interlude by Michel Balke

Graphic interlude by Michel Balke

Christian Bauer

The Varieties of Goodness Or: How Meta-Ethicists Recognize Good Graphic Design

Introduction

How do we normally know what is good? Usually, the term 'good' is used because a thing, fact, or situation is 'good for' something else. Apparently, the attribution 'good' comes into play when it comes to relations between means and ends, in which the respective ends can be unavailable, transcendent, or abstract.

Since we want to think about criteria of good graphic design, we have to deliberately limit ourselves. My way of deliberate limitation is to bring up a certain doubt. In the Western sphere of values we feel an unhindered urge to optimize everything—world, society, and the self. Designs for the world are made as a matter of course. One discipline that seems to work well in this *ideology of design and optimization* is design. But why *ideology* of optimization, one might ask. If it were an optimization *philosophy*, we would be able to say more about what is good or optimal. But does anyone really know what is good for people?

There are certainly authorities on questions of form who dare to make hypotheses about what 'good form' is. Like Max Bill, who taught people what the 'good form' is—for example, in the shape of an exhibition design. Then this is a lesson in aesthetic assertion philosophy. However, there is a risk of making an argumentative mistake that the Roman logicians and legal theorists called 'subreption' (*vitium subreptionis*). The error arises in the 'scope of sensory knowledge' and consists specifically in the confusion of empirically accessible and non-empirical—that is, noumenal—ideas, which Kant described with the adjective 'transcendental.'[1] Subreption can take different forms in different cases. Structurally they show the element of involuntarily or unwittingly mixing up or deliberate deception.

Thus, in order to gain an overview, it makes sense to go beyond the aesthetically good form of presenting other meanings of 'good' and to consider which meaning of 'good' is and should be claimed sometimes explicitly and sometimes implicitly. This approach, which involves a critique of knowledge and the philosophy of language, is an expression of skepticism toward an all too lax use of the word 'good' in the context of design. By referring to the 'varieties of goodness' I aim to suggest a systematic approach to our problem.

1. Prolegomena on Ethics

The successor to Ludwig Wittgenstein's chair in Cambridge, Georg Henrik von Wright, made it plausible that, above all, the moral use of the expression 'good' still requires some previous attempts at definition. In David Hume's tradition of moral philosophy, it is common to distinguish between 'is' and 'should.' A somewhat different line of tradition differentiates conceptually between norms and facts. The aim is to distinguish the areas of normative and descriptive ethics. In the area of the descriptive, existing struc-

1   'Transzendental; das Transzendente,' in: *Historisches Wörterbuch der Philosophie*, vol. 10, p. 1381.

2   Cf. Georg Henrik von Wright, *Normen, Werte und Handlungen* (Frankfurt/M, 1994), p. 19.

tures are described; in the area of the normative, ethical judgments are made and value judgements come into play, which can range from mere recommendations to precepts.

In the social sciences, people usually stay away from the evaluative function; it is common to refer to Max Weber's postulate of the freedom from value judgments.[2] A mixing of facts with normative questions should be avoided, although by now one should know that evaluative elements sneak into the system of fact making.

If one asks about the meaning of ethically relevant expressions such as 'good,' 'advisable,' or 'expected,' one is engaging with meta-ethical questions. On this level I would like to argue on the basis of Von Wright's work *The Varieties of Goodness* in the following. In this way, I aim to make the different meanings of 'good' visible and bring a meta-ethical and language-reflective level into the discourse.[3] Graphic designers and philosophers share this search for meaning as well as the conceptual approach. A common vanishing point is the question of how we want to and should lead our lives. This question calls for standards. Here, too, designers and ethicists meet: without recourse to standards and norms, there is little they can accomplish.

2. The Meaning of a Word Is Its Use

Von Wright followed in the philosophical tradition of Wittgenstein, according to which we find out what a word such as 'good' means when we look at the rules of its use. The *reasons* why a word is used in a certain way are themselves an aspect of the meaning of that word.[4] In the case of speaking of good, I will now show that there are not just one, but different ways of using it.

1. Something is instrumentally good *for* a certain purpose. As a rule, it is the goodness *of a*

3   Cf. Georg Henrik von Wright, *The Varieties of Goodness* (London/New York, 1963), p. 10.
4   Ibid., p. 5.

kind. This type represents a unity, for example the unity of function, morphology (i.e., appearance or shape) or 'form.' How the connections between function, appearance, and form are designed determines whether something appears to be 'good' or 'poor.' There are no instrumentally bad things; there are only things that are 'good' in terms of an intended functionality and thus represent an enrichment or not. Something is 'good' within a class of objects: we speak of a good knife or good hammer because an artifact serves its purpose as an instrument. A good house can provide functions that promise instrumental goodness. *If you sort some works of graphic design into a group of objects to which you assign a specific purpose, it becomes possible to decide whether it is 'good graphic design.'*

2.   Technical goodness relates to groups of people. Graphic designers can be good at their job, as can doctors. They have in common the fact that they master techniques so that others can say: this doctor is a good surgeon or this designer has mastered his craft, design; in a technical sense, his work can be said to be 'well done.'

3.   On the other hand, it is a different form of goodness when one says "my heart works well" or "your mind works well." The goodness of organs and intellectual capacities allows for a medical concept of goodness. How good the interaction of the individual capabilities is, determines how healthy or how sick someone *feels.*

4.   The term 'beneficial' is related to the medical concept of goodness.[5] Well-being is more than physiological functioning and cognitive perfor-

5   Ibid., p. 9.

mance. After all, well-being depends on the interaction of heterogeneous forces that work in a part of society, for example. If a person has 'good manners,' it is usually good for everyone involved. Well-being or what is agreeable is a subcategory of the useful.

5.   The good in the sense of the useful or the generally advantageous. When someone talks about a 'good plan' or a 'good opportunity,' they usually have their own advantage or individual benefit in mind. The generally useful differs from the concept of the good in the sense of well-being in that the latter has to do with the particular conditions of well-being of a particular person, whereas the useful usually refers to a more general purpose.

6.   Hedonic goodness relates to our well-being. We speak of 'good taste,' a 'good meal,' we appreciate the 'good company' of a 'good friend.' The 'good weather' can be 'good' in a hedonic sense because it warms a person and therefore 'does good.' The weather can also be 'good' in a useful sense because it helps plants grow. The hedonic good is what someone enjoys or likes, while the absolutely useful is good for a purpose or need. Hedonic good thus seems to be located in the realm of aesthetic perception. This makes it the bearer of a *value index*, which states that increased aesthetic perception can be a special characteristic of 'good graphic design.' Hedonically good things such as a pleasantly stimulating sight of a graphic design or the entertaining progress of an opera production share the fact that they give us pleasure.[6]

7.   The moral good comes into play in connection with human action, personal intentions,

6   Ibid., p. 11.

and stirrings of the will. We often assume that a person's moral goodness is related to their character and behavior. A person's moral life is reflected in expressions such as 'good manners' or 'good ideas'; depending on the context, these phrases can also have a meaning that extends beyond the moral.

These seven points provide an overview of linguistic usages and semantic subtleties, some of which are mutually exclusive, and some of which are complementary. The respective meaning lies in the use, a certain linguistic pragmatism, in which graphic design is also embedded as a means of communication, through which they become readable and understandable.

Is a good graphic designer like a good ophthalmologist, who, in the sense of *technical goodness*, ensures that certain things can be clearly recognized? It may be so for adepts at the Swiss Style. But isn't a graphic designer also a good therapist who ensures that people change their behavior and realize what is really 'good' for them? If the readers of this text think it is good, does that mean that they liked it in an aesthetically pleasing, maybe even hedonic sense? Do you think more people should read this text? Does it make statements about well-being in the sense of the common good? Hopefully, all of these possibilities exist, because for the common good we need variance and not simple definitions. No one can know what will happen tomorrow and what we need the day after tomorrow—hence, 'varieties of goodness.' A good graphic designer in Bangalore will have to master different skills than a designer who works in Ulm, for example.

3. Summation

If we agree on good graphic design, our starting point is an uncertainty: first we should determine what good graphic design is, how you can recognize it, how it is made. This is a theoretical and methodological task. That is why books are written that deal with determining what is good graphic design. But it remains bad taste to say, "Good design is this and that." As if a Moses had received salutatory commandments on Mount Sinai: "You can recognize good form, my son, by the fact that it makes you happy!" "My sister, you can recognize good content by the fact that it sets you free!" Nothing good is guaranteed to come from this!

It would be a pleasure for me to have made no rules on what good graphic design is. To me, this appears to tend toward the authoritarian and forgetting history. In the words of Samuel Butler: "He who would do good must do so in minute particulars [intervento minimo!]; the general good is the plea of patriots, politicians and knaves."[7] As an ethicist, I can only recommend refraining from making general judgments, which are mostly questions of attitude. The fact that graphic designers who work in advertising create refined print products and ensure the legibility of character systems does not make them good or bad people; probably it makes them technically skilled designers.

For a 'truly' good graphic design (whatever that means), society would have to radically change. Perhaps ethically good graphic design is only possible in a society in which doing business is possible without advertising. If we inquire in this direction, good graphic design is not something isolated, but embedded in the context of a more general economy of needs.

The political person in us gets advice about psychological drives, looks for direction, for security, is appealed to by advertising for fashion, cosmetics, and travel all over the world. Is advertising graphic design to blame for the fact that people live in such a society? I think we would do well to answer this question in the negative. The aim of differentiating between the 'varieties of goodness' was to show that the different meanings of 'good graphic design' are based on very

7   Quoted from: Paul Watzlawick, *Vom Schlechten des Guten oder Hekates Lösungen* (Munich/Zurich, 1993), p. 101.

different uses ('aspects'). We should be careful not to claim all the meanings when we talk about good design. This is particularly important when it comes to ethical challenges. Designers may create ethically important accents on a small scale. However, always wanting to inscribe an all-encompassing ethical mandate ('design for the world') in their work often not only remains far too unspecific, but also runs the risk of becoming a source of ethical overload.

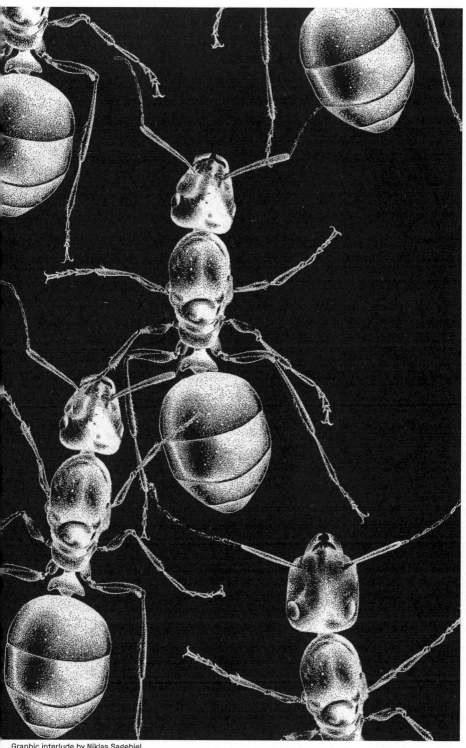

Graphic interlude by Niklas Sagebiel

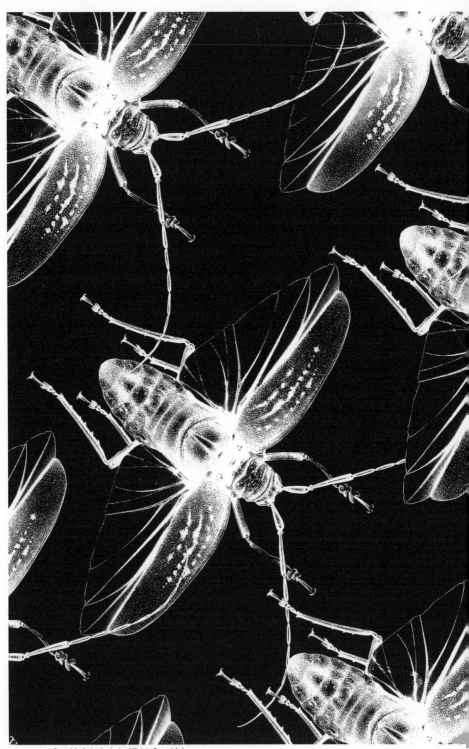

Graphic interlude by Niklas Sagebiel

Daniel Martin Feige

Aesthetics of Graphic Design

In the course of the debates that have been gaining momentum in recent years in Anglo-American aesthetics and more recently also in German aesthetics about questions of a philosophy of design, it is striking that, with a few exceptions, graphic design receives little attention.[1] This may be due to the fact that, unlike objects of industrial design, it perhaps forms our everyday practice in a less visible way and also has a genealogically relatively clear relation to the history of the visual arts. Under the title 'Aesthetics of Graphic Design,' I would like to develop two ideas were that are connected to two relevant texts on the theory of design: Vilém Flusser's *The Shape of Things: A Philosophy of Design* and Jean-François Lyotard's *Paradox on the Graphic Artist*.[2] Overall, I am concerned with the question of what exactly 'good' in terms of 'good' graphic design could mean if we also ask this question from an aesthetic perspective.

The following sketch is based on further ideas that I cannot develop here deeply, but which I would like to mention at least briefly.[3] Fundamentally, I assume that questions about the aesthetics of graphic design cannot be dealt with independently of questions about the ethics of graphic design. The relationship between the two is misunderstood if one sees the aesthetic characteristics of objects simply as an extension or reinforcement and thus ultimately as a rhetoric of the ethical. Rather, we should assume that

[1] The following works, among others, are central: Andreas Dorschel, *Gestaltung: Zur Ästhetik des Brauchbaren* (Heidelberg, 2003); Glenn Parsons and Allen Carlson, *Functional Beauty* (Oxford, 2008); Jakob Steinbrenner and Julian Nida-Rümelin (eds.), *Ästhetische Werte und Design* (Stuttgart, 2011); Jane Forsey, *The Aesthetics of Design* (Oxford, 2013).
[2] Cf. Vilém Flusser, *The Shape of Things. A Philosophy of Design* (London 1999); Jean-François Lyotard, 'Paradox of the Graphic Artist', in: *Postmodern Fables* (Minneapolis, 1997), pp. 33–47.
[3] Cf. also Daniel M. Feige, *Design: Eine philosophische Analyse* (Berlin, 2018), especially chapters 4 and 8; as well as: Daniel M. Feige, *Zur Dialektik des Social Designs: Ästhetik und Kritik in Kunst und Design*, in: *Studienhefte Problemorientiertes Design* (vol. 9), (Hamburg, 2019).

questions of aesthetics are always related to questions about the *role* of corresponding objects in our way of life—and thus to the question of a good life.[4] The difficulty is to qualify more precisely what this could mean in terms of graphic design. In my opinion, the line of demarcation between graphic design and art that operates with graphic means runs exactly in relation to ethical questions. In the case of artworks, the standards of assessment must be derived from the examination of the works themselves, since they serve no tangible purposes and, if they serve purposes, they tend to be a reflection on the meaning of these purposes, rather than simply fulfilling them.[5] This also means that an ethical assessment simpliciter of artworks is categorically wrong. When art is related to ethical questions, it always articulates something that cannot be translated into ethical terms precisely due to the fact that what it says cannot be separated from its form. By contrast, the objects of *graphic design* are more tangibly involved in practical matters: books are published by certain publishers on certain subjects; posters often announce events and products from certain companies or cultural institutions; developing a corporate design not only means accepting the market-based form of our society, but also giving a company a graphic face. For me, these definitions are not about neatly sorting all objects into either art or design. Rather, I want to insist that we are dealing with two different forms of practice, whose differences must be profiled against the background of their commonalities. And the fact that graphic design has something tangible to do with purposes means that the question of 'good' graphic design requires a different kind of answer than the question of powerful art.

Two Forms of the 'Good'

In Flusser's *Philosophy of Design* the author comes to a rather sobering result in regard to the question of what 'good' design is: if design is good, it is ethi-

4   Cf. also Christian Bauer's ideas in this book.
5   Cf. also Daniel M. Feige, *Computerspiele: Eine Ästhetik* (Berlin, 2015), chapter 4.

cally just as bad as if it is bad. He writes: "Since the technicians had to apologize to the Nazis for their gas chambers not being good enough—i.e., not killing their 'clients' quickly enough—we have once more been made aware what is meant by the Devil. We realize once more what is lying in wait behind the notion of *good design*."[6] He explains this as follows: "Between pure good ('moral' good), which is good for nothing, and applied good ('functional' good) there can be absolutely no compromise, because in the end everything which is good in the case of applied good is bad in the case of moral good. There can be no such thing as a bad designer acting out of nothing but pure good, because even the intention of producing a bad design is functional and not pure. If therefore a designer claims that he only designs objects that correspond to his idea of pure good (eternal values and all that), he is mistaken."[7] Flusser's idea thus means the following: something that is good for *something* cannot be good *in itself*; instrumental goodness *counteracts* pure goodness. In this view, design operates only in regard to the question of the implementation of given purposes, but not on the level of the purposes themselves.

The fact that Flusser's distinction between means and ends is fundamentally convincing can be demonstrated in terms of recent debates in the philosophy of action as follows. There are actions that are not performed for their own sake, but must be explained instrumentally.[8] For example, I usually cross the street not because I like to walk across streets, but, for example, because I am currently shopping, visiting someone, have to leave the city, or something similar; in this case, walking across the street is a *phase* (a temporal part) of my going shopping or visiting friends, and its goodness is measured by the contribution it makes to the purpose it serves. Purposes themselves can of course be pursued in the name of other purposes, namely when we can reasonably ask

6   Flusser, *The Shape of Things*, p. 34.
7   Ibid., p. 33.
8   For background on the following ideas, cf. G.E.M. Anscombe, *Intention* (Cambridge US, 2000); as well as recent further developments, for example in Sebastian Rödl, *Kategorien des Zeitlichen: Eine Untersuchung über die Formen des endlichen Verstandes* (Berlin, 2005).

the 'why' question about them. For example, I go shopping to cook something for myself because I am hungry or because I am expecting friends that evening. Non-instrumental purposes, unconditional purposes, on the other hand, are those for which any further question about the 'why' would be one question too many. For example, if you ask why you should help your friends or keep promises, you are asking the wrong question. To say that you help your friends in order to benefit from their help in certain situations simply means that you have not understood what friendship is (and perhaps even that you have no friends at all).

I think that Flusser's distinction between instrumental and pure goodness can be made understandable within the context of these brief action-theoretical considerations. The crucial point is: Flusser places design exclusively at the level of instrumental goodness, so that unconditional purposes are eliminated in advance as something that has to do with the design. However, we do not have to share this idea. On the one hand, we can understand objects of design as 'good' in the sense of a means to achieve a given purpose—a brochure can be good because it leads to many sales of a car; a poster be good due to the fact that it fills a concert hall or leads to reviews of an event in the culture sections of newspapers. On the other hand, we can view them as 'good' in the sense of the purposes themselves and not simply the means: a poster for an NGO can be good because the purpose it serves— namely, to promote awareness of the problems that this NGO addresses or its work—is good.

However, an assessment of the means or the ends still has a crucial flaw when it comes to the question of what the 'good' of graphic design is. The specific elements of the design no longer appear in it—and I do not think Flusser sees this. What is missing in the distinction between instrumental goodness and the goodness of purposes is the goodness of the objects of graphic design themselves.

Daniel Martin Feige

...and the 'Good' of Graphic Design

What does it mean that something is 'good' *as an object of graphic design* (as a poster, as typography, as a book, and so on)? If this goodness were identical to instrumental goodness, graphic design could in principle also be replaced with other things (such as politics or laws); if it were identical to the purposes, an assessment of graphic design would be identical to an ethical or moral assessment.

At this point, an obvious answer comes to mind: namely, to understand goodness in graphic design in the sense of the *well-crafted* (as belonging to the genus of graphic design). And such a practice of assessment is often one that is still used in commissions for master's exams in design. To be clear: of course a poster or a book can be good in that it is an expression of the craftsmanship of its designers. However, in my opinion, the following thought experiments speak against seeing the goodness of graphic design in them: we would not only say that a work of graphic design that is poorly crafted but serves ethically desirable purposes is not 'good' graphic design. Rather, I think that we would also not say about well-made posters or video spots that serve as propaganda for a totalitarian regime or are intended to promote terrorist attacks on behalf of ISIS that they are 'good graphic design' (as well as, for other reasons, in the case that we are dealing with a demagogic poster for a politically desirable goal or, for still other reasons, with posters reproduced by hand through child labor; in the first case it is the means and in the second case it is an aspect of the causal history of the object that prevents us from treating them as 'good' objects). My point is this: if we do not understand the ethical goodness of graphic design itself as part of what it does well, then, as Flusser in fact argues, graphic design becomes a *purely instrumental category*. Then it would be the case that the question of ethically good graphic design would have to be explained with regard to questions of the personality of the designer and one would have to agree with Flusser to say that graphic design is bad per se. By contrast, I would like to suggest that graphic design that does not also ask what its objects are for and in what way they are made for something is a *privation* of graphic design—a practice that does not do justice to a full understanding of what graphic design could achieve in our society. This is because, in such a position, the quality of the craftsmanship is only *coincidentally* linked to the ethical quality.

In my opinion, it is precisely the concept of an aesthetic of graphic design that attempts to conceive of this interconnection. After all, aesthetics in graphic design does not mean merely the external appearance, the sensual idiosyncrasies of the objects, or even whether the objects are 'beautiful.'[9] A correctly understood aesthetics of graphic design does not mean (unlike in the case of artworks) a self-contained consideration of how its logic works (even if one can learn much from it in teaching and should often do something like this), but a consideration of the means and ends *in their particular forming* through the objects of graphic design. In opposition to Flusser, it must be said that a correctly understood graphic design is by no means external to its purposes; rather, *the objects of graphic design themselves work on the determination of their purposes.* In and through every graphically relevant work, the ends it serves and the means are simultaneously renegotiated. What a poster is and what it means that it is made for an anonymous and mostly not entirely undefined public is renegotiated in and through every successful poster. This is precisely why objects of graphic design are aesthetic objects and require judgment on the part of those who produce them and who view them. With this reconstruction, the question still arises of what purposes the respective objects serve and how they serve them. However, it now arises *internally from an aesthetic perspective.* After all, an assessment of the graphic

9   The fact that a sensualist interpretation even of art is insufficient has been shown convincingly by, among others, Arthur C. Danto. Cf. Arthur C. Danto, *Die Verklärung des Gewöhnlichen: Eine Philosophie der Kunst* (Frankfurt/M, 1999).

design is an assessment of the ends and means in the light of their formation in and through graphic work.

Coda

I plead guilty that my considerations up to this point were ultimately of a general nature with regard to design. In conclusion, for this reason I would like to make recourse to Lyotard's motives to suggest aspects that are specific to the way in which these insights could be developed in regard to graphic design. Lyotard claims that graphic designers are subject to various constraints between which they must maneuver: moderations between the demands of 'persuasiveness,' 'aesthetic quality,' and 'truthfulness,' and their currencies are to 'intrigue' (to stop the restless gaze of the anonymous public), 'surprising' (which consists of the visual establishment of unusual relationships), and the flash of the evidence of a truth (which arises in the appropriateness of the graphic work with regard to what is articulated).[10] Lyotard thus makes two things clear. On the one hand, graphic design, even if it serves purposes and works on the form of the purposes, is *categorically different from advertising*, because unlike graphic design, advertising belongs to the area of demagogy and does not aim to convince, but to persuade. On the other hand, graphic design is an aesthetic practice *aimed at a specifically modern public*: an anonymous and heterogeneous mass, within which the work of graphic design attempts to briefly captivate its restless gaze. Even if this purpose does not apply to everything that is done in the field of graphic design, Lyotard seems to be on the right track with his idea when he cites the restless public as a particular aspect to which graphic designers respond, and points to the fact that the graphic work can cause parts of this public to reflect for a short moment. In this way, 'good' graphic design that lives up to its own idea would not be advertising or rhetoric, but precarious work on truth, which itself is precarious.

10   Lyotard, 'Das Paradox des Graphikers,' p. 34f.

Univesal suffrage effering

Graphic interlude by Saki Ho

Sandra Doeller

Graphic Design Conceives Between Individual and Collective Authorship

As graphic design is increasingly recognized for its artistic practice, a romanticized view has gained ground about what graphic designers are set to achieve: many believe that only those who work in the cultural field or can devote themselves to independent projects are living up to their artistic aspiration. But why does this idea seem so attractive? First, cultural and independent projects promise a level of self-determination and creative freedom that goes beyond the traditional (self-)image of the profession. Such projects offer the potential to work not 'only' as a designer, but also as a curator, artist, author, or producer. At the same time, independent projects make it possible to critically engage with political or social issues and thus open up the possibility of creating 'meaning' that is relevant to society. However, graphic designers are faced with a dilemma: commissioned jobs in the cultural sector are often not well paid, and independent projects are usually done as pro-bono work or for self-promotion. How can designers fulfill their own standards under these conditions and at the same time ensure their livelihood?

The obvious tensions between independent and applied work, between individual fulfillment and working according to commercial terms, are nothing new. For example, the self-publishing movement in graphic design at the beginning of the 2000s can be seen as a move away from commissioned work and toward independent projects allowing designers to express their own authorship. More recently, however, a different tendency can be observed in the self-perception of many designers—especially in a change in positioning that can be described as a shift from *what* to *how*.

For a long time, graphic designers have concentrated on a factual self-description—for instance, focusing on certain means or media, such as typography, corporate identities, books, or websites to promote their practices. Nowadays, many take a broader approach, emphasizing *how* they arrive at a result, rather than speaking about *what* they offer. This involves an account of the design process and, more importantly, all the processes preceding and accompanying the conceptual phase of a project. The services offered range from "concepts and designs" (Atlas Studio)[1] to "conceptual design" (Bureau David Voss)[2] to "more than design: consultation, concept and implementation" (L2M3).[3]

While the phrase "more than" hints at a distancing from a supposedly traditional formalistic approach to design, in other cases the extensive approach to design is articulated more explicitly. The studio Daily Dialogue puts it this way: "We develop bespoke design and strategic solutions for clients that are willing to work in close collaboration towards a common goal. Our work is based on a meticulous attention to detail and ideas to create holistic concepts. We are diametrically opposed to formulaic uninspired work."[4]

1   Atlas Studio, *About* www.atlasstudio.ch/about (accessed on 18 December 2018).
2   Bureau David Voss, *About*, bureau-david-voss de/about (accessed on 18 December 2018).
3   L2M3 communication design, www.l2m3.com (accessed on 18 December 2018).
4   Daily Dialogue, *About* dailydialogue.cc/about (accessed on 18 December 2018).

Beyond the specific quotes, statements of these kinds not only reflect an expanded understanding of what designers offer, but a desire for participation and co-determination in the relationship with their clients. Collaboration and the ability to engage in dialogue are cited as the basis for such a cooperative approach. Typical formulations can be found in designers' 'mission statements,' ranging from "collaborative design studio" (ok-rm)[5] to "working 'with' instead of 'for' somebody" (Lamm & Kirch)[6] to the desire to be involved at an early stage, "before any design is involved" (Julia).[7] As in the statements by L2M3 and Daily Dialogue, these formulations speak to the view that good graphic design requires the participation of graphic designers in conceptual if not strategic questions, always in close cooperation with the clients. While established design agencies have long since developed into communications and design consultancy, smaller studios are increasingly taking up this approach.

The expressly distancing of many designers from formalistic approaches, combined with the claim to be involved in conceptual and strategic questions, suggests that the traditional understanding of graphic design as 'making things look nice' does not match the designers' own professional self-image. In this respect, the statements cited are, above all, an expression of expanded participatory standards of competence and a virulent desire for emancipation. As such, these statements aim to relate the designer's own role to the social relevance of graphic design and its ubiquitous presence.

The increasing self-awareness of graphic designers is reflected not least in their desire for authorship. At the same time, such aspiration also points to a fundamental uncertainty about the value of their own work and a supposed lack of recognition for it. It is the author who is generally viewed as the 'creator' by the wider public. The role of graphic designers is

5   OK-RM, *About*, www.ok-rm.co.uk/about-the-studio/introduction,(accessed on 18 December 2018.)
6   Lamm & Kirch, *About us*, lamm-kirch.com/contact (accessed on 18 December 2018).
7   Julia, *Info*, julia.studio/info (accessed on 18 December 2018).

often understood as assisting the authors in bringing their work into a publishable form—an attribution that inevitably leads to a hierarchical gap between content and form. Furthermore, the etymological proximity of the term 'author' in literary works underscores this distinction and has led to misunderstandings. This became clear, for example, when Michael Rock made an attempt to free graphic design from the misery of low esteem in 'Designer as Author' (1996).[8] The essay was largely understood as a call to work as a designer *and* author instead of viewing the designer *as* an author.

On the contrary, the design studios' mission statements relate to the idea of the 'designer as author,' committing to a conceptual approach in graphic design. In this spirit, conceptual design can be paraphrased as getting to the 'heart of the matter.' Such an approach requires an analysis of the issue at hand leading to a process of interpretation and translation, where the choice of formal means depends equally on context and objectives. One of the goals of a conceptual approach—its communicative and aesthetic effectiveness—is to develop a theme that resonates with the recipient's perceptions and understanding. This requires not a mere act of illustrating pre-existing content, but one that uses the power of artistic means to create something original.

An important element is the search for possible references and associations that can serve the development of original imagery corresponding to the objective. Here, too, the focus is on *how* to select and condense certain elements, rather than the formal traits as such. Even the editing of visual materials and the handling of text by the designer aims—more or less consciously—at a specific effect and thus inevitably requires a form of authorship, which implies a corresponding joint responsibility.[9] This is why it is essential not to think of content and form in terms of hierarchies or competition. Just as graphic design

8   Michael Rock, 'Fuck Content,' (New York, 2009)
9   cf. Eva Linhart, 'Grafikdesign Design,' in: *Lerchenfeld* no. 48 (Hamburg, 2019), pp. 3–7.

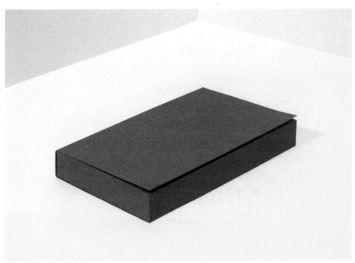

Book design *Martin Schmitz-Kuhl, Books & Bookster: Die Zukunft des Buches und der Buchbranche* by Sandra Doeller, 2015.

Graphic Design Conceives

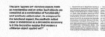

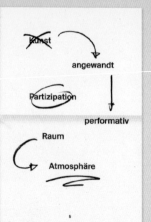

Newspaper design by Sandra Doeller. Newspaper as a catalog for the exhibition
'Give Love Back: Ata Macias and Partners. An exhibition on the question of what applied
art can be today,' Museum für Angewandte Kunst, 2014.

gives the objective its appearance, it is the message that turns graphics into design.

At the same time, this view entails a dilemma: how far should designers go in conceptualizing their work? How can they set the right cues and references that suit the subject matter without overusing them? These questions crystalize in particular when working with artists. There can be a great temptation to visually refer to the artistic strategy and expression or even to adopt it, as observed especially in book design. James Goggin describes this dilemma in his essay 'The Matta-Clark complex' along publications about the sculptor Gordon Matta-Clark. Many of these printed matters mimic the artist's interventions, such as 'building cuts' applied to a book by cutting the spine or cover. But 'where does the designer draw the line between engagement with content and pure decoration?'[10] A reflection on this question primarily requires an awareness of the designer's own role in relation to the artist's work, avoiding "the attempt to compete with the artist".[11]

With a conceptual approach, the challenges in day-to-day work also change. While the processes in purely implementation-oriented work are often easier to foresee and plan, conceptually oriented work requires deliberately open processes, which are rarely linear. Especially in the struggle for a good idea, the participants develop, discard, and condense their thoughts, distance themselves, consider the options, and sometimes start all over again. A higher complexity in the work processes therefore also requires expanded skills, both in speaking about creative approaches and strategies as well as in integrating the various perspectives of all involved.

Reflecting on the respective roles and areas of competence is just as crucial for a successful collaboration as mutual recognition of differences in perspectives. In other words, real dialogue requires designers and clients to listen to each other. This also

10   cf. James Goggin, 'The Matta-Clark Complex,' in: The Form of the Book Book (London, 2009), pp. 23–31.
11   Ibid., p. 30.

means that the desire for greater participation, especially in the conceptual phase of a project, cannot be reserved for just one side. Graphic designers are not the only ones who have a desire for authorship: Nowadays it is not unusual for clients to question their own roles and claim creative authorship with the label 'creative direction.' When clients want to be more closely involved in the design process, graphic designers should not fear a threat to their creative authorship. On the other hand, if this logic were taken to its conclusion on various levels, it would mean that creative positions—whether graphic design or editing of text or photography—would dissolve into a collective nothingness, regardless of the required skills. The conceptual approach understands precisely this balancing act as a challenge and an opportunity.

But how can the shares of authorship of different project participants be determined and evaluated? For example, how important is the decision for or against a design? And isn't the foundation already laid with the selection and commissioning of specific partners? Every exchange has a moment that shapes the result. The closer different parties work together, the less it is possible to clearly identify the authorship of individuals. A practice that can already be observed in some cases in the cultural field could serve as a constructive model: a comprehensive and sensitive crediting of all those involved in a project—including the 'conception' work—would do justice to individual contributions, while at the same time recognizing the collective effort.

To understand graphic design first and foremost as 'authored' work in its various facets does not preclude a close partnership between all those involved. On the contrary, the emphasis of a conceptual approach to graphic design requires an ever-closer dialogue and collaboration between clients and designers, as well as mutual recognition of different competencies and perspectives. In this sense, the statements discussed at the beginning reflect one thing that numerous designers demand above all else: to recognize graphic design in its relevance and participatory dimension.

designing

designing is useless
designing is not useless
not designing is useless
not designing is not useless
useless designing is useless
useless designing is not useless
not useless designing is useless
not useless designing is not useless

Original text: *Struggling*, H.N. Werkman, *The Next Call 9*, 1926.
The text *Struggling* is replaced with *Designing*.

Martin Ludwig Hofmann

Semantic Battles
Or: Why Design Cannot Be Innocent

Design is not innocent. And certainly not communication design. Because design takes sides, it deliberately places itself in the service of a cause. Its entire system of language and symbols is suggestive. Its close relative is emotional seduction, not rational argumentation. "By its double message, the connoted language of advertising reintroduces the dream into the humanity of the purchaser: the dream: i.e., no doubt, a certain alienation (that of competitive society), but also a certain truth (that of poetry)," writes Roland Barthes (1915–1980), the great philosopher of semiotics.[1] In other words, communication design only appeals to the recipient superficially on a conscious level of visual and haptic perception. A deeper analysis reveals that design is primarily aimed at the unconscious areas of our cognition. It speaks the language of poetry, appeals to our dreams, and has the power to control behavior—without all of this being apparent at first glance.

The tools available to designers for these aspects of their work are becoming increasingly nuanced. Miles Young, former longtime CEO of Ogilvy & Mather, recently stated: "The arrival of the digital age coincided with big leaps in neuroscience."[2] And he makes clear that he sees a central driver of the dynamic developments of our time in the coincidence of these two elements. He is by no means the only one to arrive at this diagnosis. And it is almost always

1   Roland Barthes, 'Der Werbespot,' *Das semiologische Abenteuer* (Frankfurt/M., 1988), p. 184; Roland Barthes, 'The Advertising Message,' *The Semiotic Challenge* (Berkeley, 1988).
2   Miles Young, *Ogilvy über Werbung im digitalen Zeitalter* (München, 2019), p. 236 [Miles Young, Ogilvy on Advertising in the Digital Age, New York, 2018].

emphasized that the potential of neuroscientific and cognitive-psychological research combined with practical design techniques is immense. "Neuroscience helps us persuade better; behavioral economics assists people to make choices," Miles Young explains.[3]

Neuro design (design based on neuroscience) is becoming an established term. In such a situation, it is first necessary to define the term: neuro design refers to forms of design that use insights from neuroscience, psychology, sociology, and behavioral science to design more effective solutions. The designation 'more effective' is understood in the sense of achieving the goal of actually triggering certain behaviors that are meant to be induced in the user by the design intervention. Neuro design places particular emphasis on the mental processes that have a major influence on users' behavior, but which largely take place unconsciously. The concept of design in the context of neuro design is deliberately broadly defined and refers to all interventions in the real and virtual environment of the users, regardless of whether these are visual, verbal, haptic, or other interventions.[4]

Bombing the Mind

The sea turns blood red. It is a particularly cruel and repulsive spectacle, and yet it is still practiced to this day. We are talking about whaling—or, to be more precise, the industrially organized slaughter of some of the most intelligent and largest mammals in the world. The images associated with it have burned themselves into our collective memory, as have those of resistance to it. Who does not recall the images of inflatable boats steered by courageous activists between the harpooners of the whalers and the defenseless marine mammals? Several decades ago, with its 'Save the Whales' campaign, Greenpeace grew from an ecological splinter group on the Canadian Pacific coast into a global environmental protection organization.

3   Ibid., p. 242.
4   The paragraph in which this definition appears and the following sections are taken from my book on neuro design: Martin Ludwig Hofmann, *Neuro-Design: Was Design und Marketing von Neurowissenschaft und Psychologie lernen können* (Paderborn, 2019), p. 27 and pp. 200–211.

Martin Ludwig Hofmann

A few years ago I visited Rex Weyler in Vancouver to talk to him about the communications activities in the early years of Greenpeace.[5] As one of the early Greenpeace activists, Weyler was the group's communications director, one of the heads of the first 'Save the Whales' campaign in 1975, and a few years later one of the founders of Greenpeace International. Weyler had been a media man, as they were called at the time. His friend Bob Hunter (1941–2005), the charismatic founding director of Greenpeace, was one too. The former was a photographer, and the latter a copywriter and journalist. Together with other activists from these early days, many of whom previously worked in the media, they advocated for the techniques of modern brand communications and public relations to be used in the emerging environmental movements. Inspired by the writings of media theorist Marshall McLuhan (1911–1980), Hunter even developed his own concept for it: the principle of 'mind bombs.' And one of the first and to this day most powerful mind bombs was their 'Save the Whales' campaign.

It was a bold campaign in every respect. "We went right between the whales and the harpooners—our speedboats jumped over the waves and we had to hold on to ropes so that we wouldn't be thrown overboard," Rex Weyler recalled at the time. "The explosions from the harpoon cannons were so loud that we had to cover our ears. It was hell on earth. But when I looked through the lens, I saw exactly the image that we had been looking for for three years: the back of a whale with a deadly harpoon stuck in it."[6] After all, this was what the activists wanted: to show the world what actually lies behind the sober term of whaling. They wanted to use the emotional power of images that captured this cruel activity after the mere exchange of rational arguments had done so little for so long.

Upon their return, Weyler and Hunter wrote: "We returned 85 days after leaving Vancouver. On our trip we had rescued eight whales, unsettled the Russian

5   Cf. Martin Ludwig Hofmann, *Mindbombs: Was Werbung und PR von Greenpeace & Co. lernen können* (Munich, 2008) [2nd edition, 2012].
6   Quoted from ibid., p. 17.

whaling fleet, and were 40,000 dollars in debt."[7] In addition to the debt, however, they brought with them the essentials they needed for their campaign: images that served to detonate their mind bomb and generated a worldwide response in the media. The importance of this and subsequent campaigns by Greenpeace and other organizations in the fight against whaling can hardly be overestimated. They marked the turning point when people began to take a new look at the industrialized practice of slaughtering these marine mammals.

The International Whaling Commission (IWC) was founded in 1946, although it was powerless to actually protect whales. "The commission specified the minimum size of the animals that could be caught, closed hunting seasons, protected areas, and catch quotas," explains Marliese Kübler.[8] It was not until 1982, after the various campaigns for the protection of whales had developed their global impact, that the majority of the member nations of the IWC were able to agree on a ban on commercial whaling. This so-called international moratorium came into force in the mid-1980s and soon yielded successes.

The populations of most endangered whale species have stabilized in recent decades, even though countries such as Japan, Norway, and Iceland still hunt whales. In regard to Japan alone, the International Fund for Animal Welfare explains: "The exemption for scientific whaling allows them to kill up to 1,000 minke whales and 50 fin whales. In the North Pacific, each year Japan kills up to 200 minke whales, 50 Bryde's whales, 100 sei whales, and 10 sperm whales in the name of science."[9] Norway now kills several hundred minke whales per year, and the small country of Iceland, which is a member of the IWC but does not recognize the moratorium, allows itself a quota of around 200 minke whales and around 150 fin whales. Most of the time, however, it must be added, it does not reach these quotas

7   Bob Hunter, Rex Weyler, *Rettet die Wale: Die Fahrten von Greenpeace* (Frankfurt/M., Berlin, Wien, 1982), p. 58 [Bob Hunter, Rex Weyler: *To Save a Whale*, San Francisco, 1978].
8   Quoted from ibid., p. 137f.
9   ifaw.org/deutschland/unsere-arbeit/wale/welche-länder-betreiben-heute-noch-walfang (accessed on 18 June 2018).

Martin Ludwig Hofmann

Chamberlin's Path

Several thousand kilometers from Vancouver and a few years after my visit to Rex Weyler, I am again seeking to examine the cruel activity of whaling, in Iceland's capital Reykjavik, where most Icelandic whalers are based, and in Húsavík, a town of 2,000 inhabitants on the country's rugged north coast. This is where the Húsavík Whale Museum, tellingly located in a former slaughterhouse, is located. The metaphors this suggests can be understood in two different ways. Iceland is one of the few remaining countries in the world to slaughter the gentle marine mammals, so the cynicism of locating its oldest whale museum in a former slaughterhouse might seem unsurprising. But this interpretation would by no means do justice to the work that the museum's founder Ásbjörn Björgvinsson invested in his institution and that Valdimar Halldórsson and his team continue to do today.

The metaphor can also be interpreted completely differently, in a forward-looking way. Times are changing, and former whaling infrastructure, such as this slaughterhouse, is deliberately being repurposed. This interpretation stems from a small sign in the back of the exhibition space, which refers to Chuck Chamberlin. Chamberlin, an American fisherman on the coast of San Diego, California, was a simple man who went about his business year in and year out—and at the same time a man who, with a clever business idea, laid the foundation for something that would change the world in the mid-1950s.

'Whale watching one Dollar' reads the sign in the exhibition at the Húsavík Whale Museum. It is a reproduction of a sign that Chamberlin displayed in front of his fishing boat. "In 1955, the first commercial whale watching operation was started by fisherman Chuck Chamberlin, who charged US $1 to view gray whales on their winter migration off the coast of San Diego," is printed in slightly smaller type under the sign in the museum. Chamberlin thus (perhaps unconsciously) made a significant contribution that, along with the various 'Save the Whales' campaigns, may have been decisive for the survival of the whales in our oceans. He gave the impetus for offerings, products, and processes to be designed which had behavior-changing effects on several levels. Taking up Chamberlin's legacy, the aggressive advertising campaigns in the style of mind bombs were joined by the seemingly gentler behavior-changing impetuses in the sense of neuro design. And only together—according to the thesis presented here—were they strong enough to make lasting changes in human behavior on a global scale.

Changing Behavior

Whale watching builds on and transforms behaviors learned over generations. It is not uncommon for the operators of whale watching boats to be descendants of fishers and whalers. The protests that showed their fathers the cruelty of their activities were important—even if the whalers themselves mostly dismissed these as 'crazy hippie actions' and thus further solidified their position. Despite these negative reactions, the protests created a new framework that, combined with the option of being able to maintain their accustomed lifestyle on the coast under different conditions, ensured that over the years this solidified position could be softened among many whalers and their families.

Whale watching and whaling are also antipodes in Iceland. Together with various environmental protection organizations, the Icelandic whale watching lobby organization IceWhale has been campaigning for an end to whaling for many years. Most recently, it launched the 'Meet us, don't eat us!' campaign, which is used to advertise the alternative economic use of whales on the coast of Iceland—and which designates restaurants that choose not to serve whale. In fact, whaling in Iceland has steadily declined in recent years. In 2016, 46 minke whales were hunted, and in 2017 only 17. The hunt for the larger fin whales even ceased completely in these two years—not due to animal protection considerations, but because it was simply no longer profitable.[10] Japan, the only remaining market for fin whale products, had raised concerns about the high levels of pollution measured in the meat of fin whales killed off Iceland.

Analytically speaking, a wide variety of elements of neuro design can be seen at work in the triumphant progress of whale watching, starting with *framing*, which put the centuries-old profession of whaling in a new, completely different context. Moby-Dick romanticism, which heroized whaling as the mythical struggle of brave men against a violent nature, was replaced with the image of the cowardly and bloodthirsty slaughter of gentle marine mammals by industrialized killing machines. Words create reality! And images support this emotionally controlled process.

This has to do with the way our brain works. The amygdala, which is connected to the hippocampus, serves a central function in the emotional processing of experiences. When it is active, we tend to be guided by emotions. Functional magnetic resonance imaging (fMRI) has revealed increased activity in the amygdala when test subjects succumb to framing effects. The situation can also be stated more simply: In general, rational arguments are of little use against emotionally controlled processes. According to neuroscientific experience, emotional constructs are more efficiently countered with other emotional constructs. "If here is a choice between the objectively true and the subjectively interesting, the factual always loses," as the advertising icon Howard Luck Gossage (1917–1969) once described this situation.[11]

Between Anchoring and Pressure to Conform

These framing efforts are flanked by the use of the *anchoring effect*. When whales were mentioned in recent

10   UnterWasserWelt: 'Waljagd 2018—Walfang in Europa,' unterwasserwelt.de/waljagd-2018-in-europa (accessed on 20 June 2018).
11   Howard Luck Gossage, *Ist die Werbung noch zu retten?* (Norderstedt, 2017), p. 174 [original publication 1967].

decades, very often the attributes 'gentle' and 'intelligent' preceded the respective descriptions: "The gentle and intelligent marine mammals ..." No matter what comes next, it will be outshone by these attributes. Psychologists call this the *halo effect*. If, for example, it is argued that whales in the seas should be viewed like red deer in the forests, meaning that excessively large whale populations would decimate fish stocks—a frequently cited argument by the defenders of whaling—then most people will barely listen, let alone rationally examine this argument. The image of the gentle and intelligent marine mammals has anchored itself in our brains and overshadows everything else.

This effect is reinforced by the targeted use of the *representativeness heuristic*. Our brain is constantly unconsciously comparing what we perceive with the stereotypical images that we have in our mind. The following rule applies: coherence beats logic. What is consistent with the images in our mind convinces us faster and more lastingly, regardless of what the facts are or how the probabilities are distributed. For this reason, cleverly used *storytelling* is often more successful than factual arguments. The image of whales as eating machines that threaten fish stocks does not fit with the image of gentle and intelligent mammals which has been implemented very successfully in our minds.

The marketing strategies of whale watching operators almost always prominently feature stories of very impressive encounters with whales. These stories are often embedded in a larger narrative context consisting of the stories of the seafaring operator family, historical events in the bay in which the family runs their whale watching operation, and scientific clichés about the highly developed social behavior and intelligence of whales.

Last but not least, the subtle power of statistics is regularly used—what social psychologists refer to as the *pressure to conform*. "If decision architects want to get people to change their behavior, then they can simply tell them what others do in the same situation," Richard H. Thaler and Cass R. Sunstein explain.[12] And that is exactly what makes opponents of whaling together with whale watching lobbyists very successful. For example, Icelandic whaling advocates argue that whaling is part of Icelandic culture, justifying the need to oppose the international whaling moratorium. On the other hand, the environmental protection organization International Fund for Animal Welfare regularly publishes survey results such as these: "Contrary to the popular belief that eating whale meat is traditional in Iceland, a Gallup survey last October showed that actually only 1.5 percent of Icelanders regularly eat whale meat."[13]

The publication of these survey results serves two functions. Outwardly, it seems to accuse whaling defenders of making false statements. One point five percent of the population is negligible. Almost no one in Iceland consumes whale meat today. Thus, according to the subtext implicit in this and similar publications of survey results, there can no longer be any question about whether whaling is deeply anchored in Icelandic culture. Inwardly, it reinforces the trend that on the surface it only seems to document. 98.5 percent of people in Iceland do not eat whale meat. The conclusions that Icelanders draw from this are obvious. Virtually no one does this, so neither should I. From this perspective, the statement that the International Fund for Animal Welfare added to the publication of these figures is quite telling: "The domestic consumption of whale meat has never been so low."[14] In other words, the trend is clear—and it is self-reinforcing.

Design Based in Human Science

This trend has much to do with that well-designed 'product' that competes directly with whaling. After

12   Richard H. Thaler, Cass R. Sunstein, *Nudge. Wie man kluge Entscheidungen anstößt* (Berlin, 2011), p. 97 [Richard H. Thaler, Cass R. Sunstein: *Nudge: Improving Decisions About Health, Wealth, and Happiness*, New York, 2009].
13   ifaw.org/ deutschland/aktuelles/ freiwillige-aus-aller- welt-gesucht-kommt- nach-island-um-wale- zu-retten (accessed on 19 June 2018).
14   Ibid.

all, what began as a small side job for an American fisherman has since turned into a global multi-million-dollar business. In Iceland alone, a country with a population of just 330,000, the whale watching industry generates more than twenty million dollars annually[15]—significantly more than is currently being earned from whaling.

Whale watching offers many former fishing families opportunities to work in an area they know well: the coast and the sea. It uses both existing infrastructures and existing skills. And it opens up new opportunities to improve the lives of local coastal communities. "One way to get people to try something new is to build on behaviors that are familiar to them," emphasizes Tim Brown,[16] CEO of the design agency IDEO. While the anti-whaling campaigns attracted attention, whale watching opened up an economically viable alternative for whalers to make lasting changes to their behavior.

Húsavík is a good example of this. In contrast to Reykjavik, whales are no longer hunted from Húsavík. The city has dedicated itself entirely to professional whale watching and proudly calls itself 'Europe's whale watching capital.' In addition to several providers of various whale-watching tours, the small port town on the north coast of Iceland has developed a considerable tourism infrastructure in recent years: there are cafes, restaurants, museums, shops, hotels, and even a golf course nearby. "While governments continue to debate the future of whaling, the bottom line is increasingly clear: responsible whale watching is the most sustainable, environmentally friendly and economically beneficial 'use' of whales in the twenty-first century," says Patrick R. Ramage, senior director of outreach and program collaboration at the International Fund for Animal Welfare.[17]

In other words, the key to success is not only that whale watching is an environmentally friendly alternative to whaling, but above all an economically viable one. Whale watching is an intelligently designed product that uses existing skills on the supply side and arouses desire in the target group on the demand side. In the words of management icon Peter Drucker, it is a product that is able to convert needs into demand. Every year, whale watching gives hundreds of thousands of tourists a special experience for which they are willing to pay significant sums. This gives the former whalers economic incentives to realign their behavior in a sustainable manner. "At a time when the global economy, our planet's great whales, and international whale conservation measures are all under threat, it is encouraging to see coastal communities the world over continuing to reap increasing benefits from this rapidly developing form of ecotourism," Ramage adds.[18]

The example of whale watching illustrates what designers already knew: "We can use our empathy and understanding of people to design experiences that create opportunities for active engagement and participation," says Tim Brown.[19] So is the use of findings from neuroscience and other human sciences in design legitimate? Should designers be allowed to use such insights? It is certainly difficult to answer these questions. A short version could be: it depends on how they are used and what they are used for. In the words of Roland Barthes: "If it is 'good,' advertising enriches; if it is 'bad,' advertising degrades."[20] Miles Young is even clearer: to him it would simply be

15   Cf. ifaw.org/ deutschland/unsere-arbeit/wale/walbeobachtung-walfangländern (accessed on 19 June 2018).
16   Tim Brown, *Change by Design. Wie Design Thinking Organisationen verändert und zu mehr Innovation führt* (München, 2016), p. 98 [Tim Brown: *Change*

by Design: How Design Thinking Transforms Organizations and Inspires Innovation, New York, 2009].
17   Simon O'Connor, Roderick Campbell, Hernan Cortez Tristan Knowles, *Whale Watching Worldwide: Tourism Numbers, Expenditures and Economic Benefits, A Special Report from*

the *International Fund for Animal Welfare* (Yarmouth Port, USA), 2009, p. 8.
18   Ibid.
19   See note 16, p. 37.
20   See note 1, p. 184.

"a great mistake to blame these methods for something much more fundamental you disagree with. Like
any other tool in life—including a spade—they can be
used for good or ill purposes."[21]
      Only one thing is clear: design does not remain
innocent.

Graphic interlude by Natalie Andruszkiewicz

Graphic interlude by Natalie Andruszkiewicz

Pierre Smolarski

Common-Sense Design
On the Rhetorical Limits of What Can Be Designed

Introduction

Recently, major questions have been regularly scattered across the field of design. Should designers conquer the public or not? Should they take responsibility or admit their powerlessness? Should they even ask these questions, or is asking these questions already part of their staging, a kind of whitewashing? The field of design is expanding, partly in real terms, and partly only conceptually, because German design theory often uses terms like advertising slogans.

I want to try to counteract these excessive design terms as well as the exaggerated expectations of design. Throughout history, *sensus communis*—which I will discuss at length—has often been praised as an everyday lifeline against excessive metaphysical speculations. In this sense, it is about common-sense design. With this as a starting point, I would like to propose that design is not content, not a point of view, not an opinion, but a technique, a craft of emphasizing. For centuries this technique has been described in all its facets—very much like the current discussions in design—as *techne rhetorike*, rhetorical art; and the rhetorical term for social transformation is persuasion, the ability to convince. That is what I will focus on. I will return to this point.

If design is not content, but a technique, then it becomes clear: the question "How do we win over the public?" is a question of rhetorical design; the

Common-Sense Design

question "What do we have to say to the public?" is not. In this regard, design contrasts with all political, social, and emancipatory movements with which a social, political, or civic design would like to adorn itself. These have something to say and ask *how*; designers know *how*, and now they are looking for content of their own making. This is understandable—and possibly also gratifying—since it could be useful for democratizing the rhetorical means of power, and it would correspond to the spirit of a radical pluralism. If only this pluralism were not so difficult to define; if only the imaginary roots of the social would not push through again and again. Then people talk about 'the' society as if it simply existed, singular, a monolith, a noun that is there in substance, waiting to be determined by an adjective.

I would like to talk about such an imaginary thing, about *sensus communis*, common sense, which *does not* exist and yet is effective. I will do this from a rhetorical point of view, based on rhetorical theory, which asks questions about the appropriateness of design under the term aptum.

Easy Demarcation: Identification, Affirmation

The rhetorical boundaries of what can be designed are basically easy to draw. As Aristotle says, it is not difficult to praise Athenians in Athens, and so ultimately what is most convincing is what no one doubts.[1] That is quite trivial, but, as Kenneth Burke emphasizes, if it is systematically expanded, it is the core of rhetorical design: a "persuasion by flattery."[2] The art of convincing is a flattering art, and rhetorical design is a flattering seduction of the user or viewer. Even if the rhetorical competition of opinions continually conceals and obscures this core, the same principle at least applies to the successful *rhetor* as to the successful designer, which Umberto Eco identifies as a characteristic of rhetoric in general:

1 Aristotle, Rhet. I, 2. 1357a2–9.

On the one hand, rhetoric tends to focus attention on a speech that seeks to convince the listener in an unusual (informative) way of something that they *did not yet* know. On the other hand, it achieves this goal by starting from something that the listener already knows and wants and trying to prove how the conclusion can be derived *naturally* from it.[3]

The core of persuasion is ultimately not a total, but nevertheless a fundamental affirmation of what already exists with the audience, so that this can help the audience identify with what has been presented. As Gian Battista Vico never tires of emphasizing, finding what the audience already knows, wants, believes, or hopes in the matter at hand is the task of topics.[4] And the constant use of what is found in this way is ultimately nothing other than an unceasing appeal to *sensus communis*, to what Antonio Gramsci calls "common sense." Common sense is not a closed system or a homogeneous ensemble of beliefs, but *in the best sense* the "philosophy of the non-philosophers,"[5] *in the worst sense* common sense is "an ambiguous, contradictory, manifold concept" to which to "refer to as a measure of truth," as Gramsci says, "is foolishness."[6] But truth is not the topic of rhetoric or of design—at most of philosophy. After all, it is obviously clear that the rhetorical measure in design generally cannot be evaluated with the categories 'true,' 'right,' or 'wrong.' What would a right poster or a wrong teapot be? And how should such a question strengthen creative judgment? Ultimately, it is more about—and can also be grasped and expressed as such—whether a certain result is better or worse than another in relation to certain goals. The parameters required for this can be determined by questions of functionality, the client's desires, success, and others. However, a design product is never better or worse independent of parameters of judgement and its context of use.

2   Burke 1969, p. 55.
3   Eco 2002, p. 184.
4   Vico 1974.
5   Gramsci 1995, §13, p. 1393.
6   Ibid., p. 1397.

A well-designed and tailored campaign for a certain audience can be bad in a different context, when presented to a different, heterogeneous audience. David Kaufer and Brian Butler put it this way: "What makes an outcome better or worse has to do with *the fit* of the design to the client's purpose."[7] Although the addressee is the rhetorically most important parameter in the design process, they are neither a uniform quantity—as the quotation suggests—nor the only point of reference. Christopher Alexander expresses the precept of appropriateness expressed here better, though much more generally:

> The form is a part of the world over which we have control, and which we decide to shape while leaving the rest of the world as it is. The context is part of the world which puts demands on this form; anything in the world that makes demands of the form is context. Fitness is a relation of mutual acceptability between these two.[8]

The acceptability of the relation between context and form, as suggested here by Alexander, is mirrored in the category of appropriateness, which is central to rhetorical theory and especially to design rhetoric: the *aptum*. As Bernhard Asmuth emphasized in his article on appropriateness in rhetoric, this category is considered "a kind of super-principle"[9] of rhetoric. He aptly combines this principle with the biological principle of adaptation, as "the ability of living things to adapt to changing environmental requirements for the purpose of survival.[10] Against the background that rhetorical efforts (also in design) are always about creating possibilities for identification, appropriateness refers to the possibility of being able to provide a specific audience with a kind of 'adaptation behavior' for identification. But this also means that the specific guidelines of appropriateness can vary greatly

7   Kaufer/Butler 1996, p. 40.
8   Alexander 1964, p. 18f.
9   Asmuth 1992, col. 579.
10   Ibid.

depending on the audience and the rhetorical setting. The *aptum* thus refers to a major category—and
in this sense is a super-principle—that brings together different elements: appropriateness is ascribed
in relation to the subject of speech, as well as the
speaker's reference to this subject—but also in relation to the requirements and desires of the audience
as well as their horizon of understanding and ethical and aesthetic ideas. Questions about adequacy
should therefore be addressed to design not only from
a political, ethical, or moral perspective, but also in regard to design, expression, and structure. The latter
is sometimes referred to as the inner aptum and is
distinguished from the former, the outer *aptum*. This
is a distinction that ultimately takes into account the
fact that products of rhetorical art always seek to address two audiences: the external audience, the target group, and an internal audience, the expert group
of the art itself. Indeed, these two levels can be distinguished within rhetoric (as well as in design). A rhetorical effort can be recognized as a great achievement in the sense of rhetorical technique, even if it
may not have been successful in relation to the target
audience. It is probably easy to find examples of successful and 'revolutionary' design that were not well
received by the user and yet are canonized in design
history; or even, as with many award-winning advertising campaigns, were never intended for an external
audience, but only for publication in annual reports,
competition catalogs, or lookbooks. This is a dubious
achievement of design.

But back to the drawing of boundaries!

Sensus communis

In addition to the view of the *aptum* as a super-principle of rhetoric, *aptum* can also be understood as the
limit of what can be said, justified, and thus designed,
which constitutes rhetorical space as the space in
which the rhetorically possible can occur in the first

place. *Aptum* is then primarily a category of morality and the space defined by it is ultimately the area of what is referred to as *sensus communis*, or common sense, in terms of the history of rhetoric and philosophy. As Thomas Leinkauf emphasizes, *sensus communis* is

> ...understood as a kind of collective term for certain phenomena of the perceptual and emotional horizon which are difficult to specify and which suggest the instinctive and pre-reflective forms of moral or aesthetic knowledge to the individual within a group or socio-cultural unit, to which the individual can see themselves as belonging of their own accord.[11]

This 'belonging' refers to the basis of possible rhetorical efforts, insofar as they always rely on identification and thus ultimately to a certain extent on affirmation. Common sense therefore also coincides with the outer *aptum*, at least when it comes to drawing boundaries, and gives the *rhetor*, as Vico among others emphasizes, a real-life orientation in the areas of practical knowledge, which includes politics, morality, and the arts as well as rhetoric.[12] It is also Vico who sees this area of real-life wisdom through an overemphasis on scientific methods of insight as a danger and therefore sees *sensus communis* in dissolution. Hannah Arendt takes up this idea and opposes a translation of the term as 'common sense,' which for her expresses the worldlessness of pure intellectual activities. As she points out in agreement with Vico, it is not about a structure of understanding that—if it is 'healthy'—produces binding results, but a principle that creates a community which can—at least sufficiently—guarantee a shared world. *Sensus communis* and the rhetorical orientation toward it by the *aptum* is thus a sense of reality.[13] This real-world sense of reality also makes the boundary tangible in design, in

11   Leinkauf 1995, col. 629f.
12   Vico 1974.
13   Arendt 2015, p. 359f.

which the rhetorical sense of possibility can potentially develop successfully.

If one understands the outer *aptum* to mean above all the above-described demarcation of the rhetorical space of possibility by a sense of reality, then classical rhetorical theory offers three methods above all to recognize this space and thus to find what is possibly credible: the status doctrine, the doctrine of degrees of justifiability, and especially topics.[14]

Frictions, or, What Pushes the Designer to the Limits?

So far, I have spoken about the necessary rhetorical foundation in *sensus communis* to find the basis of identification that is essential for every rhetorical transformation process. An affirmation by *sensus communis* clearly will not transform anything. As convincing as the connection to what is already believed is, ultimately it pushes the designer to the limits of what can be said, justified, and thus also shaped. More precisely: striking design does not simply take place *within* the limits of what can be designed, but always *at the limits themselves*. The reasons that drive the designer not to settle in the heartland of *sensus communis* can be diverse. The design 'dogma of the new,' the creativity imperative[15] of the creative industries, and the personal drive for recognition surely play important roles. Sometimes rhetorically aimed innovation may also be borne by a genuine political interest, by convictions and the imagination of a common good. From a rhetorical point of view, however, the standard case seems to me to be simply that of potential market success: particularly in advertising design, the rhetorical balancing act must succeed in balancing two conflicting principles. On the one hand, it can be said that attention must be gained at all costs. This is done primarily through repetition. Not much rhetorical art is necessary if the possibility for media omnipresence and ceaseless repetition

14 Smolarski 2017.
15 This dogma has been emphasized by countless parties. The term 'creativity dispositive' and the related 'creativity imperative' were coined mainly by Reckwitz (2012).

exists or can be afforded. In addition, provocation, the easy crossing of boundaries, and other forms of ironically or comically challenging *sensus communis* are also extremely effective means of directing attention. On the other hand, without a solid basis for identification and thus without a fixed position within what is already believed, desired, hoped for, one cannot successfully operate rhetorically. These two motives, creating a connection and attracting attention, result in a problem of two extremes in which attempts are repeatedly made to achieve maximum control of attention without really leaving the rhetorical space of possibilities. In this way, people operate on the rhetorical boundaries of what can be said and justified and thus designed, and, if successful, these boundaries are also shifted. This shifting of boundaries is undoubtedly a transformation on a social level, and designers operate on a central, socially imagined root, an ensemble of common beliefs, which is not least also the basis for what can be postulated as the common good. To conclude: if, from this position, we pose the question of the relationship between responsibility and design, then it must be repeated: design is not content, design is not a position, and design is not an opinion. The expansive operation at the limits of what can be designed is borne and caused by the political and social attitude of the designer. Or it is simply not borne, not caused. Thus, it is a question of an attitude of the designer, which one would hope would not see the expansion of boundaries merely as a key position for generating attention, and instead—at least sometimes—would not move a boundary, an area of the sacred without market stalls. Where this attitude is lacking, and the boundaries are shifted only for the purpose of generating attention, design becomes playfully hollow; it becomes ironic in today's common misunderstanding of the word. And this irony is a total rejection of any principle of responsibility.

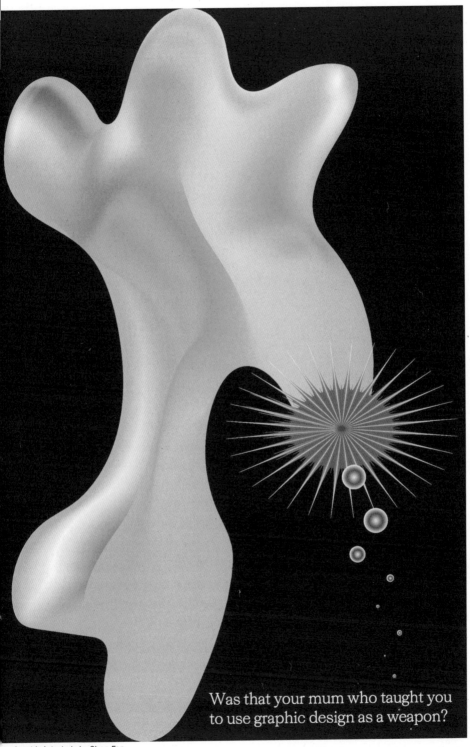

Was that your mum who taught you to use graphic design as a weapon?

Graphic interlude by Shen Fan

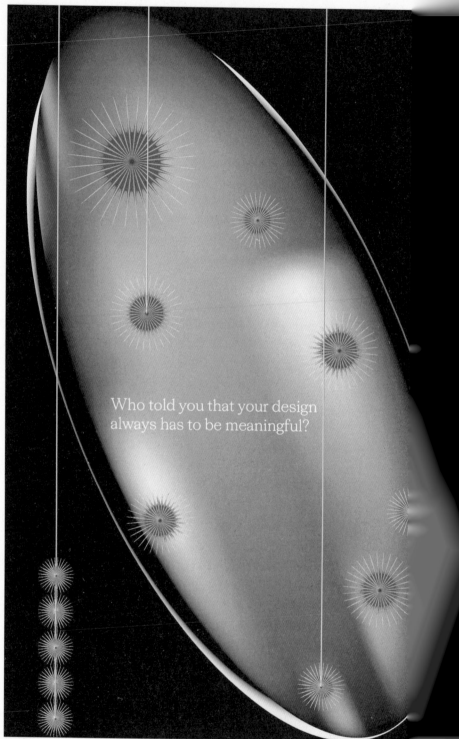

Who told you that your design always has to be meaningful?

Graphic interlude by Shen Fan

Graphic Design | 3-in-1

Most readers will be familiar with 3-in-1 shampoo, which combines shampoo, conditioner, and anti-dandruff treatment into one hair care product. What constitutes great design can also be based on the idea of 3-in-1. One of my favorite designers, Eiko Ishioka, looks for three qualities when evaluating design; great design should be "original, revolutionary, and timeless."[1] Over the years, I have found Ishioka's definition to be best. 'Original' refers to the imagination behind the design, while 'revolutionary' pushes the boundaries of technological innovation. Lastly, 'timeless' encapsulates the designer's contemplation of time, their attitude toward history. Together with the first two elements, the designer is able to create a design that may transcend the boundaries of time—another 3-in-1 concept that is as beneficial as it is effective.

In the 1930s, Chinese essayist and philosopher Hu Shih often expounded upon his understanding of 'good literature.' He wrote that good literature should possess three qualities. "First, it should be clear and understandable. Second, it should be moving. Third, it should be beautiful."[2] Coincidentally, Ishioka's 3-in-1 is similar to Hu's. Graphic design must convey information. This act must be masterful and clear—the information must be correct, and the design must not cause misunderstanding. This is the foundation. Without it, design is pointless. How then, do you ensure that the method used to convey a message stands

1   Jianping He (ed.) *Master of Design: Eiko Ishioka*, 2006 (Vicoroa, 2006), p 4.
2   Hu Shih, 'What is Literature?' in: *Collected Essays of Hu Shih*, 1921.

out enough to snag the viewers' attention in today's cacophony of information?

The means of conveyance must be powerful. Such power is not a matter of the wrist, but of the intellect. A transformation of the mind made possible by skillful expression and a powerful imagination. As for the third aspect—beauty, this builds on the foundation of the two preceding concepts. If a designer can satisfy the previous points while also conveying beauty, then they have reached the heights of design. The third element is also the most elusive. Much like style and temperament, it is formless and shapeless, but it surely exists.

3-in-1 condenses the designer's thoughts while it also helps organize them. The boundaries set by the number 3 allow us to eliminate the cumbersome while maintaining focus. Every designer has a different 3-in-1, a trinity that comprises their own understanding of design. My trinity is thinking, technology, and experimentation.

Thinking

Design is thinking made visual.
Saul Bass[3]

I want to carve these words into marble, and then place that slab of marble in the middle of a plaza at the city center. It is unfortunate that graphic design is not as important to society as I imagine it to be. I doubt many would support my effort to center this statement. Yet I constantly worry this phrase will be forgotten in this era, when information flows like flood water and images are as countless as the grains of sand on a beach.

Perhaps life is moving faster, or perhaps design cycles have shrunk. A designer's understanding of visual communication has been reduced to the single metric of the visual image. As a creator of visual images, the designer no longer has time to contemplate *how* information is conveyed. A century ago, images

[3]   Saul Bass (1920–1996), American typographer, graphic designer, photographer, and filmmaker.

were not easily accessible, contrary to today's world, where digital cameras and smartphones churn out massive amounts of junk images.

Dutch artist and designer Erik Kessels understands the crisis created by the flood of visual images in our era. His project, *24 Hrs in Photos*[4] posits that image-sharing platforms such as Flickr and the image search engines behind Facebook and Instagram are generating excessive volumes of images. For his project, Kessels invited people from around the world to send him photos taken in real time. As soon as he received the images, he printed them in an empty gallery space. Within twenty-four hours, he had printed over 350,000 photographs. These 9 × 13 cm photos were piled up high throughout the exhibition space, filling the entire room.

The birth of any new image can be drowned out by this frenzy of information. If there is no thought behind the creation of an image, it will disappear all the faster. If the information we attempt to convey is not bolstered by thought, if the image itself is but a mish-mash of bright colors and bold text—it will not convey a message. Thought imbues design with intelligence. That intelligence sparks a connection in the viewer's mind the moment they see the design. It makes them think. This act of thinking creates a memory in the viewer—a record of their thoughts when they perceived the design. This record is the greatest thing that graphic design can create.

Technology

Deng Xiaoping once said: "Science and technology are primary productive forces."[5] Advancements in technology shorten production cycles and change our values. In the field of graphic design, technological advancements also disrupt traditional procedures and transform industry categories. The people who make up this industry transcend boundaries—they are art-

4   Erik Kessels (b. 1966), Dutch artist, designer and curator. For more information on his project *24 Hrs in Photos*, visit, www.erikkessels.com/24hrs-in-photos.

5   Deng Xiaoping (1904–1997) was the leader of the People's Republic of China from the late 1970s to the late 1980s. He opened China to the West at the end of the 1970s. The quote "Science and technology are primary productive forces" was put forward by Deng in the government report of the Third Plenary Session of the Thirteenth Central Committee in September, 1988.

ists, designers, technologists, new media artists, and more. It is imperative that graphic design opens up the scope of a designer's work in order to assist in the completion of the work of other industries. Working with diverse groups of people has transformed the relative uniformity of who may be classified as a designer, and in the future, designers will by definition need to possess technical expertise.

The development of contemporary technology is a double-edged sword. With more information to convey, design must be faster. Under such time pressure, the human brain's ability to generate new ideas cannot keep up. Yet the effectiveness of design undergoes more and more specific measuring and evaluation with big data. So, is it outdated and unrealistic to expect design to continue to emphasize creativity and aesthetics? If matters continue along this trajectory, will technology ultimately dig the grave of graphic design?

In 2009, retailer Alibaba's Taobao and Tmall created a new virtual holiday. Each year, November 11 is a bacchanalia of online shopping and sales. The holiday, named Double 11, has achieved unprecedented commercial success. In 2016, a total of 98,000 brands participated in Taobao's Double 11 promotions, racking up sales of 168.2 billion RMB (24 billion USD). Products were advertised on the home page of Taobao in the form of banners—changing with each click and never repeating. These banners were generated by Alibaba's AI design platform Luban,[6] which generated 40 million banners in twenty-four hours, with no two banners alike. In 2016, it created 170 million product banners for Double 11 and generated hundred percent more clicks for these products. Luban was able to achieve these results through a combination of deep learning algorithms and an evaluation network. Basically, Luban's design capabilities were achieved by humans teaching the program to learn design by putting large volumes of data through AI

6   Why was the program named Luban? The name is a double entendre. Firstly, it is derived from homophones in the phrase, "Let there be no 'Ban'-ner too difficult to churn out (lu)." Secondly, Lu Ban was a famed craftsman from China's Spring and Autumn period (5th century BC) who is revered as the patron of Chinese craftsmen.

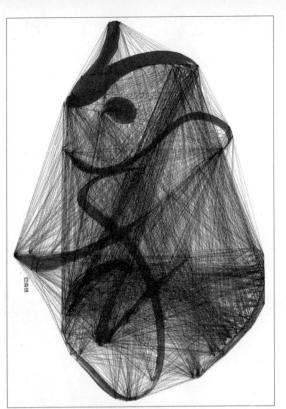

Poster design *Spirited* by Jianping He, 2011.
In 2011, Taiwanese calligrapher Ms. Tong Yang-Tze invited 40 designers from China, Taiwan, Hong Kong and Japan, to design posters by collaborating with her 24 calligraphy works, with the subject of 'imitating nature'.

Poster design *West & East* by Jianping He, 2018.

Poster design *200 years Bodoni* by Jianping He, 2018.

Poster design *Flash Back* by Jianping He, 2012.

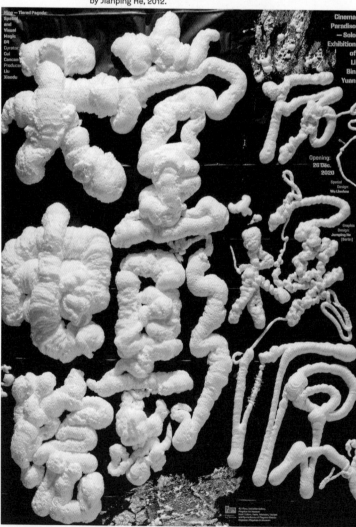

Poster design *Li Bin Yuan* by Jianping He, 2020. Poster for 'Cinema Paradiso – Solo exhibition of Li Bin Yuan' at Pingshan Art Museum in Shenzhen, China.

algorithms. If human designers had to design as many banners as Luban made in twenty-four hours, it would have taken a hundred designers 300 years at the rate of one banner every twenty minutes.

For this massive shopping bonanza, human designers were outpaced by machines in an obvious defeat. However, the program's design principles were based on examples of existing design; after these had been compiled by big data, the program created random combinations using fragments of pre-existing design. Luban lacks independent creative ability and an understanding of aesthetics. In other words, there were probably not many graphic designers on the team that developed the design software. Graphic designers are unable to join technical teams because they often lack technical knowledge about programming, AI, and so on. This deficiency comes from how designers are educated, and what they are traditionally expected to do. Coding, machine learning, and other technical knowledge are not part of most graphic design curricula. However, changing times are forcing the industry to redefine what it means to be a graphic designer.

Faced with ongoing technological developments, how should a graphic designer continue to work? Given the pressures of contemporary technology, is it necessary to change the connotations and boundaries of graphic design? Should graphic designers forsake their professional standards? Or rather, how should designers redefine their profession? What new content should be added to graphic design curricula? Which professional groups should graphic designers learn to accommodate? I believe these questions should be explored first and foremost in the education of graphic designers. This is where changes to content and teaching modes should be made.

The current graphic design curriculum is still based on the century old Bauhaus structure—the three major areas of art and design theory, profes-sional work, and workshopping. There is an emphasis on artistic training over technical training. The soft-ware that students learn to use is limited to just a few programs. Meanwhile, mass-produced devices such as mobile phones and computers have given individ-uals a direct means of transmitting information. The medium of graphic design has changed. It is time to think about how to train and strengthen graphic de-sign students in subjects such as mathematics and physics. After a basic grounding in art, this new group of students will be able to apply their STEM abilities to graphic design. If the characteristics of Bauhaus and Basel once separated graphic design from art, then today we need to create graphic designers out of mathematicians and IT specialists. Tomás Maldo-nado[7] once said: "The 'Designer' is neither engineer nor artist, nor does he stand between the engineer and the artist: his occupation is rather that of a new and independent profession."[8] Today, perhaps we find ourselves at yet another such crossroads.

Experimentation

I once spent a considerable period studying the work of Wolfgang Weingart. In terms of output, his body of work pales in comparison that of his teachers Emil Ruder and Armin Hoffman. Furthermore, most of his work was not client work, but rather the product of his own experimentation. At first, I did not understand the importance of his work in design history, but lat-er I came to realize that Weingart's self-driven experi-mentation was his contribution to graphic design as a profession. In the 1960s, Weingart's revolutionary use of photosetting instead of letterpress led many oth-ers to incorporate the technique into graphic design. In the 1970s, he began a series of experiments with multi-layered dot screens. Coincidentally, the timing of these experiments aligned with the dawning of the digital age, providing much inspiration. Weingart's work

7   Tomás Maldona-do (1922–2018), Argen-tinian artist, designer, design theorist, philos-opher, and university professor.
8   'The 'Design-er' is neither engineer nor artist, nor does he stand between the en-gineer and the artist: his occupation is rath-er that of a new and independent profes-sion Tomás Maldonado, *Wim Crouwel—Modern-ist* (Eindhoven, 2015), p. 333.

with dot screens was so pioneering that it actually anticipated the use of pixels on computer screens.
In fact, it was his work that inspired many aspects of
the graphic design software that began popping up
in the 1980s.

Experimentation generates great value for any
profession because it foretells the development of
an industry. Though the way forward may be murky
and full of detours, innovation breathes new life into
a profession and allows it to find continued growth.

In his Nobel Prize acceptance speech, Mario Vargas
Llosa said: "Without fictions we would be less aware
of the importance of freedom for life to be livable, the
hell it turns into when it is trampled underfoot by a
tyrant, an ideology, or a religion."[9] What fiction is to
literature, experimentation with graphics is to design.
Its true application unfolds in the moment people become aware of the profession's existence, while reality is the obstacle that restricts its growth. Imagination is the first step in nearly all forms of progress. An
unrelenting devotion to reality will only limit growth.
Art is not exempt from this strange loop. "Art cannot accept the realities of life. Therefore, at certain
junctures, we cannot accept art. Art is superficial, it
is vain excitement—a futile agitation."[10] Experimentation and exploration are the libido of any profession.
Without libido, there is no procreation, without procreation, there is no legacy.

9   From 'In Praise
of Reading and Fic-
tion,' Vargas Llosa's No-
bel Prize acceptance
speech, 2010.
10   Mu Xin, Ai-
mosheng jia de e ke
(Beijing, 2009).

Designers can make their biggest social and political impact by *not designing* ?

Graphic interlude by Pawel Wolowitsch

Friedrich von Borries

Writing and Violence

Dear Ingo,

Around ten years ago, when I had just arrived at the HfBK,[1] we talked about the question of whether graphic design is political. As I remember, you were of the opinion that in product design, which I feel increasingly responsible for at the university, the potential in this regard is greater than in graphic design and typography, your area of activity. This question, it seems to me, continues to occupy you, and so of course I gladly accepted your invitation to further consider this question.

So, instead of writing a conventional academic text for this publication (others can do that better than me anyway), I have chosen the format of a letter, from colleague to colleague, from friend to friend, to delve into some of these thoughts—which are still loose thoughts, sketches, fragments, half-baked ideas.

I emailed you a 'snappy' title in advance, 'Writing and Violence,' and I would now like to pursue this further.

For me, writing is always a struggle, a struggle with oneself and with the subject, but when I chose the title 'Writing and Violence' I didn't mean this inner struggle, but a more fundamental violence of the written word.

Etymologically the word 'writing' seems to be related to carving. Though I am not a historical anthropologist or classical studies scholar, when I imagine the beginnings of writing, in my mind I see stones worked upon with a chisel and skin scratched with a

1 . HfBK Hochschule für Bildende Kunst (University for the Arts, Hamburg).

knife. This first writing, as I imagine it, is absolute, ir-revocable: one's membership in a tribe is carved into the skin of one's face; God's laws are carved in stone. This irrevocability of the written word still applies today. Not without reason, a text is set before going to print.

One could argue that this has nothing to do with graphic design, but with the text that the graph-ic designer is given, but I think that such a separation of form and content is insufficient. After all, this is to overlook the fact, which seems self-evident today, that the graphic designer as a connoisseur of writing has a knowledge of power, and so is much more than just a proxy.

When we speak of graphic design today, we no longer only mean the printing of books (we could also talk about the force of the printing press and what form of violence this entails), but also new forms of communication, for which at our university the not very widely used term of 'communication and infor-mation design' has become established. Violence is also contained in the concept of information. Vilém Flusser once described information as "bringing something into form." Thus, informing something or someone does not mean delivering a message, but rather bringing the recipient into a certain form—or several of them—into a formation, to bring this mili-tary term into the associative space.

Thus, various associations of the use of vio-lence and irrevocability echo in the act of graphic de-sign. I believe it is important to bear this in mind. In my view, it makes it clear that graphic designers do not operate on neutral ground or untouched territo-ry, but are always in contaminated areas, on battle-fields where positions are taken and molds are cast.

I would also like to recall a picture that I showed in my lecture on the topic of writing: a scratched fore-arm. Cutting marks into one's own skin is a practice in youth culture that is often classified as self-harm. I have even seen it among students at our university.

This cutting is of course a violent act, an act of self-harm, but also a form of graphic design that makes protest visible. On the one hand, it has a strong communicative power. On the other hand, it refuses to be appropriated because it does not 'bring something into form' but remains formless, and it is precisely in this way that it becomes visible as a counter-position.

So, what could a graphic design be that reacts to the inherent political dimension of all graphic design?

For some time now I have been concerned with the idea of a skill of incompleteness—the idea that it could be an essence of democratic design to be never finished, never complete, to remain open so that it can be appropriated, changed, transformed. But unfinished would also mean awkward, not perfect, absolute, but incomplete. Perhaps we can teach such a 'skill of incompleteness' together at our university in the future? What could that look like? I don't know. But hopefully we have enough years left together to try this out.

Yours,
Friedrich

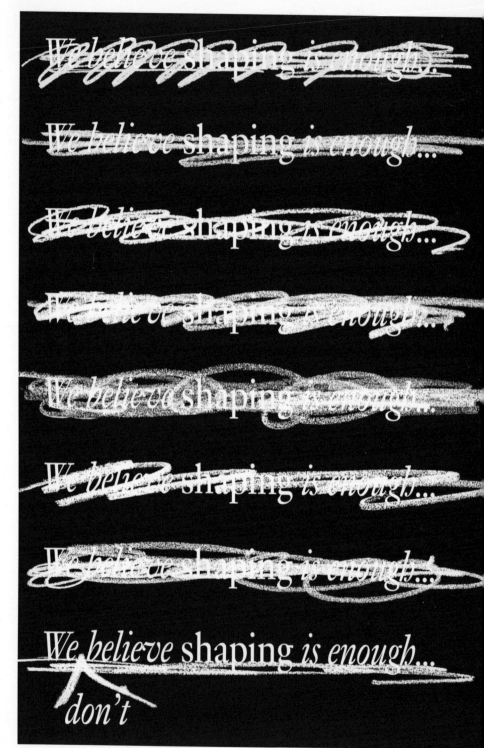

Graphic interlude by Gihong "Kiki" Park

Francisco Laranjo

Graphic Design after the New Normal

The Covid-19 pandemic had just begun, and numerous graphic designers—mainly from Europe—quickly gathered online to share posters. As usual, design hackathons spread across social media, attempting to tackle political problems with technological solutions. Contrary to the stylish pomposity with which they appeared, they were discreetly ignored. Soon after, the prefix 'post' was already circulating in Western design discourse, looking for universal applicability. What's the post-pandemic design going to be? What's it going to look like? How does all this impact future internships and job opportunities? Can we still thrive despite the adversities? Whom should we listen to and who can offer useful tips and advice? Biennials postponed, festivals turned into online 'experiences' of retrofitted content, award deadlines extended, portfolio showcasing transferred to gigantic video conferences and virtual stands. The future was reduced to 2021, too distant to grasp. Designers already lived and worked in 35sqm, but it was possible to get some air every now and then, staring at the phone, swiping up to kill time, tapping occasionally to keep friendships alive. Too much screen time showed us that perhaps the future isn't digital. That progress does not mean air-charging our devices or controlling the color of light bulbs in the living room with an app. Perhaps the future has less design—at least not as it's now being sold on a daily basis. We are in a constant state of alert, eyes wide open, but with fading attentiveness. To racism, classism, sexism, colonialism, inequality, precarity.

We're tired—too tired. We subscribe to and miss Zoom meetings, then avoid watching recorded sessions. We're spoiled by quantity in a time of generosity. Tabs pile up on an open browser, the disk is almost full and tomorrow is almost here. Our life is suspended: waiting for internships, for budgets to arrive and companies to invest, eventually preparing for a non-design job in the background. But who's doing that funny, clever meme that will make us crack a smile? Graphic designers looked numb before the pandemic and continue adrift today, waiting for an inevitable subsequent wave of the virus, or for the ripples of the first to wash us away. It's complex. All we wanted to do was play with type and image and tech, maybe work abroad in a big agency, a well-known brand that we could tag, be recognized. Is it too late, or can we still do it from home? At the same time, we want the best for everyone. Do we? Most graphic design in these circumstances is generally well-intentioned, sometimes self-indulgent and highlighting an obsession with form and style—but mostly, pathetic. This is not new, it just got worse.

In 2019, Greta Thunberg's handwriting was copied by a designer, who turned it into a typeface named Greta Grotesk. This is exactly the kind of simplistic, functional 'tribute' that throws design under the bus when it attempts to strive for meaningful contributions to society beyond the capitalist logic. Form always takes the prize. The pandemic spread across the globe and graphic design primarily focused on four approaches: signage, celebration, relief, and help. The first is the most obvious need during a pandemic. Examples include social-distancing vinyl to be applied on the pavement and general way-finding, from routes to follow, to procedures to be taken. Celebration pays visual and symbolic tributes to health professionals and care workers, as well as honoring and remembering the deceased. Relief is more self-directed, but sometimes also a form of self-care by distraction. This took form in the proliferation of memes, ranging from humorous takes on the contingencies of a confined reality to reflecting upon the impact the pandemic has had on the discipline and designers in Western societies. Selling prints and producing publications with the funds going to multiple charities, is also a hybrid manifestation of this category. Finally, 'help' applies design in a more pragmatic manner. Useful examples include DIY forms distributed in neighborhoods to exchange contacts in order for essentials to be delivered, and less abled people to be supported—forming hyper-local activism. But also open-source documents listing mutual-aid groups, and collective maps identifying places where food is available. At different levels, these approaches exposed design's redundancy, but also potential, especially when thinking beyond the typical and self-imposed limitations of the discipline.

The rest is just business as usual. Regardless of the scale of the crisis, we will see yet another Shepard Fairey poster circulating online. Adobe capitalizes on these moments: "stay connected, stay productive", while offering tips and selling Adobe Fresco, Spark, Premiere Rush, XD, Scan and Acrobat Reader. During a time of suspended consciousness such as this—a natural disaster, a political conflict—corporations enter into a state of rebranding: seeking to transmit empathy and change, while effectively reaffirming and reproducing the status quo by standardization. McDonalds may not pay workers a living wage or sick leave, but they will distance the strokes of the logo's 'M', referring to social distancing. Coca-Cola, Audi, Mercedes and countless other companies adhered to the need of showing compassion and responsibility, with design as a fundamental complicit. This state of unconsciousness is also used to reaffirm neoliberalism through the constant championing of coronapreneurialism, using new needs as business opportunities, trial and push new technology that would need further reflection, debate, evaluation, and legislation, increasing control and surveillance.

In design education, the consequences of a massive increase of virtual education were rapidly felt. There's a feeling of powerlessness—what can a group of design students do? What can they do at and with their institutions? How can they reach out to other groups of students with similar concerns to gain more leverage? And will these micro-gestures matter if political change will only likely take place through voting? This creates substantial (and additional) anxiety in students, while being bombarded with entrepreneurial discourse and the hopefulness of institutions' belief that the 'normal' will soon return. There's also a solutionist tendency ingrained in designers to be proud, flexible, and adaptable, even if it damages their education and future. This pride fades from undergraduate to graduate students, with maturity and experience. But there's a realization that degrowth in design and slowing down are possible if imposed under the circumstances of a pandemic, but unrealistic financially if the 'old', or when the announced 'new', normality arrives. What would be possible to do as graphic designers if, for example, universal basic income was a reality? What kind of practices is education promoting beyond production (print and digital)? And would educational institutions be open to radically different uses of their facilities? Under asphyxiating tech imperialism and rampant surveillance capitalism that shows no signs of slowing down, graphic design students generally see the discipline at odds with the kind of change they think it's necessary.

The #newnormal has then become the official slogan used to justify virtually any nefarious rule and political decision, disguised as necessary and unavoidable change. It benefits from the aforementioned state of shock and recovery, and can be reused under any circumstance. The term has a history dating back to the 2008 financial crisis and is particularly alluring to neoliberalism because it can be applied as a strapline to force acceptance through ad campaigns and repetition. During or immediately after a crisis, it carries both the seductiveness of newness and the comfort of normality. It can even pretend to be empathetic: "Unfortunately, it's the new normal." In education, the new normal is used to push more precarity, surveillance, and turn students and staff into Zoombies. The new normal is the imposition of a poorer condition packaged as inevitable, universal progress. Graphic design is not immune. It never was. It's shot with politics, ethics and ideology through-and-through. This pandemic exposed its fallacies, exploitative principles, redundancy, pointlessness, but also potential. It contributed to bring communities together, readapt failing systems at local and hyper-local levels, and expand the reach of its definition.

Now it's still the time for resilience. But it's not the time to be swallowed by the snowball of production. Destruction and dismantlement are just as valid. A possible list includes design festivals, design weeks and design capitals, biennials and clubs, design awards, portfolio showcasing and established canons. Universalism has been once again predominantly underlined by the discipline during 2020, with banal sentences, generic illustrations and clever visual puns. This reaffirmed privilege, lack of attention to context, politics, difference and otherness—something embedded in the foundations of the discipline, administered continuously as an addictive drug in design schools, bibliographies, methods. Created in and distributed from Europe and North America, bad habits soon become traditions in design, and then norms. The new normal appears once more during a crisis, preceding its aftermath. It is a weapon of neoliberalism with a clear, colonizing mission. This term comes from a position of power and privilege, and as such, it must be destroyed. It can make space for alternatives, other approaches, other worlds. These don't need to be invented as something new, or as product to be consumed. They exist beyond the navel-gazing of the usual Western centers where newness is sold, exported, and imposed. Places where mutual generosity and cooperation is a feature, not an exception. The pandemic has given yet another opportunity for them to listen to, and learn with and from realities that are capable of imagining otherwise, respecting people who have been working on the margins for decades. If this happens, other futures are still possible.

This publication is partly based on the symposium 'Point of No Return', Hochschule für bildende Künste Hamburg (HFBK), 2019. Since then some of these lectures have been edited and extended, new contributions have been added to build a multi-faceted discourse on key questions, potentials, limits and challenges of graphic design. This book can by no means be exhaustive or 'final', and wants to open up a constructive discussion on the role of graphic design in these times of change and turmoil.

The editor wishes to deeply thank all contributors, the assistant editors of this book Dokho Shin and Sam Kim, and his HFBK colleagues Beate Anspach and Andrea Klier.
     The publication would not have been possible without the structural and financial support of the Hochschule für bildende Künste Hamburg (HFBK). The editor would therefore also like to express special thanks to Martin Köttering, the president of the HFBK Hamburg. He would also like to thank Tim Albrecht, the head of the workshop for digital typesetting and graphics, who helped to realize this book through a generous donation from his teaching award.

H F B K
Hamburg

Editor	Ingo Offermanns
Assistant editors	Dokho Shin & Sam Kim
Contributors	Karo Akpokiere, Christian Bauer, David Bennewith, Friedrich von Borries, Clémentine Deliss, Sandra Doeller, Daniel Martin Feige, Feminist Internet, Annette Geiger, Matthias Görlich, Jianping He, Anna Lena von Helldorff, Martin Ludwig Hofmann, Kay Jun, Anoushka Khandwala, Francisco Laranjo, Degeng Li, Eva Linhart, Madoka Nishi, Ingo Offermanns, Offshore, Sophia Prinz, Konrad Renner (Knoth & Renner), Conor Rigby (Feminist Internet), Isabel Seiffert (Offshore), In-ah Shin (Feminist Designer Social Club), Pierre Smolarski, Markus Weisbeck
Translation German-English	Anthony DePasquale
Copy-editing	Leo Reijnen
Proofreading and index	Elke Stevens
Visual graphic interludes	former and current members of Klasse Grafik, HFBK Hamburg
Graphic design	Ingo Offermanns
Typesetting	Dokho Shin & Sam Kim
Typefaces	Maison, Milieu Grotesque
Paper inside	Holmen Trnd, 70 gr, 2.0
Paper cover	Natural Strongboard 265 gr
Lithography	Mariska Bijl, Wilco Art Books, Amsterdam
Printing and binding	Wilco Art Books, Amersfoort
Publisher	Valiz, Amsterdam 2022, Astrid Vorstermans & Pia Pol

Credits

This publication has been printed on FSC-certified paper by an FSC-certified printer. The FSC, Forest Stewardship Council promotes environmentally appropriate, socially beneficial, and economically viable management of the world's forests. fsc.org

For the images: © All rights reserved, Amsterdam, 2022
Since most of the images are directly related to the text, their use is permitted under citation right in this context.
We apologize for any inadvert errors or omissions. The author and the publisher have made every effort to secure permission to reproduce the listed material, texts, illustrations and photographs. Parties who nevertheless believe they can claim specific legal rights are invited to contact the publisher. info@valiz.nl

Creative Commons

The texts of this book are licensed under a Creative Commons Attribution-NonCommercial-NoDerivativesWorks 4.0 international licence.
You are free to: Share, copy and redistribute the material in any medium or format. The licensor cannot revoke these freedoms as long as you follow the license terms. Under the following terms:
— Attribution
— NonCommercial
— NoDerivatives
— No additional restrictions
The full license can be found at creativecommons.org/licenses/by-nc-nd/4.0

International distribution

BE/NL/LU Centraal Boekhuis, www.centraal.boekhuis.nl
Europe/Asia (except GB/IE) Idea Books, www.ideabooks.nl
GB/IE consult Valiz, www.valiz.nl
USA/Canada/Latin America D.A.P., www.artbook.com
Australia Perimeter Books, www.perimeterbooks.com
Individual orders www.valiz.nl; info@valiz.nl

This book has been generously supported by Hochschule für bildende Künste Hamburg

H F B K
Hamburg

ISBN 978-94-92095-90-9
Printed and bound in the EU, 2022

Aesthetics of Graphic Design, pp. 213–219.
- G.E.M. Anscombe, *Intention*, Cambridge/Mass.: Harvard University Press, 2000.
- Arthur C. Danto, *Die Verklärung des Gewöhnlichen: Eine Philosophie der Kunst*, Frankfurt am Main: Suhrkamp, 1999.
- Andreas Dorschel, *Gestaltung: Zur Ästhetik des Brauchbaren*, Heidelberg, 2003.
- Daniel M. Feige, *Computerspiele: Eine Ästhetik*, Berlin, 2015, chapter 4.
- Daniel M. Feige, *Design: Eine philosophische Analyse*, Berlin, 2018.
- Daniel M. Feige, *Zur Dialektik des Social Designs: Ästhetik und Kritik in Kunst und Design*, in: *Studienhefte Problemorientiertes Design* (vol. 9), Hamburg: Adocs, 2019.
- Vilém Flusser, *The Shape of Things. A Philosophy of Design*, London, 1999.
- Jane Forsey, *The Aesthetics of Design*, Oxford, 2013.
- Jean-François Lyotard, 'Paradox of the Graphic Artist,' in: ibid., *Postmodern Fables*, Minneapolis, 1997, p. 33–47. Glenn Parsons and Allen Carlson, *Functional Beauty*, Oxford, 2008.
- Sebastian Rödl, *Kategorien des Zeitlichen: Eine Untersuchung über die Formen des endlichen Verstandes*, Berlin: Suhrkamp, 2005.
- Jakob Steinbrenner and Julian Nida-Rümelin (eds.), *Ästhetische Werte und Design*, Stuttgart 2011.
Common-Sense Design, pp. 245–253.
- Christopher Alexander, *Notes on the Synthesis of Form* (Cambridge, 1964).
- Hannah Arendt, *Vita Activa: Oder vom tätigen Leben*, 16th edition (Munich, 2015).
- Aristotle, 'Rhetorik,' in: *Werke in deutscher Übersetzung*, Ernst Grumach (ed.), Hellmut Flashar (transl.), (Berlin, 2002).
- Bernhard Asmuth, 'Angemessenheit,' in: *Historische Wörterbuch der Rhetorik*, Gerd Ueding (ed.), vol. 1 (Tübingen, 1992), col. 579–604.
- Kenneth Burke, *A Rhetoric of Motives* (Berkeley, 1969).
- Umberto Eco, *Einführung in die Semiotik* (Munich, 2002), p. 184.
- Antonio Gramsci, *Philosophie der Praxis: Gefängnishefte 10 und 11*, Wolfgang Fritz Haug (ed.), (Hamburg, 1995).
- David S. Kaufer; Butler, Brian S., *Rhetoric and the Arts of Design* (Mahwah, 1996).
- Thomas Leinkauf, *Sensus Communis: I Antike*, in: *Historisches Wörterbuch der Philosophie*, Joachim Ritter and Karlfried Gründer (eds.), (Darmstadt, 1995), col. 622–633.
- Andreas Reckwitz, *Die Erfindung der Kreativität: Zum Prozess gesellschaftlicher Ästhetisierung* (Berlin, 2012).
- Pierre Smolarski, *Rhetorik des Designs: Gestaltung zwischen Subversion und Affirmation* (Bielefeld, 2017).
- Gian Battista Vico, *De Nostri Temporis Studiorum Ratione: Vom Wesen und Weg der geistigen Bildung* (Darmstadt, 1974).
Graphic Design as a Narrative Tool, pp. 153–161.
- Jerry Brotton and Nick Millea, *Talking Maps* (Oxford, 2019).
- 'The World Geo-Graphical Atlas', *Codex 99*. www.codex99.com/design/the-world-geographical-atlas.

- Thomas Strangeways, *The Work that Helped Promote the Poyasian Fraud*, (Courtesy Daniel Crouch Rare Books, accessed 2019). www.crouchrarebooks.com/books/view/the-work-that-helped-promote-the-poyasian-fraud.
- Tony Fry, 'Book review: The Archeworks Papers,' *Design Issues*, Volume 23, Number 3 (Cambridge US, 2007), p. 88.
- Donald Lombardi, 'Mark Lombardi's Narrative Structures and Other Mappings of Power Relations' (2012). socks-studio.com/2012/08/22/mark-lombardi.
- Mark Monmonier, *How to Lie with Maps* (Chicago, 1991)
- Ruben Pater, *The Politics of Design* (Amsterdam, 2016).
- Paula Scher, 'All maps lie,' *Design Observer*, 2017. designobserver.com/feature/all-maps-lie/30828.
- Apoorva Tadepalli, 'Colonial Cartography', *Real Life Magazine*, 2019. reallifemag.com/colonial-cartography.
- Joanna Walters, 'Boston public schools map switch aims to amend 500 years of distortion,' *The Guardian*, 2017. www.theguardian.com/education/2017/mar/19/boston-public-schools-world-map-mercator-peters-projection.
- Wikipedia 'Karte (Kartografie)', 2019. de.wikipedia.org/wiki/Karte.)
- Andrew Wiseman, 'When Maps Lie,' *CityLab*, 2015. www.citylab.com/design/2015/06/when-maps-lie/396761.
- Denis Wood, *Rethinking the Power of Maps* (New York, 2010).
Graphic Design Is Fluid, pp. 105–113.
- Art Basel talk with Thomas Scheibitz and Martin Eder, 'Figuration and Abstraction', www.youtube.com/watch?v=qp2fVeFF8cE.
- Andrew Blauvelt, 'The Particular Problem of Graphic Design (History)', readings.design/PDF/problem-design-history.pdf.
- Munich Dialogue III with Simon Denny (artist) and Hans Ulrich Obrist, (artistic director, Serpentine Galleries) | DLD17.
- 'A Hard-Hitting Lightness,' conversation between Sunah Choi, Thomas Bayrle and Markus Weisbeck, SUNAH CHOI, Distanz Publishing.
- Robert Storr on Ad Reinhardt at David Zwirner, New York, on the occasion of the centennial anniversary of Ad Reinhardt's birth, www.youtube.com/watch?v=diaOT5bzRzQ.
- Big Think interview with Massimo Vignelli, ww.youtube.com/watch?v=schuTm9iuuA.
- Gerhard Richter, video interview by Fondation Beyeler, www.youtube.com/watch?v=kfzk2wYyOSM.
- George Condo interview: 'The Way I Think', Louisiana Channel, www.youtube.com/watch?v=BhRdIVcQnjk.
- A conversation with Paul Rand, *Conversations with Paul Rand*, 28 minutes, a film by Preston McClanahan.
- Michael Bierut on how to think like a designer, *Design Week*, www.designweek.co.uk/issues/21-27-september-2015/how-to-be-michael-bierut.
- Alexandra Midal, *Design by Accident: For a New History of Design*, (London, 2019).

Sources

- Bernd Scherer, Olga von Schubert and Stefan Aue (eds.), *100 Years of Now Library*, (Berlin, 2019).
On the Encroachment of Modernism, pp. 59–65.
- Louise Benson, *How Middle Class Modernism Took Over the World* (2020). elephant.art/how-middle-class-modernism-took-over-the-world-07092020/ (accessed on 17 September 2020).
- Elizabeth Critchlow, *Why Minimalism is a Class Issue and You Might Not Need That Expensive Adobe Subscription* (2018). eyeondesign.aiga.org/why-minimalism-is-a-class-issue-you-might-not-need-that-expensive-adobe-subscription (accessed on 17 September 2020).
- Ishwara Giga, *Gentrification, A Continued Colonisation*, unpublished BA thesis (University of the Arts London, 2020).
- Emily Gosling, E *New Zine by Ian Lynam Looks At The 'Opposite of Solving Design Problems'* (2019). www.creativeboom.com/inspiration/the-opposite-of-solving-design-problems, (accessed on 17 September 2020)./
- Anoushka Khandwala, *Decolonizing Means Many Things to Many People: Four Practitioners Discuss Decolonizing Design* (2020). eyeondesign.aiga.org/decolonizing-means-many-things-to-many-people-four-practitioners-discuss-decolonizing-design (accessed on 17 September 2020.
- Amber Newman, *Troll Palayan: Clara Balaguer on Design, Decolonization and Trolling Duterte* (2018). walkerart.org/magazine/troll-palayan-clara-balaguer-on-design-decolonization-trolling-duterte (accessed on 17 September 2020).

Contributors

Karo Akpokiere (b. 1981) is an artist whose practice focuses on fusing experiences and observations gleaned from everyday life with his interests in drawing, textiles, printmaking, and graphic design to tell stories of a personal and/or political nature. He studied Graphic Design in Hamburg (DE) and Lagos (NG).
Recent exhibitions and projects include 'The World is White no Longer,' Museum der Moderne, Salzburg, 2021; 'Die Vergangenheit ist ein Weg' (The Past is a Path), MARKK Museum, Hamburg, 2020.
Akpokiere lives and works in Hamburg, Germany.
www.karoakpokiere.com

Christian Bauer (b. 1979) is a design theorist, design historian and rector of the Hochschule für Bildende Künste in Saarbrücken (DE). His research interests include the interrelation between design, ethics, and democracy as well as the education for sustainable development. He is co-editor of the 'Würzburger Beiträge zur Designforschung' (Springer VS); latest publication in this series *Aufklärung durch Gestaltung digitaler Umwelten* (Wiesbaden 2021). He lives in Cologne (DE).
www.hbksaar.de/personen/details/bauer

David Bennewith (b. 1977) is an Aotearoa/New Zealand-born graphic designer and design researcher based in Amsterdam. Under the name Colophon, he works on research and commissioned projects focused on type design and typography. He has done extensive research into New Zealand type design, particularly the work of Joseph Churchward, publishing a monograph on him in 2009. Bennewith is the head of the graphic design department at the Gerrit Rietveld Academie, Amsterdam.
www.colophon.info

Friedrich von Borries (b. 1974) is an architect and professor of design theory at HFBK / University of Fine Art Hamburg. His work focuses on the relation between politics and design, architecture and art.
Recent exhibitions include: 'Friedrich von Borries: Politics of Design, Design of Politics,' The Design Museum, Munich, 2018–2019; 'School of No Consequences,' Museum of Arts and Crafts (MK&G), Hamburg, 2021–2021
Recent publication: *The World as Project. A Political Theory of Design* (2020)
Friedrich von Borries lives and works in Berlin, Hamburg and Havelberg, Germany.
www.friedrichvonborries.de

Clémentine Deliss (b. 1960) is a curator, publisher, and cultural historian. From 2002–2009 she ran the international transdisciplinary collective Future Academy. Between 1996–2007 she published the independent artists' and writers' organ *Metronome*. Between 2010–2015, she directed the Weltkulturen Museum in Frankfurt, instituting a new research lab to remediate collections within a post-ethnological context. She was co-curator of the exhibition 'Hello World: Revising a Collection,' Hamburger Bahnhof, Berlin (2018). In 2018–19, she was Interim Professor of Curatorial Theory and Dramaturgical Practice at the Karlsruhe University of Arts and Design. Since 2020 she is associated curator at KW Institute for Contemporary Art, Berlin. Her latest publication is *The Metabolic Museum*, 2020.
www.clementinedeliss.academia.edu/

Sandra Doeller (b. 1983) is a graphic designer. Since 2013 she runs the studio Bureau Sandra Doeller in Frankfurt (DE). Her work focuses on typographical graphic design, using a clear and reduced design language. Sandra is co-founder of the Design Verein Frankfurt e.V., which has organized self-publishing fairs for young designers and publishers. She taught typography at the University of Applied Sciences Darmstadt and the University of the Arts Bremen. Her works have received numerous awards, such as The Most Beautiful German Books.
www.sandradoeller.com

Daniel M. Feige (b. 1976) is a professor of philosophy and aesthetics in the design group at the Staatliche Akademie der Bildenden Künste Stuttgart (DE). He first studied jazz piano in Amsterdam, then philosophy, German literature, and psychology in Germany. In 2009 he received his doctorate with a thesis on Hegel's art theory and was a research assistant in the collaborative research center 626 from 2009 to 2015 at the Freie Universität Berlin. In 2018 he was a visiting professor for design theory at Burg Giebichenstein Halle. His research focuses on the intersection of aesthetics and theoretical philosophy. His publications include: *Kunst als Selbstverständigung* (2012); *Philosophie des Jazz* (2014); *Computerspiele: Eine Ästhetik*, (2015); *Design: Eine philosophische Analyse*, 2018; *Die Natur des Menschen: Eine dialektische Anthropologie* (in preparation, 2022).

Feminist Internet is a creative collective based in Europe that seeks to advance internet equalities through critical practice. The collective was formed in 2017 following a series of workshops at the University of the Arts London which sought to understand what a feminist internet might look like. Recent projects include 'Antisemitism and the Internet,' Mozfest, 2021; 'Queering AI,' Tech and Power, London, 2020; 'Designing an Ecological Alexa,' Impact Festival, Utrecht, 2019; 'Tomorrow's Nipple,' The Photographers Gallery, London, 2018.
www.feministinternet.com

Annette Geiger is professor of Theory and History of Design at the Hochschule für Künste Bremen. After studying communication science and cultural studies in Berlin, Grenoble, and Paris, she completed her doctorate thesis *Urbild und fotografischer Blick* (Munich, 2004) on aesthetics and image theory in the eighteenth century, at the Institute for Art History, University of Stuttgart. Since 2009, she teaches and researches in Bremen and Berlin about design history, visual culture and aesthetic theories about art, design and everyday life. Recent monograph: *Andersmöglichsein: Zur Ästhetik des Designs* (2018).

Matthias Görlich is a communication designer, teacher, and researcher. In 2000, he set up his de-

Contributors

sign studio as a platform for critical research, education, and design development. He is co-editor of the *Civic City Cahiers* (with Jesko Fezer), *Studienhefte Problemorientiertes Design* (with Jesko Fezer & Oliver Gemballa) and *Vergessene Schulen* (with Philipp Misselwitz and Nina Gribat). Since 2017, he is a professor for Information Design at the University of Art and Design, Burg Giebichenstein in Halle (DE).
www.mgoerlich.com; www.truth.design

Jianping He (b. 1973, CN) is a graphic designer, professor, and publisher. He studied graphic design at the China Academy of Art in Hangzhou, Meisterschule of Fine Arts in Berlin University of Arts and obtained his PhD in cultural history at Free University of Berlin in 2011. In 2002, he established his own design studio and publishing house, hesign, in Berlin and in Hangzhou in 2008. His works have won international awards and his art is represented in many art collection organizations worldwide.
In 2021, his book *daydream* was published and his 'daydream' exhibition took place in the V&A Museum in Shenzhen, China. He is also a member of the AGI, Alliance Graphique Internationale. He lives and works in Berlin (DE).
www.hesign.com

Anna Lena von Helldorff (b. 1977) studied at the Academy of Fine Arts Leipzig, and works as an independent collaborator and designer. Her praxis is based on the principle of collaboration in varying constellations and formats—reflecting on forms of exhibiting, editing, presenting, publishing, making public. She is member of the AGI, Alliance Graphique Internationale. Recent publication: *Kunstpavillon, 1950–2020*, newspaper, co-edited with Frauke Zabel, 2021.
Anna Lena von Helldorff lives and works in Munich (DE).
www.ingebrauch.de

Martin Ludwig Hofmann (b. 1972) is a professor of human sciences in the context of design at the OWL University of Applied Sciences and Arts (Technische Hochschule Ostwestfalen-Lippe, DE) and an award-winning creative director. At OWL he also is the dean of the faculty of interior design and architecture. Recent publications include: *Neuro-design: What Design and Marketing Can Learn from Neuroscience and Psychology*, 2019; *Human-Centered Design: Developing Innovations instead of Following Trends*, 2017; and *Mindbombs: What Advertising and PR Can Learn from Greenpeace & Co.*, 2008.
Hofmann lives and works in Detmold and Freiburg (DE).
www.martin-ludwig-hofmann.de

Kay Jun (b. 1975) is a design writer, researcher, lecturer, and publisher. Having studied German Literature and Visual Communication in Seoul (KR), she now lives in Daegu (KR) running Aprilsnow Press, a publishing platform at the intersection of text, image and graphic design. As a researcher and writer, her recent focus of research is the history of modern Graphic Design in Korea and its historiography.

Projects and publications include: 'Voices from St.Gallen: Book Design of Jost Hochuli,' Platform P, Seoul (2021) (curator); *Ways of Working*, Aprilsnow (2021) by Richard Hollis and Stuart Bertolotti-Bailey (editor); *Design Archive 2: The Search for Korean Design at the Turn of the Century 1998–2007* (co-author) (2020).

Anoushka Khandwala is a designer, writer, and educator. She teaches on the Graphic Communication Design course at Central Saint Martins, in a role that challenges the canon of graphic design. Her work takes critical approaches to the intersection of design, culture, and identity. This manifests through design projects that prioritize cultural and social intervention, writings published in Elephant and AIGA *Eye on Design*, as well as the development of a lecture series entitled 'Radical Recipes,' which unearths hidden design histories. Khandwala lives and works in London (GB).
www.anoushkakhandwala.com.

Klasse Grafik is the course for graphic design at the University of Fine Arts (HFBK) Hamburg. Its students have produced the series of opening images (graphic interludes) of each chapter in this book. Since a connection between society and design is only possible if design reflects the spirit of society and society reflects the spirit of design, Klasse Grafik focuses on the visual examination of e.g. the public sphere, individuality, image/language, foreignness and authorship. Based on the students' artistic projects, the relationship between these factors are explored individually to formulate a personal design position in the field of tension between social contexts.
www.hfbk-hamburg.de

Christoph Knoth (b. 1985) is a graphic designer who studied at Burg Giebichenstein, University of Art and Design Halle (DE), Gerrit Rietveld Academie (Amsterdam, NL) and ECAL (Lausanne, CH). He is a professor in digital graphics at the HFBK / University of Fine Arts Hamburg. Together with Konrad Renner he runs the graphic design studio Knoth & Renner in Berlin and Leipzig. Recent projects include websites for artists such as Simon Denny and !Mediengruppe Bitnik; publishers such as Sternberg Press, *ARCH+* Magazine and Spector Books; cultural institutions like Kunsthalle Zurich and HGB Academy of Fine Arts Leipzig.
www.knoth-renner.com

Francisco Laranjo is a graphic designer and researcher. His writings have been published in *Design Observer*, *Eye*, *Creative Review*, *Grafik*, *Público*, and others. He has been a guest lecturer at the Sandberg Instituut (NL), CalArts (US), Royal College of Art, London College of Communication, Kingston University (UK), Zürich University of the Arts, University of the Arts Bern (Switzerland) and speaker many universities all over the world. Francisco has a PhD in graphic design methods and criticism from the University of the Arts London and an MA in Visual Communication from the Royal College of Art. He is an Associate Lecturer at Central Saint Martins, editor of the design criticism journal *Modes of Criti-*

Contributors

cism, and co-director of the design research center Shared Institute, and director of the Center for Other Worlds.
www.modesofcriticism.org; www.shared.institute; www.otherworlds.pt

Degeng Li (b. 1973) is a designer and an associate professor at Tsinghua University, Beijing China, specializing in design theory and narrative design.

Recent publications include: *Liquid Museum* (2020); *Design Edge: Inside Outside* (2014); *Social Energy: Dutch Graphic Design Meets China Graphic Design at 2008/2009*, co-edited with Jianghua and Luoyi (2010).

Recent projects include: the narrative design of the 'Shenzhen Urban Planning' exhibition, co-designed with Zhu Rongyuan, Atelier Brueckner, Silk Road Ltd. (2020); the narrative design of Taste Museum in Shenyang (2019); the narrative design of Museum of Zhang Zhidong in Wuhan (2017).

Eva Linhart is director of the book art and graphics department at the Museum Angewandte Kunst in Frankfurt am Main. Her most important exhibitions include 'Almir Mavignier: Additive Plakate' and 'Tobias Rehberger: Flach: Plakate, Plakatkonzepte und Wandmalereien'. Her latest exhibition, 'Michael Riedel: Grafik als Ereignis,' focused on the interface between applied and artistic graphic design. She studied art history, philosophy, and archeology in Frankfurt am Main and earned her doctorate in Basel under Gottfried Boehm on the subject of 'Artists and Passion.' Her research areas include 'the aesthetics of genius,' the question of the 'aesthetic limit,' and the positioning of the artistic book object as a 'performative art space.' She has been and continues to serve as a lecturer at various universities, where she addresses the double talent of the book in the context of the problem of fine and applied art.

Madoka Nishi (b. 1987) is the editor-in-chief of *IDEA* (since 2018), a quarterly magazine published in Tokyo, that focuses on graphic design and typography. After earning a Master's degree in Art management from Musashino Art University (Kodaira, Tokyo, JP), she worked as an editor for exhibition catalogs and is currently editing design magazines and books for *IDEA* at the Seibundo Shinkosha *IDEA* editorial department. She has collaborated with designers from Japan and abroad to organize exhibitions linked to the magazine, as well as special features that connect graphic design with various topics such as MANGA, games, fashion and gender.

Ingo Offermanns (b. 1972) is a graphic designer who studied at the University of Fine Arts, Munich (DE), and at the Werkplaats Typografie, Arnhem (NL). Since 2001, he has worked as an independent designer specializing in books and printing for a number of museums, publishing houses and artists in Germany and abroad. His research focuses on analytical graphic design. Since 2006, Ingo Offermanns lectures at the University of Fine Arts Hamburg. He lives and works in Kirchtimke and Hamburg (DE).
www.ingooffermanns.com

Offshore Studio is a Zurich-based design studio founded by Isabel Seiffert (b. 1986, DE) and Christoph Miler (b. 1988, AT). Their projects have a strong focus on typography, bold imagery as well as research-driven design and visual narratives. Next to commissions and collaborations, they engage in design education and investigate critical issues within the fields of design, media, ecology and globalization in self-initiated projects. Their work has been published, exhibited, and awarded internationally. www.offshorestudio.ch

Sophia Prinz (b. 1979) is a cultural sociologist and theorist and currently professor for Design Theory and History at ZHdK Zürich (CH). Her work focuses on sociology of design, practice theory of form, and transcultural design in global modernity. Recent exhibitions include: 'World Exhibition.' Johann Jacobs Museum, Zurich (2019); 'Mobile Worlds,' MK&G, Hamburg (2018). Recent publications include: *The Migration of Form* (with Roger M. Buergel); *Ästhetik und Gesellschaft* [Aesthetics and Society], co-edited (2015); *Die Praxis des Sehens* [The Practice of Seeing] (2014).

Prinz lives and works in Berlin and Zurich.

Konrad Renner (b. 1982) is a graphic designer, studied at Burg Giebichenstein, University of Art and Design Halle (DE) and is a professor for digital graphics at HFBK / University of Fine Arts Hamburg. Based on a deep appreciation of technology and its visual echo, he is running the graphic design studio Knoth & Renner together with Christoph Knoth in Berlin and Leipzig. Recent projects include websites for artists such as Simon Denny and !Mediengruppe Bitnik; publishers such as Sternberg Press and Spector Books; cultural institutions such as Kunsthalle Zurich and the German pavilion at the Venice art biennial. Recent publications include *Para-Platforms: On the Spatial Politics of Right-Wing Populism*, edited by Markus Miessen and Zoë Ritts (2020) and *100 beste Plakate 19* (2020).
www.knoth-renner.com

In-ah Shin (b. 1985) is a graphic designer based in Seoul, South Korea. Her primary interest lies in understanding authenticity in contemporary Korean culture and translating it into design practice. She runs 'Scenery of Today,' an independent design studio and publisher, and collaborates with social and cultural institutions/individuals of all sizes. She co-founded the Feminist Designer Social Club, a community and a platform providing a space to reimagine and transform the Korean design industry from a feminist perspective.
www.fdsc.kr; instagram.com/sceneryoftoday

Pierre Smolarski (b. 1984) is a design theorist who studied philosophy, art history and ancient history at the University of Jena (DE). He currently works as a research assistant in the Master's program 'Public Interest Design' at the University of Wuppertal (DE). His research focuses on rhetorical theory and practice and the transfer of rhetorical theory to the field of design, as well as the aesthetics of everyday life, especially on the aesthetics of work.

Contributors

He is co-editor of the publication series 'Post-Wert-Zeichen' (on philately as a historical science) and 'Public Interest Design.' He is the author of several books on the rhetoric of design.

Markus Weisbeck (b. 1965) is an artist and designer, and teaches as Professor for Graphic Design at the Bauhaus University in Weimar where he founded the Space for Visual Research. He is a member of the AGI, Alliance Graphique Internationale.

His projects include art direction for the MMK Frankfurt; Forsythe Company; corporate Identity for Zumtobel; Städelschule Architecture Class; Bundesfinanzministerium; ARTE; Deutsche Bank; documenta 12; Biennale di Venezia (German Pavilion, 2007); Manifesta 7; German Design Award; Greene Naftali NY & Sternberg Press; and over a hundred books for various artists and institutions. Weisbeck also lectures at numerous international conferences and Universities. He lives and works in Frankfurt and Weimar (DE).
www.markusweisbeck.studio;
www.herbert.gd

Editor and assistant editors

Ingo Offermanns, see his short biography on p. 281.

Sam Kim (b. 1984) is a graphic designer who specializes in the design and art direction of visual identities. He works with a focus on strong visual language and systematic implementation. His projects are often developed in close collaboration with the client, from the initial concept to the final realization. He studied at University of the Arts Berlin, and now works as a freelance designer in Berlin (DE).
www.samkim.de

Dokho Shin (b. 1986) is a graphic designer who has been working as a freelance designer since he graduated from Dankook University (Yongin, KR) with a major in Visual Communication Design. He enjoys working with various artists and designers in the cultural field. He also works for GRAPHIC magazine as a co-editor and designer. He has been working in Berlin since 2017.
www.shindokho.kr

Publisher

Valiz is an independent international publisher, based in Amsterdam, addressing contemporary developments in art, design, architecture, and urban affairs. Their books provide critical reflection and interdisciplinary inspiration in a broad and imaginative way, often establishing a connection between cultural disciplines and socio-economic questions. Valiz is headed by Astrid Vorstermans (1960) and Pia Pol (1985).
www.valiz.nl; @valiz_books_projects

Index of Names

Index of Names

ell this book.

Critique of
Commodity Aesthetics

Appearance, Sexuality and
Advertising in Capitalist Society

Wolfgang Fritz Haug
Translated by Robert Bock

Polity Press

d this free PDF.

y Max Weinland

EMBRACE
EMBRACE
EMBRACE
EMBRACE

EMBRACE
EMBRACE
EMBRACE
EMBRACE
EMBRACE
EMBRACE
EMBRACE

CHANGE
CHANGE
CHANGE
CHANGE
CHANGE
CHANGE
CHANGE

CHANGE
CHANGE
CHANGE
CHANGE

Graphic interlude by Cyrill Kuhlmann